The Complete Israeli Cookbook

Quick, Easy and Delicious Homemade Recipes From Israeli Cuisine

BY: LINDA L. KENNEDY

TABLE OF CONTENTS

RECIPES

1.Hummus with Tahini:

Prep Time: 10 mins

Cook Time: 0 mins

Total Time: 10 mins

Servings: 6

Ingredients:

- 2 cups of canned chickpeas, drained and rinsed
- 1/3 cup of tahini
- 1/4 cup of fresh lemon juice
- 2 cloves garlic, chop-up
- 1/2 tsp ground cumin
- Salt as needed
- 3 tbsp olive oil
- 2 tbsp water
- Paprika and olive oil for garnish

Instructions:

1. Combine chickpeas, tahini, lemon juice, garlic, cumin, and salt in a mixer.
2. Blend till smooth, adding olive oil and water gradually while blending.
3. Drizzle with olive oil and sprinkle with paprika before serving.
4. Serve with fresh vegetables or pita bread.

Nutrition (per serving):

Cals: 220 kcal, Fat: 15g, Carbs: 18g, Fiber: 5g, Protein: 6g

2.Falafel with Pita and Salad:

Prep Time: 15 mins

Cook Time: 20 mins

Total Time: 35 mins

Servings: 4

Ingredients:

- 1 cup of dried chickpeas, soaked overnight
- 1 mini onion, roughly chop-up
- 3 cloves garlic
- 1 cup of fresh parsley leaves
- 1 tsp ground cumin
- 1 tsp ground coriander
- 1/2 tsp baking soda
- Salt and pepper as needed
- Vegetable oil for frying
- Pita bread
- Lettuce, tomatoes, cucumbers, and pickles for salad
- Tahini sauce (from the Hummus recipe above) for serving

Instructions:

1. The soaked chickpeas Must be drained and rinsed. With a towel, pat them dry.
2. Blend chickpeas, onion, garlic, parsley, cumin, coriander, baking soda, salt, and pepper in a mixer up to a coarse texture forms.
3. Make little balls or patties out of the Mixture.
4. In a pan, heat the vegetable oil and fry the falafel till golden brown and crispy on both sides.
5. Serve the falafel with lettuce and tahini sauce on pita bread.

Nutrition (per serving, excluding pita and salad):

Cals: 320 kcal, Fat: 15g, Carbs: 35g, Fiber: 8g, Protein: 13g

3.Shakshuka with Feta Cheese:

Prep Time: 10 mins

Cook Time: 25 mins

Total Time: 35 mins

Servings: 4

Ingredients:

- 2 tbsp olive oil
- 1 onion, thinly split
- 1 red bell pepper, thinly split
- 3 cloves garlic, chop-up
- 1 tsp ground cumin
- 1 tsp ground paprika
- 1/2 tsp ground cayenne pepper (adjust as needed)
- 1 can (400g) diced tomatoes
- 1 can (400g) crushed tomatoes
- Salt and pepper as needed
- 4-6 Big eggs
- 100g feta cheese, cut up
- Fresh parsley, chop-up, for garnish

Instructions:

1. In a Big skillet over medium heat, heat the olive oil. Sauté the onions and bell peppers up to tender.
2. Combine the chop-up garlic, cumin, paprika, and cayenne pepper in a combining bowl. Cook for a few mins, or up to aromatic.
3. Combine the chop-up and crushed tomatoes in a combining bowl. Season with salt and pepper as needed. Let the sauce to thicken for about 10-15 mins.
4. Make mini wells in the sauce and place the eggs inside. Cover the skillet and cook the eggs up to they are done to your liking (runny or set).
5. Sprinkle with cut up feta cheese and garnish with chop-up parsley.
6. Serve warm with pita or crusty bread.

4.Israeli Salad with Lemon Dressing:

Prep Time: 10 mins

Cook Time: 0 mins

Total Time: 10 mins

Servings: 4

Ingredients:

- 2 cucumbers, diced
- 2 tomatoes, diced
- 1 red bell pepper, diced
- 1 yellow bell pepper, diced
- 1/4 cup of fresh parsley, chop-up
- 1/4 cup of fresh mint, chop-up
- 1/4 cup of red onion, lightly chop-up
- Juice of 1 lemon
- 2 tbsp olive oil
- Salt and pepper as needed

Instructions:

1. Combine chop-up cucumbers, tomatoes, red and yellow bell peppers, parsley, mint, and red onion in a Big combining dish.
2. To make the dressing, whisk together lemon juice, olive oil, salt, and pepper in a separate mini bowl.
3. Toss the salad with the dressing up to completely incorporated.
4. Serve chilled as a light side dish or as a complement to other courses.

Nutrition (per serving):
Cals: 110 kcal, Fat: 7g, Carbs: 11g, Fiber: 3g, Protein: 2g

5.Sabich Sandwich with Eggplant and Hard-Boiled Eggs:

Prep Time: 15 mins

Cook Time: 20 mins

Total Time: 35 mins

Servings: 4

Ingredients:

- 1 Big eggplant, slice into thin slices
- 4 hard-boiled eggs, split
- 4 pita bread
- 1 cup of shredded lettuce
- 1 cucumber, thinly split
- 1 tomato, thinly split
- 1/2 cup of pickles, split
- Tahini sauce (from the Hummus recipe above)

- Amba sauce (non-compulsory, a tangy mango pickle sauce)

Instructions:

1. Preheat the oven to 200 Ds Celsius (390 Ds Fahrenheit). Arrange the eggplant slices on a baking sheet and brush with olive oil. Roast for 15-20 mins, or up to tender and slightly browned.
2. Heat the pita bread in the oven or in the microwave.
3. Spread a sufficient amount of tahini sauce on every pita bread before assembling the sandwich.
4. Inside every pita, layer roasted eggplant slices, split hard-boiled eggs, lettuce, cucumber, tomato, and pickles.
5. Drizzle more amba sauce on top if desired for extra flavor.
6. Fold the pita in half and serve warm.

Nutrition (per serving):
Cals: 380 kcal, Fat: 15g, Carbs: 50g, Fiber: 8g, Protein: 15g

6.Shawarma with Tahini Sauce:

Prep Time: 20 mins (+ marinating time)

Cook Time: 25 mins

Total Time: 45 mins (+ marinating time)

Servings: 4

Ingredients:

- 500g boneless chicken thighs or beef, thinly split
- 2 tbsp olive oil
- 2 tbsp lemon juice
- 2 cloves garlic, chop-up
- 1 tsp ground cumin
- 1 tsp ground paprika
- 1/2 tsp ground coriander
- 1/4 tsp ground turmeric
- Salt and pepper as needed
- 4 pita bread
- Split tomatoes, cucumbers, and onions
- Tahini sauce (from the Hummus recipe above)

Instructions:

1. Combine the split meat, olive oil, lemon juice, chop-up garlic, cumin, paprika, coriander, turmeric, salt, and pepper in a combining bowl. Let it to marinade for at least 1 hr (overnight is preferable).
2. Melt the butter in a skillet or grill pan over medium-high heat. Cook up to the marinated meat is fully cooked and slightly browned.
3. Heat the pita bread in the oven or in the microwave.
4. Spread some tahini sauce on every pita bread before assembling the shawarma.

5. Top with the cooked meat and split tomatoes, cucumbers, and onions.
6. Serve the pita neatly rolled up.

Nutrition (per serving):
Cals: 450 kcal, Fat: 18g, Carbs: 35g, Fiber: 5g, Protein: 35g

7.Tahini Cookies with Sesame Seeds:

Prep Time: 15 mins
Cook Time: 12 mins
Total Time: 27 mins
Servings: 24 cookies

Ingredients:

- 1/2 cup of (1 stick) unsalted butter, melted
- 1/2 cup of tahini
- 1 cup of granulated sugar
- 1 Big egg
- 1 tsp vanilla extract
- 1 1/2 cups of all-purpose flour
- 1/2 tsp baking soda
- 1/4 tsp salt
- 1/4 cup of sesame seeds

Instructions:

1. Preheat the oven to 180 Ds Celsius (350 Ds Fahrenheit) and line a baking sheet with parchment paper.
2. Cream together the melted butter, tahini, and sugar in a Big combining basin up to light and fluffy.
3. Combine in the egg and vanilla extract up to fully combined.
4. Whisk together the flour, baking soda, and salt in a separate bowl. Gradually combine the dry and wet components, combining up to a dough forms.
5. Roll the dough into mini balls and set them on a baking sheet lined with parchment paper, leaving space between every cookie.
6. Flatten every ball with the back of a fork, then top with sesame seeds.
7. Bake the cookies for 10-12 mins, or up to the edges are faintly brown.
8. Let the cookies to cool for a few mins on the baking sheet before moving them to a wire rack to cool fully.

Nutrition (per cookie):
Cals: 110 kcal, Fat: 6g, Carbs: 13g, Fiber: 1g, Protein: 2g

8.Malabi with Rosewater Syrup:

Prep Time: 5 mins (+ chilling time)
Cook Time: 10 mins
Total Time: 15 mins (+ chilling time)
Servings: 4

Ingredients:

- 4 cups of milk (can be substituted with coconut milk for a vegan version)
- 1/2 cup of cornstarch
- 1/2 cup of sugar
- 1 tsp rosewater
- Chop-up pistachios and shredded coconut for garnish

Instructions:

1. In a mini bowl, combine the cornstarch and a mini amount of the milk to make a homogeneous paste.
2. Warm the remaining milk in a saucepan over medium heat. Stir in the sugar up to it dissolves.
3. Whisk in the cornstarch paste slowly, continually swirling to avoid lumps. Cook, stirring constantly, up to the Mixture thickens and coats the back of a spoon.
4. Take out from the heat and add the rosewater.
5. Fill individual serving dishes or glasses with the Mixture.
6. Refrigerate the malabi up to totally set and cool (at least 2 hrs or overnight).
7. Before serving, garnish with chop-up pistachios and shredded coconut.

Nutrition (per serving):
Cals: 280 kcal, Fat: 6g, Carbs: 48g, Fiber: 0g, Protein: 5g

9.Israeli Couscous with Vegetables and Herbs:

Prep Time: 10 mins
Cook Time: 15 mins
Total Time: 25 mins
Servings: 4

Ingredients:

- 1 cup of Israeli couscous (pearl couscous)
- 1 3/4 cups of vegetable or chicken broth
- 1 tbsp olive oil
- 1 mini onion, lightly chop-up
- 1 zucchini, diced
- 1 red bell pepper, diced
- 1 cup of cherry tomatoes, halved
- 1/4 cup of fresh parsley, chop-up
- 1/4 cup of fresh mint, chop-up
- Juice of 1 lemon
- Salt and pepper as needed
- Cut up feta cheese (non-compulsory, for serving)

Instructions:

1. Warm the olive oil in a saucepan over medium heat. Sauté the chop-up onion up to melted and transparent.
2. Toast the Israeli couscous in the pot for a few mins, up to it turns slightly golden.
3. Bring to a boil with the vegetable or chicken broth. Reduce the heat to low, cover, and cook for 10-12 mins, or up to the couscous is soft and the liquid has been absorbed.
4. Meanwhile, prepare the vegetables. Sauté the diced zucchini, red bell pepper, and cherry tomatoes in a separate skillet up to just soft.
5. When the couscous is done, fluff it with a fork and place it in a serving bowl.
6. To the couscous, add the sautéed veggies, chop-up parsley, chop-up mint, and lemon juice. Toss everything together up to everything is fully intefinely finely grated.
7. Season as needed with salt and pepper.
8. Before serving, top with cut up feta cheese if desired.

Nutrition (per serving, without feta cheese):
Cals: 270 kcal, Fat: 5g, Carbs: 48g, Fiber: 4g, Protein: 8g

10. Matbucha with Roasted Peppers and Tomatoes:

Prep Time: 15 mins

Cook Time: 45 mins

Total Time: 1 hr

Servings: 6

Ingredients:

- 3 red bell peppers
- 3 ripe tomatoes
- 3 tbsp olive oil
- 1 onion, lightly chop-up
- 3 cloves garlic, chop-up
- 1 tsp ground cumin
- 1 tsp paprika
- 1/4 tsp cayenne pepper (adjust as needed)
- Salt and pepper as needed
- 1 tbsp tomato paste
- 1/4 cup of water
- Fresh parsley, chop-up, for garnish

Instructions:

1. Preheat the oven to 220 Ds Celsius (425 Ds Fahrenheit). On a baking sheet, sprinkle 1 tbsp olive oil over the red bell peppers and tomatoes. Roast for 25-30 mins, or up to the skins of the peppers and tomatoes are browned and blistered.

2. Let the roasted veggies to cool after they have been take outd from the oven. When the peppers and tomatoes have cooled, peel off the skins, take out the seeds from the peppers, and slice them into mini pieces. Place aside.
3. Heat the remaining 2 tbsp olive oil in a Big skillet over medium heat. Sauté the chop-up onion up to melted.
4. Combine the chop-up garlic, ground cumin, paprika, cayenne pepper, salt, and pepper in a combining bowl. Cook for a few mins, or up to aromatic.
5. Cook for another min after adding the tomato paste.
6. Add the roasted peppers and tomatoes, along with 1/4 cup of water, to the skillet. Simmer for about 10-15 mins, or up to the sauce thickens and the flavors combine.
7. Before serving, adjust the seasoning and garnish with chop-up fresh parsley.

Nutrition (per serving):
Cals: 90 kcal, Fat: 7g, Carbs: 7g, Fiber: 2g, Protein: 1g

11. Sufganiyot with Raspberry Jam Filling:

Prep Time: 1 hr

Cook Time: 20 mins

Total Time: 1 hr 20 mins

Servings: 12

Ingredients:

- 2 1/4 tsp (1 packet) active dry yeast
- 1/4 cup of warm water
- 3 1/2 cups of all-purpose flour
- 1/4 cup of granulated sugar
- 1/2 tsp salt
- 3/4 cup of warm milk
- 3 Big egg yolks
- 2 tbsp unsalted butter, melted
- Vegetable oil for frying
- Raspberry jam for filling
- Powdered sugar for dusting

Instructions:

1. Combine the active dry yeast and warm water in a mini basin. Let it to sit for 5 mins, or up to frothy.
2. Whisk together the flour, sugar, and salt in a Big combining basin.
3. To the dry ingredients, add the bubbly yeast Mixture, warm milk, egg yolks, and melted butter. Combine everything together up to a dough forms.

4. Knead the dough for 5-7 mins on a floured surface, or up to smooth and elastic.
5. Place the dough in a greased bowl, cover with a moist cloth, and let aside for 1 hr, or up to doubled in size.
6. Punch the dough down and roll it out to about 1/4 inch thickness on a floured surface.
7. Slice out circles of dough with a round cookie sliceter or a glass. Roll the leftovers again to produce more circles.
8. Half of the circles Must have a mini tbsp of raspberry jam in the center. Place another circle on top of every and push the sides together to seal.
9. In a deep saucepan or fryer, heat the vegetable oil to 180°C (350°F).
10. Fry the sufganiyot in batches up to both sides are golden brown.
11. Drain the sufganiyot on a paper towel after removing it from the oil.
12. Before serving, dust with powdered sugar.

Nutrition (per serving):
Cals: 240 kcal, Fat: 7g, Carbs: 39g, Fiber: 1g, Protein: 5g

12.Bourekas with Cheese and Spinach:

Prep Time: 30 mins
Cook Time: 25 mins
Total Time: 55 mins
Servings: 12

Ingredients:
- 2 sheets refrigerate puff pastry, thawed
- 1 cup of refrigerate chop-up spinach, thawed and drained
- 1 cup of feta cheese, cut up
- 1 cup of ricotta cheese
- 1 Big egg, beaten
- 1 tsp dried oregano
- 1 tsp dried parsley
- Salt and pepper as needed
- Sesame seeds for sprinkling (non-compulsory)

Instructions:
1. Preheat the oven to 200 Ds Celsius (400 Ds Fahrenheit) and line a baking sheet with parchment paper.
2. Combine the chop-up spinach, feta cheese, ricotta cheese, beaten egg, dried oregano, dried parsley, salt, and pepper in a combining dish.
3. Roll out every sheet of puff pastry to about 1/8 inch thickness on a floured surface.
4. Slice the puff pastry into squares about 4 inches in size.

5. Fill every square with a tbsp of the cheese and spinach Mixture.
6. Fold the pastry over the filling and press the sides together to seal.
7. Brush the bourekas with the beaten egg and place them on the prepared baking sheet.
8. If desired, top with sesame seeds.
9. Bake for 20-25 mins, or up to the bourekas are golden brown and puffy, in a preheated oven.

Nutrition (per serving):
Cals: 250 kcal, Fat: 16g, Carbs: 19g, Fiber: 1g, Protein: 8g

13.Baba Ganoush with Grilled Eggplant:

Prep Time: 10 mins
Cook Time: 30 mins
Total Time: 40 mins
Servings: 6

Ingredients:
- 2 Big eggplants
- 3 tbsp tahini
- 3 tbsp lemon juice
- 2 cloves garlic, chop-up
- 1/4 cup of extra-virgin olive oil
- Salt and pepper as needed
- Chop-up parsley and olive oil for garnish

Instructions:
1. Heat the grill or the oven to medium-high.
2. To let steam to escape during cooking, prick the eggplants with a fork.
3. Grill or roast the eggplants for 20-25 mins, or up to the skin is toasted and the flesh is tender and cooked through.
4. Let the eggplants to cool somewhat before peeling off the charred skin and discarding it.
5. Blend the grilled eggplant flesh, tahini, lemon juice, chop-up garlic, and olive oil in a mixer up to smooth.
6. Season as needed with salt and pepper.
7. Transfer the baba ganoush to a serving plate and top with chop-up parsley.
8. Serve with fresh vegetables or pita bread.

Nutrition (per serving):
Cals: 150 kcal, Fat: 12g, Carbs: 11g, Fiber: 5g, Protein: 2g

14.Jerusalem Bagel with Za'atar Seasoning:

Prep Time: 15 mins
Cook Time: 15 mins
Total Time: 30 mins
Servings: 8

- 2 cups of all-purpose flour
- 1 tsp active dry yeast
- 1 tsp sugar
- 1 tsp salt
- 3/4 cup of warm water
- 2 tbsp olive oil
- 1/4 cup of za'atar seasoning

Instructions:

1. Warm water, sugar, and active dry yeast Must all be combined in a mini bowl. Let it to sit for 5 mins, or up to frothy.
2. Whisk together the flour and salt in a Big combining dish.
3. To the dry ingredients, add the frothy yeast Mixture and olive oil. Combine everything together up to a dough forms.
4. Knead the dough for 5 mins on a floured surface, or up to smooth and elastic.
5. Place the dough in a greased bowl, cover with a moist cloth, and let aside for 1 hr, or up to doubled in size.
6. Preheat the oven to 200 Ds Celsius (400 Ds Fahrenheit) and line a baking sheet with parchment paper.
7. Divide the dough into 8 equal sections and roll every into a 10-inch-long rope.
8. Make a circle out of every rope and pinch the ends together to seal.
9. Coat every bagel equally with the za'atar seasoning.
10. Place the za'atar-coated bagels on the baking sheet that has been prepared.
11. Bake for about 15 mins, or up to the bagels are golden brown, in a preheated oven.

Nutrition (per serving):
Cals: 180 kcal, Fat: 5g, Carbs: 29g, Fiber: 2g, Protein: 5g

15.Kibbeh with Spiced Lamb and Bulgur:

Prep Time: 30 mins

Cook Time: 25 mins

Total Time: 55 mins

Servings: 8

Ingredients:

- 1 cup of fine bulgur wheat
- 500g ground lamb or beef
- 1 Big onion, lightly chop-up
- 2 tbsp pine nuts
- 1 tsp ground cinnamon
- 1/2 tsp ground allspice
- Salt and pepper as needed

- Vegetable oil for frying

Instructions:

1. Drain the bulgur wheat and rinse it in cold water.
2. Combine the drained bulgur wheat, ground lamb or beef, onion, pine nuts, ground cinnamon, ground allspice, salt, and pepper in a combining dish.
3. Knead the Mixture up to it is well combined.
4. Shape a part of the Mixture into an oval or football shape.
5. In a deep saucepan or fryer, heat the vegetable oil to 180°C (350°F).
6. Fry the kibbeh in batches up to golden brown and well done.
7. On a paper towel, drain the fried kibbeh.
8. Serve the kibbeh hot, accompanied with tahini sauce or yogurt dip.

Nutrition (per serving):
Cals: 350 kcal, Fat: 18g, Carbs: 18g, Fiber: 3g, Protein: 26g

16.Falafel Wrap with Hummus and Pickles:

Prep Time: 20 mins (+ soaking time for chickpeas)

Cook Time: 15 mins

Total Time: 35 mins (+ soaking time)

Servings: 4

Ingredients:

- 1 cup of dried chickpeas, soaked overnight
- 1 mini onion, roughly chop-up
- 3 cloves garlic
- 1 cup of fresh parsley leaves
- 1 tsp ground cumin
- 1 tsp ground coriander
- 1/2 tsp baking soda
- Salt and pepper as needed
- Vegetable oil for frying
- 4 pita bread
- Hummus (from the Hummus recipe above)
- Pickles, split
- Split tomatoes and cucumbers

Instructions:

1. The soaked chickpeas Must be drained and rinsed. With a towel, pat them dry.
2. Blend chickpeas, onion, garlic, parsley, cumin, coriander, baking soda, salt, and pepper in a mixer up to a coarse texture forms.
3. Make little balls or patties out of the Mixture.
4. In a pan, heat the vegetable oil and fry the falafel till golden brown and crispy on both sides.
5. Heat the pita bread in the oven or in the microwave.

6. Spread hummus on every pita bread before assembling the falafel wrap.
7. Toss in the fried falafel, pickles, tomatoes, and cucumbers.
8. Serve the pita neatly rolled up.

Nutrition (per serving, excluding hummus and pickles):

Cals: 320 kcal, Fat: 15g, Carbs: 35g, Fiber: 8g, Protein: 13g

17. Shakshuka with Spinach and Feta:

Prep Time: 10 mins

Cook Time: 25 mins

Total Time: 35 mins

Servings: 4

Ingredients:

- 2 tbsp olive oil
- 1 onion, thinly split
- 3 cloves garlic, chop-up
- 1 red bell pepper, thinly split
- 2 cups of fresh spinach leaves
- 1 tsp ground cumin
- 1 tsp ground paprika
- 1/2 tsp ground cayenne pepper (adjust as needed)
- 1 can (400g) diced tomatoes
- Salt and pepper as needed
- 4-6 Big eggs
- 100g feta cheese, cut up
- Fresh parsley, chop-up, for garnish

Instructions:

1. In a Big skillet over medium heat, heat the olive oil. Sauté the onions and bell peppers up to tender.
2. Combine in the chop-up garlic, cumin, paprika, and cayenne pepper. Cook for a few mins, or up to aromatic.
3. Cook up to the fresh spinach leaves are wilted.
4. Add the diced tomatoes. Season with salt and pepper as needed. Let the sauce to thicken for about 10-15 mins.
5. Make mini wells in the sauce and place the eggs inside. Cover the skillet and cook the eggs up to they are done to your liking (runny or set).
6. Sprinkle with cut up feta cheese and garnish with chop-up parsley.
7. Serve warm with pita or crusty bread.

Nutrition (per serving, without bread):

Cals: 280 kcal, Fat: 19g, Carbs: 14g, Fiber: 3g, Protein: 13g

18. Challah Bread with Honey Glaze:

Prep Time: 20 mins (+ rising time)

Cook Time: 25 mins

Total Time: 2 hrs 15 mins (+ rising time)

Servings: 8

Ingredients:

- 4 cups of all-purpose flour
- 1/4 cup of granulated sugar
- 2 tsp active dry yeast
- 1 tsp salt
- 3/4 cup of warm water
- 1/4 cup of vegetable oil
- 2 Big eggs
- 1 egg yolk (for glaze)
- 1 tbsp water (for glaze)
- 2 tbsp honey (for glaze)
- Sesame seeds for sprinkling

Instructions:

1. Warm water, sugar, and active dry yeast Must all be combined in a bowl. Let it to sit for 5 mins, or up to frothy.
2. Whisk together the flour and salt in a Big combining dish.
3. To the dry ingredients, add the frothy yeast Mixture, vegetable oil, and eggs. Combine everything together up to a dough forms.
4. Knead the dough for about 10 mins on a floured surface, or up to smooth and elastic.
5. Place the dough in a greased bowl, cover with a moist cloth, and let aside for 1 hr, or up to doubled in size.
6. Punch the dough down and divide it into three equal parts.
7. Make a long rope out of every section, then braid the ropes together to form a loaf.
8. Place the braided challah on a parchment-lined baking pan.
9. Preheat the oven to 180 Ds Celsius (350 Ds Fahrenheit).
10. For the glaze, combine together the egg yolk, water, and honey in a mini basin.
11. Brush the challah with the glaze and sprinkle with sesame seeds.
12. Bake for approximately 25 mins, or up to the challah is golden brown and sounds hollow when tapped on the bottom.

Nutrition (per serving):

Cals: 340 kcal, Fat: 11g, Carbs: 52g, Fiber: 2g, Protein: 8g

19. Stuffed Grape Leaves with Rice and Herbs:

Prep Time: 45 mins

Cook Time: 1 hr

Total Time: 1 hr 45 mins

Servings: 4

Ingredients:

- 1 jar (about 30) grape leaves, preserved in brine
- 1 cup of long-grain rice, uncooked
- 1 mini onion, lightly chop-up
- 2 tbsp fresh dill, chop-up
- 2 tbsp fresh mint, chop-up
- 2 tbsp fresh parsley, chop-up
- 1/4 cup of lemon juice
- 1/4 cup of extra-virgin olive oil
- Salt and pepper as needed
- Lemon wedges for serving

Instructions:

1. Take out the preserved grape leaves from the brine and carefully separate them with cold water.
2. Combine the uncooked rice, chop-up onion, dill, mint, parsley, lemon juice, and olive oil in a combining bowl. Season as needed with salt and pepper.
3. Place a grape leaf, glossy side down, on a flat surface. If the stem is excessively thick, slice it off.
4. Place a tsp of the rice filling near the bottom of the grape leaf, then fold the sides inward and tightly roll it up like a cigar.
5. Fill and roll all of the grape leaves up to the rice Mixture is gone.
6. Arrange the packed grape leaves in a single layer in a big pot, seam side down.
7. Cover the grape leaves with water, then set a heat-resistant plate on top to weigh them down while cooking.
8. Bring the water to a boil, then reduce to a low heat, cover the pot, and leave the grape leaves to simmer for 1 hr, or up to the rice is tender.
9. Take out the platter and let aside to cool before serving the packed grape leaves.
10. With lemon slices, serve.

Nutrition (per serving):

Cals: 250 kcal, Fat: 10g, Carbs: 38g, Fiber: 2g, Protein: 4g

20. Israeli Breakfast Spread with Various Salads and Breads:

Prep Time: Varies for every salad and bread

Cook Time: Varies for every salad and bread

Total Time: Varies for every salad and bread

Servings: 4

Ingredients:

- Hummus (from the Hummus recipe above)
- Baba Ganoush (from the Baba Ganoush recipe above)
- Israeli Salad (diced cucumbers, tomatoes, bell peppers, red onions, parsley, lemon juice, and olive oil)
- Labneh or Greek yogurt
- Olives (green and black)
- Pickles (cucumber and combined vegetables)
- Assorted cheeses (feta, halloumi, etc.)
- Fresh herbs (mint, cilantro, etc.)
- Freshly baked pita bread, Jerusalem bagels, and challah bread

Instructions:

1. Prepare every salad and bread according to the recipes provided above.
2. Arrange everything on a big serving platter or individual plates.
3. Serve the Israeli breakfast spread among the salads, breads, cheeses, and condiments.
4. This tasty and nutritious breakfast spread features a range of flavors and textures.

Nutrition (per serving, will vary depending on servings and chosen portions):

Cals: Varies, Fat: Varies, Carbs: Varies, Fiber: Varies, Protein: Varies

21. Maqluba with Chicken and Rice:

Prep Time: 30 mins

Cook Time: 1 hr

Total Time: 1 hr 30 mins

Servings: 6

Ingredients:

- 1 whole chicken, slice into pieces
- 2 cups of basmati rice
- 2 Big onions, thinly split
- 3 Big carrots, peel off and split
- 2 Big potatoes, peel off and split
- 1 cup of cauliflower florets
- 1/4 cup of vegetable oil
- 1 tsp ground cinnamon
- 1 tsp ground cumin
- 1/2 tsp ground turmeric
- Salt and pepper as needed
- 4 cups of chicken broth or water

1. Warm the vegetable oil in a big pot over medium heat. Sauté the split onions up to melted and golden.
2. Cook up to the chicken is browned on all sides in the pot.
3. Sprinkle the chicken and onions with the cinnamon, cumin, turmeric, salt, and pepper. Stir in the spices to coat the chicken.
4. On top of the chicken, arrange the split carrots, potatoes, and cauliflower.
5. Rinse the basmati rice in cold water and sprinkle it evenly over the vegetables.
6. Pour the chicken stock or water over the rice, ensuring sure it completely covers everything.
7. Bring the Mixture to a boil, then reduce to a low heat, cover, and leave to stew for 40-45 mins, or up to the rice and veggies are fully cooked and soft.
8. Let the pot to cool for 10 mins before carefully tipping it over onto a Big serving plate. The rice Must now be on the bottom, followed by the chicken and vegetables.
9. Serve the maqluba hot and savor the layered tastes.

Nutrition (per serving):

Cals: 600 kcal, Fat: 25g, Carbs: 55g, Fiber: 5g, Protein: 38g

22.Israeli Vegetable Soup with Lentils:

Prep Time: 15 mins

Cook Time: 45 mins

Total Time: 1 hr

Servings: 6

Ingredients:

- 1 cup of red lentils, rinsed and drained
- 1 onion, chop-up
- 2 carrots, peel off and diced
- 2 celery stalks, diced
- 2 zucchini, diced
- 1 cup of chop-up tomatoes (canned or fresh)
- 6 cups of vegetable broth or water
- 2 tbsp olive oil
- 2 cloves garlic, chop-up
- 1 tsp ground cumin
- 1 tsp ground coriander
- Salt and pepper as needed
- Fresh parsley or cilantro, chop-up, for garnish

Instructions:

1. Warm the olive oil in a big pot over medium heat. Combine in the onion, carrots, celery, and zucchini. Sauté up to the vegetables have melted slightly.
2. Combine in the chop-up garlic, cumin, and coriander. Cook for a few mins, or up to aromatic.
3. Combine the diced tomatoes and red lentils in a combining bowl.
4. Bring the vegetable broth or water to a boil in a saucepan.
5. Reduce the heat to low, cover the saucepan, and cook for 30-35 mins, or up to the lentils and vegetables are cooked.
6. Season the soup as needed with salt and pepper.
7. Serve the Israeli vegetable soup immediately, garnished with fresh parsley or cilantro.

Nutrition (per serving):

Cals: 220 kcal, Fat: 6g, Carbs: 30g, Fiber: 10g, Protein: 10g

23.Rugelach with Chocolate and Nuts:

Prep Time: 30 mins (+ chilling time for the dough)

Cook Time: 20 mins

Total Time: 50 mins (+ chilling time)

Servings: 24

Ingredients:

- 2 cups of all-purpose flour
- 1/2 tsp salt
- 1 cup of unsalted butter, melted
- 8 ozs cream cheese, melted
- 1/4 cup of granulated sugar
- 1 tsp vanilla extract
- 1 cup of chocolate chips or lightly chop-up chocolate
- 1 cup of chop-up nuts (walnuts, pecans, or almonds)
- 1/4 cup of apricot preserves (or other fruit preserves)
- Powdered sugar for dusting

Instructions:

1. Whisk together the all-purpose flour and salt in a combining dish.
2. Cream together the melted butter, cream cheese, granulated sugar, and vanilla extract in a separate Big combining bowl up to light and fluffy.
3. Add the flour Mixture to the creamed Mixture gradually, combining up to a dough forms.
4. Divide the dough into four equal parts, form every into a disk, wrap in plastic wrap, and place in the refrigerator for at least 2 hrs, or up to firm.
5. Preheat the oven to 180 Ds Celsius (350 Ds Fahrenheit) and line a baking sheet with parchment paper.

6. Roll out one cold dough disk into a circle approximately 1/8 inch thick on a floured surface.
7. Sprinkle with chocolate chips or chop-up chocolate and chop-up nuts after spreading a thin layer of apricot preserves over the dough.
8. Slice the circular into 6-8 triangular wedges using a sharp knife or pizza sliceter.
9. To make a rugelach shape, roll every triangle up from the wide end.
10. Repeat with the remaining dough and filling, placing the rugelach on the prepared baking sheet.
11. Bake for 18-20 mins, or up to the rugelach are golden brown, in a preheated oven.
12. Take out from the oven and place on a wire rack to cool.
13. Before serving, dust with powdered sugar.

Nutrition (per serving):
Cals: 200 kcal, Fat: 13g, Carbs: 17g, Fiber: 1g, Protein: 3g

24.Kanafeh with Sweet Cheese Filling:

Prep Time: 30 mins

Cook Time: 40 mins

Total Time: 1 hr 10 mins

Servings: 8

Ingredients:
- 1 box/pkg (500g) kadaif or kataifi dough (shredded phyllo dough)
- 1 cup of unsalted butter, dilute
- 2 cups of sweet cheese (such as Akkawi, mozzarella, or ricotta), shredded or cut up
- 1 cup of semolina or fine breadcrumbs
- 1/2 cup of granulated sugar
- 1 cup of water
- 1 tbsp lemon juice
- 1/4 cup of chop-up pistachios or almonds
- Rosewater or orange blossom water (non-compulsory)

Instructions:
1. Preheat the oven to 180°C (350°F) and coat a circular baking dish with cooking spray.
2. Separate the strands of kadaif dough in a bowl with your fingertips to make it fluffy and airy.
3. Dilute butter and semolina or fine breadcrumbs Must be combined in a separate basin.
4. Half of the kadaif dough Must be layered in the bottom of a greased baking dish, gently pressed down.
5. Drizzle half of the kadaif layer with the butter-semolina Mixture.

6. Combine the sweet cheese with the granulated sugar in a separate bowl and spread it evenly over the kadaif layer.
7. Add another layer of kadaif bread on top of the sweet cheese.
8. Pour the remaining butter and semolina Mixture over the top layer.
9. Slice the kanafeh into little squares or diamonds with a sharp knife.
10. Bake for 35-40 mins, or up to the kanafeh is golden brown and crispy on top, in a preheated oven.
11. Prepare the sugar syrup while the kanafeh is baking. Bring the water and sugar to a boil in a saucepan. Simmer for a few mins, stirring occasionally, up to the syrup thickens somewhat. Non-compulsory: For added taste, add a few drops of rosewater or orange blossom water to the syrup.
12. Take out the kanafeh from the oven and evenly pour the hot sugar syrup over the top.
13. Over the syrup-soaked kanafeh, scatter chop-up pistachios or almonds.
14. Before serving, let the kanafeh to cool somewhat. Enjoy it while it's still warm!

Nutrition (per serving):
Cals: 450 kcal, Fat: 30g, Carbs: 40g, Fiber: 1g, Protein: 8g

25.Israeli Pickles with Cucumbers and Dill:

Prep Time: 15 mins (+ pickling time)

Cook Time: 5 mins

Total Time: 20 mins (+ pickling time)

Servings: 8

Ingredients:
- 6-8 mini cucumbers, split
- 2 cups of water
- 1 cup of white vinegar
- 2 tbsp kosher salt
- 2 tbsp granulated sugar
- 4-6 cloves garlic, crushed
- 2 tbsp fresh dill, chop-up
- 1 tsp black peppercorns
- 1/2 tsp mustard seeds
- 1/4 tsp red pepper flakes (non-compulsory)

Instructions:
1. Warm the water, white vinegar, kosher salt, and granulated sugar in a saucepan over medium heat. Stir up to the salt and sugar have completely dissolved.
2. Turn off the heat and let the brine to cool to room temperature.

3. Layer the split cucumbers, smashed garlic, chop-up dill, black peppercorns, mustard seeds, and red pepper flakes (if using) in a clean glass jar or pickling container.
4. Pour the cooled brine over the cucumber Mixture, ensuring sure it completely covers the cucumbers.
5. Refrigerate the jar or container for at least 24 hrs to let the flavors to develop.
6. Israeli pickles can be kept in the fridge for up to two weeks.
7. Serve the pickles as a zesty side dish or as a garnish for sandwiches and burgers.

Nutrition (per serving):
Cals: 15 kcal, Fat: 0g, Carbs: 3g, Fiber: 1g, Protein: 1g

26.Sabich Bowl with Roasted Eggplant and Chickpeas:

Prep Time: 20 mins

Cook Time: 25 mins

Total Time: 45 mins

Servings: 4

Ingredients:
- 1 Big eggplant, slice into cubes
- 1 can (400g) chickpeas, drained and rinsed
- 2 tbsp olive oil
- 1 tsp ground cumin
- 1/2 tsp ground paprika
- Salt and pepper as needed
- 2 cups of cooked quinoa or rice
- 4 pita bread, warmed
- 1 cup of hummus (from the Hummus recipe above)
- 1 cup of Israeli salad (diced cucumbers, tomatoes, bell peppers, red onions, parsley, lemon juice, and olive oil)
- 1/4 cup of tahini sauce (from the Tahini Sauce recipe above)
- Fresh parsley or cilantro, chop-up, for garnish

Instructions:
1. Preheat the oven to 200 Ds Celsius (400 Ds Fahrenheit) and line a baking sheet with parchment paper.
2. Toss the eggplant cubes and chickpeas in a basin with the olive oil, cumin, paprika, salt, and pepper.
3. Spread the seasoned eggplant and chickpeas in a single layer on the prepared baking sheet.
4. Roast for 20-25 mins, or up to the eggplant is soft and slightly browned, in a preheated oven.

5. Divide the cooked quinoa or rice among four bowls to make the sabich bowls.
6. Serve with roasted eggplant and chickpeas on top of every bowl.
7. Top with a big scoop of hummus, Israeli salad, and tahini sauce.
8. With warmed pita bread on the side, serve the sabich bowls.
9. Garnish with fresh parsley or cilantro, if desired.

Nutrition (per serving):
Cals: 500 kcal, Fat: 25g, Carbs: 50g, Fiber: 12g, Protein: 15g

27.Lachuch with Date Syrup:

Prep Time: 10 mins

Cook Time: 15 mins

Total Time: 25 mins

Servings: 6

Ingredients:
- 2 cups of all-purpose flour
- 1 tbsp granulated sugar
- 1 tsp active dry yeast
- 1 tsp baking powder
- 1/2 tsp ground cumin
- 1/2 tsp ground turmeric
- 1/4 tsp ground cardamom
- 1/4 tsp salt
- 1 1/4 cups of warm water
- 1 Big egg
- 2 tbsp vegetable oil
- Date syrup (silan) for serving

Instructions:
1. Whisk together the all-purpose flour, granulated sugar, active dry yeast, baking powder, ground cumin, ground turmeric, ground cardamom, and salt in a Big combining basin.
2. Whisk together the warm water, egg, and vegetable oil in a separate basin.
3. Add the wet components to the dry ones gradually, combining up to a homogeneous batter emerges.
4. Let the lachuch batter to rest for about 10 mins after covering it with a moist cloth.
5. Melt butter in a nonstick skillet or griddle over medium heat.
6. Spread about 1/4 cup of the lachuch batter into a thin circle on the hot skillet.
7. Cook for 2-3 mins on every side, or up to golden brown and heated through.
8. Repeat with the remaining batter to make extra lachuch pancakes.

9. Serve the lachuch warm with date syrup (silan) poured on top for a sweet and delicious topping.

Nutrition (per serving):
Cals: 240 kcal, Fat: 6g, Carbs: 40g, Fiber: 2g, Protein: 6g

28. Tahini Brownies with Halva Swirl:

Prep Time: 15 mins

Cook Time: 25 mins

Total Time: 40 mins

Servings: 12

Ingredients:

- 1/2 cup of unsalted butter, dilute
- 1 cup of granulated sugar
- 2 Big eggs
- 1 tsp vanilla extract
- 1/2 cup of all-purpose flour
- 1/4 cup of cocoa powder
- 1/4 tsp salt
- 1/2 cup of tahini paste
- 1/2 cup of halva, cut up (non-compulsory)

Instructions:

1. Preheat the oven to 180°C (350°F) and coat a square baking pan with cooking spray.
2. Whisk together the dilute butter, granulated sugar, eggs, and vanilla extract in a combining bowl up to well blended.
3. To the wet ingredients, add the all-purpose flour, cocoa powder, and salt. Combine up to everything is just blended. Take care not to overcombine.
4. Spread the brownie batter evenly in the prepared baking sheet.
5. Warm the tahini paste in a mini microwave-safe bowl for a few seconds, up to it becomes more fluid.
6. Drizzle the warmed tahini over the brownie batter, swirling it in with a knife or skewer.
7. Non-compulsory: For added taste and texture, top the brownie batter with cut up halva.
8. Bake for 20-25 mins, or up to a toothpick inserted into the center comes out with a few wet crumbs.
9. Let the tahini brownies to cool before Cuttinginto squares and serving.

Nutrition (per serving):
Cals: 280 kcal, Fat: 15g, Carbs: 33g, Fiber: 1g, Protein: 4g

29. Israeli Shakshuka Pizza:

Prep Time: 20 mins

Cook Time: 25 mins

Total Time: 45 mins

Servings: 4

Ingredients:

- 1 lb pizza dough (store-bought or homemade)
- 1/4 cup of olive oil
- 1 onion, thinly split
- 1 red bell pepper, thinly split
- 1 yellow bell pepper, thinly split
- 2 cloves garlic, chop-up
- 1 tsp ground cumin
- 1 tsp ground paprika
- 1/2 tsp ground cayenne pepper (adjust as needed)
- 1 can (400g) diced tomatoes
- Salt and pepper as needed
- 1 cup of shredded mozzarella cheese
- 4-6 Big eggs
- Fresh parsley, chop-up, for garnish

Instructions:

1. Preheat the oven to 220°C (425°F) and prepare a Big baking sheet with cooking spray.
2. Roll out the pizza dough to the desired thickness on a floured surface.
3. Place the rolled-out dough on the baking sheet that has been prepared.
4. Warm the olive oil in a pan over medium heat. Cook up to the onions and bell peppers are melted.
5. Combine in the chop-up garlic, cumin, paprika, and cayenne pepper. Cook for a few mins, or up to aromatic.
6. Add the diced tomatoes and combine well. Season with salt and pepper as needed. Simmer for 10 mins to let the sauce to thicken.
7. Cover the pizza dough with the tomato and pepper Mixture.
8. Sprinkle with shredded mozzarella cheese on top.
9. Make little wells for the eggs in the sauce and cheese.
10. Crack the eggs into the wells with care.
11. Bake for 15-20 mins, or up to the crust is golden brown and the eggs are cooked to your liking, in a preheated oven.
12. Garnish the shakshuka pizza with freshly chop-up parsley.
13. Slice and serve the pizza while the egg yolks are still runny.

Nutrition (per serving):
Cals: 580 kcal, Fat: 32g, Carbs: 50g, Fiber: 3g, Protein: 22g

30. Falafel Burger with Avocado and Tahini Mayo:

Prep Time: 30 mins (+ chilling time for the falafel Mixture)

Cook Time: 15 mins

Total Time: 45 mins (+ chilling time)

Servings: 4

Ingredients:

- 1 can (400g) chickpeas, drained and rinsed
- 1/2 onion, chop-up
- 3 cloves garlic, chop-up
- 1/4 cup of fresh parsley, chop-up
- 1 tsp ground cumin
- 1 tsp ground coriander
- 1/2 tsp baking soda
- 2 tbsp all-purpose flour
- Salt and pepper as needed
- Vegetable oil for frying
- 4 burger buns
- 1 ripe avocado, split
- Lettuce leaves
- Tomato slices
- For Tahini Mayo:
- 1/4 cup of tahini paste
- 2 tbsp lemon juice
- 2 tbsp water
- 1 clove garlic, chop-up
- Salt as needed

Instructions:

1. Combine the chickpeas, chop-up onion, chop-up garlic, chop-up parsley, ground cumin, ground coriander, baking soda, all-purpose flour, salt, and pepper in a mixer.
2. Pulse the Mixture up to it forms a coarse paste, but don't overwork it into a smooth hummus-like consistency.
3. Place the falafel Mixture in a bowl, cover, and place in the refrigerator for at least 30 mins to firm up.
4. Meanwhile, make the tahini mayo by whisking the tahini paste, lemon juice, water, chop-up garlic, and salt together up to smooth and creamy. If necessary, adjust the consistency by adding more water.
5. In a Big skillet or pot, heat the vegetable oil over medium-high heat.
6. Form the refrigerated falafel Mixture into patties and gently fry up to golden brown and crispy on both sides in hot oil. Use a paper towel to absorb any excess oil.
7. If desired, toast the burger buns.

8. Spread a Big amount of tahini mayo on the bottom bun and assemble the falafel burgers.
9. Combine a falafel patty, avocado slices, lettuce leaves, and tomato slices in a bowl.
10. Put the top bread on the burger and it's ready to go!

Nutrition (per serving):

Cals: 550 kcal, Fat: 27g, Carbs: 61g, Fiber: 12g, Protein: 17g

31. Israeli Malawach with Cheese and Tomatoes:

Prep Time: 20 mins

Cook Time: 15 mins

Total Time: 35 mins

Servings: 4

Ingredients:

- 1 box/pkg malawach dough (store-bought or homemade)
- 1 cup of shredded cheese (such as mozzarella or cheddar)
- 2-3 ripe tomatoes, thinly split
- 2 tbsp olive oil
- Salt and pepper as needed

Instructions:

1. Roll the malawach dough out into a Big circle or rectangle that is about 1/8 inch thick.
2. Brush olive oil into a pan or griddle over medium heat.
3. Cook the rolled-out malawach dough for about 2-3 mins on every side, or up to golden and crispy.
4. Place the malawach on a serving platter after removing it from the skillet.
5. While the malawach is still warm, sprinkle it with shredded cheese to slightly melt it.
6. Season with salt and pepper and top with thinly split tomatoes.
7. Serve the malawach warm, slice into slices or squares.

Nutrition (per serving):

Cals: 400 kcal, Fat: 25g, Carbs: 30g, Fiber: 2g
Protein: 15g

32. Bourekas with Potato and Mushroom Filling:

Prep Time: 30 mins

Cook Time: 30 mins

Total Time: 1 hr

Servings: 8

- 1 box/pkg puff pastry sheets (store-bought or homemade)
- 2 Big potatoes, boiled and mashed
- 1 cup of mushrooms, lightly chop-up
- 1 onion, lightly chop-up
- 2 tbsp olive oil
- 1 tsp dried thyme
- Salt and pepper as needed
- 1 egg, beaten (for egg wash)

Instructions:

1. Preheat the oven to 200 Ds Celsius (400 Ds Fahrenheit) and line a baking sheet with parchment paper.
2. Warm the olive oil in a pan over medium heat. Sauté the chop-up onion up to transparent.
3. Cook up to the mushrooms release their moisture and become soft in the skillet with the lightly chop-up mushrooms.
4. In a combining dish, add the mashed potatoes, sautéed mushrooms, dried thyme, salt, and pepper.
5. On a floured board, roll out the puff pastry sheets and slice them into squares or rectangles, depending on your preference.
6. Fill every pastry square with a dollop of the potato and mushroom filling.
7. Fold the pastry over the filling to make a triangle or rectangle shape, then seal the edges with a fork.
8. Place the bourekas on the prepared baking sheet and brush the tops with beaten egg to give them a golden color.
9. Bake for 20-25 mins, or up to the bourekas are puffy and golden brown in a preheated oven.

Nutrition (per serving):

Cals: 350 kcal, Fat: 20g, Carbs: 35g, Fiber: 3g, Protein: 8g

33.Shakshuka with Harissa and Cilantro:

Prep Time: 10 mins

Cook Time: 25 mins

Total Time: 35 mins

Servings: 4

Ingredients:

- 2 tbsp olive oil
- 1 onion, thinly split
- 1 red bell pepper, thinly split
- 1 yellow bell pepper, thinly split
- 2 cloves garlic, chop-up
- 1 tsp ground cumin
- 1 tsp ground paprika

- 1/2 tsp ground cayenne pepper (adjust as needed)
- 1 can (400g) diced tomatoes
- 2 tbsp harissa paste (adjust as needed)
- Salt and pepper as needed
- 4-6 Big eggs
- Fresh cilantro, chop-up, for garnish

Instructions:

1. Heat the olive oil in a big skillet or frying pan over medium heat.
2. Cook up to the onions and bell peppers are melted.
3. Combine in the chop-up garlic, cumin, paprika, and cayenne pepper as needed. Cook for a few mins, or up to aromatic.
4. Combine the diced tomatoes and harissa paste in a combining bowl. Season with salt and pepper as needed.
5. Simmer the tomato Mixture for 10-15 mins, or up to the flavors blend and the sauce thickens slightly.
6. Make mini wells in the tomato sauce and delicately place the eggs inside.
7. Cover the skillet and cook the shakshuka for 5-7 mins, or up to the eggs are cooked to your liking.
8. Before serving, garnish the shakshuka with chop-up fresh cilantro.

Nutrition (per serving):

Cals: 250 kcal, Fat: 15g, Carbs: 20g, Fiber: 5g, Protein: 10g

34.Jachnun with Silan Syrup:

Prep Time: 15 mins (+ overnight soaking)

Cook Time: 6-8 hrs (overnight baking)

Total Time: 6-8 hrs 15 mins (+ soaking time)

Servings: 6

Ingredients:

1. 500g puff pastry sheets or phyllo dough (about 1 lb)
2. 1/2 cup of unsalted butter, dilute Silan syrup (date syrup)
3. Instructions:
4. Stack puff pastry sheets together and roll into a log form if using. Stack the sheets of phyllo dough together if using.
5. Wrap the pastry log or stack in plastic wrap and refrigerate it overnight.
6. Preheat the oven to 90 Ds Celsius (190 Ds Fahrenheit) and prepare a baking dish with parchment paper.
7. Brush the moistened pastry with dilute butter, being sure to cover every layer.

8. Roll the pastry back into a log and set it in the baking dish that has been prepared.
9. Cover the baking dish with aluminum foil and bake the jachnun for 6-8 hrs, or up to golden brown and flaky.
10. Serve the jachnun warm with silan syrup drizzled on top for a sweet and pleasant flavor.

Nutrition (per serving):
Cals: 350 kcal, Fat: 25g, Carbs: 25g, Fiber: 1g, Protein: 5g

35.Israeli Breakfast Pita with Egg and Za'atar:

Prep Time: 10 mins

Cook Time: 10 mins

Total Time: 20 mins

Servings: 4

Ingredients:
- 4 pita bread
- 4 Big eggs
- 2 tbsp olive oil
- Za'atar spice combine
- Salt and pepper as needed

Instructions:
1. In a skillet over medium heat, heat the olive oil.
2. Crack one egg into the skillet, being careful not to break the yolk. Continue with the remaining eggs.
3. Sprinkle every egg with za'atar spice combine, salt, and pepper.
4. Cook for 2-3 mins, or up to the whites are set but the yolks are still runny.
5. Warm the pita bread in the oven or toaster.
6. On every pita bread, place one fried egg.
7. Drizzle with more olive oil and sprinkle with more za'atar for more flavor.
8. Fold or roll the pita bread in half like a wrap.
9. Serve the warm Israeli morning pita with the delectable combination of egg and za'atar.

Nutrition (per serving):
Cals: 300 kcal, Fat: 15g, Carbs: 30g, Fiber: 2g, Protein: 12g

36.Bamba with Peanut Butter Snack:

Prep Time: 5 mins

Cook Time: None

Total Time: 5 mins

Servings: 4

Ingredients:
- 1 bag (150g) Bamba (peanut-flavored puffed corn snacks)

- 1/4 cup of creamy peanut butter

Instructions:
1. Combine the Bamba and creamy peanut butter in a Big combining dish.
2. Toss the Bamba in the peanut butter up to covered evenly.
3. As a delectable and crunchy snack, serve the Bamba with peanut butter Mixture.

Nutrition (per serving):
Cals: 200 kcal, Fat: 12g, Carbs: 18g, Fiber: 2g, Protein: 6g

37.Sabich Salad with Combined Greens and Pickled Vegetables:

Prep Time: 15 mins

Cook Time: None

Total Time: 15 mins

Servings: 4

Ingredients:
- 4 pita bread
- 1 Big eggplant, roasted and split
- 2 Big tomatoes, diced
- 1 cucumber, diced
- 1 cup of combined salad greens (such as lettuce, spinach, or arugula)
- Pickled vegetables (cabbage, carrots, etc.)
- Tahini sauce (from the Tahini Sauce recipe above)

Instructions:
1. Warm the pita bread in the oven or toaster.
2. Place roasted eggplant slices, chop-up tomatoes, split cucumber, combined salad greens, and pickled veggies in every pita.
3. Drizzle the tahini sauce on top of the filling.
4. Roll the pita into a wrap and serve with the sabich salad for a light and tasty lunch.

Nutrition (per serving):
Cals: 300 kcal, Fat: 10g, Carbs: 45g, Fiber: 6g, Protein: 8g

38.Israeli Fish Stew with Tomato and Cilantro:

Prep Time: 15 mins

Cook Time: 25 mins

Total Time: 40 mins

Servings: 4

Ingredients:
- 500g white fish fillets (such as cod or tilapia), slice into chunks
- 2 tbsp olive oil
- 1 onion, chop-up
- 2 cloves garlic, chop-up

- 2 bell peppers (red, yellow, or orange), diced
- 1 can (400g) diced tomatoes
- 2 cups of fish or vegetable broth
- 1 tsp ground cumin
- 1 tsp ground paprika
- Salt and pepper as needed
- Fresh cilantro, chop-up, for garnish

Instructions:

1. Warm the olive oil in a big pot or Dutch oven over medium heat.
2. Sauté the chop-up onion up to transparent.
3. Combine the chop-up garlic and diced bell peppers in a combining bowl. Cook for a few mins, or up to the vegetables are melted.
4. Add the diced tomatoes, fish or vegetable broth, cumin, paprika, salt, and pepper as needed.
5. Bring the stew to a simmer and cook for about 10-15 mins to enable the flavors to blend.
6. Add the fish chunks to the stew gently and cook for another 5-7 mins, or up to the fish is cooked through and flakes readily with a fork.
7. Before serving, garnish the Israeli fish stew with chop-up fresh cilantro.

Nutrition (per serving):
Cals: 250 kcal, Fat: 10g, Carbs: 15g, Fiber: 4g, Protein: 25g

39.Rugelach with Apricot Jam and Walnuts:

Prep Time: 20 mins

Cook Time: 20 mins

Total Time: 40 mins

Servings: 12

Ingredients:

- 2 cups of all-purpose flour
- 1/2 cup of granulated sugar
- 1 cup of unsalted butter, melted
- 1 tsp vanilla extract
- 1/2 cup of apricot jam
- 1/2 cup of chop-up walnuts
- Powdered sugar for dusting

Instructions:

1. Preheat the oven to 180 Ds Celsius (350 Ds Fahrenheit) and line a baking sheet with parchment paper.
2. Cream together the melted butter and granulated sugar in a Big combining combiner up to light and fluffy.
3. Incorporate the vanilla extract.
4. Add the all-purpose flour gradually to the creamed Mixture, combining up to a dough forms.

5. Divide the dough into four equal parts, form every into a disk, wrap in plastic wrap, and place in the refrigerator for at least 2 hrs, or up to firm.
6. Preheat the oven to 180 Ds Celsius (350 Ds Fahrenheit) and line a baking sheet with parchment paper.
7. Roll out one cold dough disk into a circle approximately 1/8 inch thick on a floured surface.
8. Sprinkle with chop-up walnuts after spreading a thin layer of apricot jam over the dough.
9. Slice the circular into 6-8 triangular wedges using a sharp knife or pizza sliceter.
10. To make a rugelach shape, roll every triangle up from the wide end.
11. Repeat with the remaining dough and filling, placing the rugelach on the prepared baking sheet.
12. Bake for 18-20 mins, or up to the rugelach are golden brown, in a preheated oven.
13. Take out from the oven and place on a wire rack to cool.
14. Before serving, dust with powdered sugar.

Nutrition (per serving):
Cals: 250 kcal, Fat: 15g, Carbs: 25g, Fiber: 1g, Protein: 3g

40.Kadaif with Pistachios and Orange Blossom Syrup:

Prep Time: 30 mins

Cook Time: 30 mins

Total Time: 1 hr

Servings: 8

Ingredients:

- 1 box/pkg (500g) kadaif or kataifi dough (shredded phyllo dough)
- 1 cup of unsalted butter, dilute
- 1 cup of crushed pistachios
- 1/2 cup of granulated sugar
- 1 cup of water
- 1 cup of orange blossom syrup

Instructions:

1. Preheat the oven to 180°C (350°F) and coat a circular baking dish with cooking spray.
2. Separate the strands of kadaif dough with your fingertips in a Big combining bowl to make it frothy and airy.
3. In a separate bowl, combine the dilute butter and pistachios.
4. Half of the kadaif dough Must be layered in the bottom of a greased baking dish, gently pressed down.

5. Drizzle half of the pistachio-butter Mixture over the kadaif layer.
6. In a separate bowl, combine the granulated sugar and water to make a simple syrup. Bring to a boil and continue to cook for a few mins, or up to the syrup thickens somewhat.
7. Half of the syrup Must be drizzled over the kadaif layer.
8. Add another layer of kadaif dough on top, followed by the remaining butter and pistachio Mixture and syrup.
9. Bake for 25-30 mins, or up to the kadaif is golden brown and crispy, in a preheated oven.
10. Take out the kadaif from the oven and evenly pour the orange blossom syrup over the top.
11. Before serving, let the kadaif to cool somewhat. Enjoy it while it's still warm!

Nutrition (per serving):
Cals: 400 kcal, Fat: 25g, Carbs: 40g, Fiber: 2g, Protein: 5g

41.Israeli Cabbage Salad with Lemon and Olive Oil Dressing:

Prep Time: 15 mins
Cook Time: None
Total Time: 15 mins
Servings: 4

Ingredients:
- 4 cups of shredded green cabbage
- 1 cup of shredded purple cabbage
- 1 carrot, finely finely grated
- 1/4 cup of fresh parsley, chop-up
- 2 tbsp olive oil
- 1 lemon, juiced
- Salt and pepper as needed

Instructions:
1. Combine the shredded green cabbage, shredded purple cabbage, finely finely grated carrot, and chop-up fresh parsley in a Big combining basin.
2. Drizzle the salad with olive oil and lemon juice.
3. Season as needed with salt and pepper.
4. Toss the salad with the dressing up to it is equally distributed.
5. As a pleasant and tangy side dish, serve the Israeli cabbage salad.

Nutrition (per serving):
Cals: 120 kcal, Fat: 7g, Carbs: 14g, Fiber: 4g, Protein: 2g

42.Bourekas with Spinach and Feta Filling:

Prep Time: 20 mins

Cook Time: 25 mins
Total Time: 45 mins
Servings: 8

Ingredients:
- 1 box/pkg puff pastry sheets (store-bought or homemade)
- 2 cups of fresh spinach, chop-up
- 1 cup of cut up feta cheese
- 1 egg, beaten (for egg wash)

Instructions:
1. Preheat the oven to 200 Ds Celsius (400 Ds Fahrenheit) and line a baking sheet with parchment paper.
2. On a floured board, roll out the puff pastry sheets and slice them into squares or rectangles, depending on your preference.
3. In a combining bowl, combine the chop-up fresh spinach and cut up feta cheese.
4. Fill every pastry square with a tbsp of the spinach and feta filling.
5. Fold the pastry over the filling to make a triangle or rectangle shape, then seal the edges with a fork.
6. Place the bourekas on the baking sheet that has been prepared.
7. For a golden finish, brush the tops of the bourekas with beaten egg.
8. Bake for 20-25 mins, or up to the bourekas are puffy and golden brown in a preheated oven.

Nutrition (per serving):
Cals: 220 kcal, Fat: 15g, Carbs: 15g, Fiber: 1g, Protein: 6g

43.Shakshuka with Chickpeas and Chorizo:

Prep Time: 10 mins
Cook Time: 25 mins
Total Time: 35 mins
Servings: 4

Ingredients:
- 2 tbsp olive oil
- 1 onion, thinly split
- 1 red bell pepper, thinly split
- 1 yellow bell pepper, thinly split
- 2 cloves garlic, chop-up
- 100g chorizo sausage, split
- 1 tsp ground cumin
- 1 tsp ground paprika
- 1/2 tsp ground cayenne pepper (adjust as needed)
- 1 can (400g) diced tomatoes
- 1 can (400g) chickpeas, drained and rinsed

- Salt and pepper as needed
- 4-6 Big eggs
- Fresh parsley, chop-up, for garnish

Instructions:

1. Heat the olive oil in a big skillet or frying pan over medium heat.
2. Cook up to the onions and bell peppers are melted.
3. Combine in the chop-up garlic and chorizo sausage slices. Cook for a few mins, or up to the flavors of the sausage are released.
4. Combine in the ground cumin, paprika, and cayenne pepper. Cook for another min, or up to the Mixture is aromatic.
5. Combine the diced tomatoes and chickpeas in a combining bowl. Season with salt and pepper as needed.
6. Let the tomato and chickpea Mixture to simmer for 10-15 mins to let the flavors to blend and the sauce to thicken slightly.
7. Make mini wells in the sauce and delicately place the eggs inside.
8. Cover the skillet and cook the shakshuka for 5-7 mins, or up to the eggs are cooked to your liking.
9. Before serving, garnish the shakshuka with chop-up fresh parsley.

Nutrition (per serving):
Cals: 400 kcal, Fat: 25g, Carbs: 30g, Fiber: 8g, Protein: 18g

44.Israeli Sesame Pretzels with Za'atar Dip:

Prep Time: 20 mins

Cook Time: 15 mins

Total Time: 35 mins

Servings: 8

Ingredients:

- 1 lb pizza dough (store-bought or homemade)
- 2 tbsp baking soda
- 1/4 cup of sesame seeds
- 1 egg, beaten (for egg wash)
- Za'atar spice combine (for dip)

Instructions:

1. Preheat the oven to 220 Ds Celsius (425 Ds Fahrenheit) and line a baking sheet with parchment paper.
2. Make 8 equal pieces of pizza dough.
3. Roll every piece into a long rope 12-14 inches long.
4. Make a pretzel out of every rope by making a loop, then crossing the ends over every other and pushing them onto the bottom of the loop.

5. Bring the water to a boil in a big pot and add the baking soda.
6. Boil the pretzels for about 30 seconds on every side, one or two at a time.
7. Using a slotted spoon, take out the boiling pretzels from the water and set them on the prepared baking sheet.
8. Brush every pretzel with beaten egg and top with sesame seeds.
9. Bake for 12-15 mins, or up to the pretzels are golden brown and cooked through, in a preheated oven.
10. To make a tasty pretzel dip, combine za'atar spice with olive oil or yogurt.

Nutrition (per serving):
Cals: 200 kcal, Fat: 6g, Carbs: 30g, Fiber: 2g, Protein: 8g

45.Malabi with Raspberry Coulis:

Prep Time: 10 mins

Cook Time: 10 mins

Total Time: 20 mins

Servings: 4

Ingredients:

- 4 cups of milk (dairy or plant-based)
- 1/2 cup of cornstarch
- 1/4 cup of granulated sugar
- 1 tsp rosewater (non-compulsory)
- Raspberry coulis (store-bought or homemade)

Instructions:

1. Whisk together the milk, cornstarch, and sugar in a saucepan up to completely blended.
2. Cook the Mixture, stirring constantly, over medium heat up to it thickens and begins to boil.
3. If used, stir in the rosewater.
4. Take out the pan from the heat and set aside to cool slightly.
5. Fill separate serving dishes or ramekins with the malabi.
6. Refrigerate the malabi for at least 2 hrs, or up to set.
7. Serve the malabi with a drizzle of raspberry coulis on top for a delicious and lovely flavor.

Nutrition (per serving):
Cals: 250 kcal, Fat: 8g, Carbs: 40g, Fiber: 1g, Protein: 6g

46.Israeli Date Honey Cake:

Prep Time: 15 mins

Cook Time: 50 mins

Total Time: 1 hr 5 mins

Servings: 10

Ingredients:
- 2 cups of all-purpose flour
- 1 tsp baking powder
- 1 tsp baking soda
- 1/2 tsp ground cinnamon
- 1/2 tsp ground ginger
- 1/2 tsp ground cloves
- 1/2 tsp salt
- 3/4 cup of date honey (silan)
- 1/2 cup of vegetable oil
- 1/2 cup of warm water
- 2 Big eggs
- 1 tsp vanilla extract

Instructions:
1. Preheat the oven to 180°C (350°F) and grease a 9x5-inch loaf pan with cooking spray.
2. Whisk together the all-purpose flour, baking powder, baking soda, ground cinnamon, ground ginger, ground cloves, and salt in a Big combining basin.
3. In a separate bowl, thoroughly combine the date honey, vegetable oil, warm water, eggs, and vanilla essence.
4. Gradually combine the wet and dry ingredients, combining up to the batter is smooth and no lumps remain.
5. Pour the batter into the loaf pan that has been oiled.
6. Bake for 45-50 mins in a preheated oven, or up to a toothpick inserted into the center comes out clean.
7. Let the date honey cake to cool for 10 mins in the pan before transferring it to a wire rack to cool fully.

Nutrition (per serving):
Cals: 300 kcal, Fat: 12g, Carbs: 45g, Fiber: 2g, Protein: 4g

47.Sabich Toast with Avocado and Pickles:

Prep Time: 10 mins

Cook Time: 5 mins

Total Time: 15 mins

Servings: 2

Ingredients:
- 4 slices of bread (such as pita or whole wheat bread)
- 1 ripe avocado, split
- 1 cup of Israeli salad (chop-up cucumber, tomato, and onion)
- 1/4 cup of pickles (split or whole)
- Tahini sauce (from the Tahini Sauce recipe above)

Instructions:
1. Toast the bread pieces till golden brown and crispy.
2. Place an avocado slice on every toast.
3. Serve with Israeli salad and pickles on top.
4. Drizzle the tahini sauce on top of the sabich toast.
5. Serve the sabich toast as an open-faced sandwich that is both tasty and filling.

Nutrition (per serving):
Cals: 350 kcal, Fat: 15g, Carbs: 45g, Fiber: 8g, Protein: 10g

48.Lachuch Sandwich with Labneh and Za'atar:

Prep Time: 15 mins

Cook Time: 15 mins

Total Time: 30 mins

Servings: 4

Ingredients:
- 1 batch of lachuch (Yemeni flatbread) - you can find the recipe above
- 1 cup of labneh (strained yogurt)
- Za'atar spice combine
- Fresh mint leaves
- Split cucumbers and tomatoes

Instructions:
1. Follow the steps in the recipe above to make the lachuch.
2. Spread labneh generously on every lachuch.
3. Sprinkle the labneh with the za'atar spice combine.
4. Garnish with fresh mint leaves, cucumber slices, and tomatoes.
5. Roll up the lachuch to make a tasty sandwich.
6. As a flavorful and filling supper, serve the lachuch sandwich.

Nutrition (per serving):
Cals: 300 kcal, Fat: 10g, Carbs: 40g, Fiber: 4g, Protein: 12g

49.Tahini Ice Cream with Halva Chunks:

Prep Time: 10 mins (+ chilling time for the ice cream base)

Cook Time: 20 mins (+ freezing time)

Total Time: 30 mins (+ chilling and freezing time)

Servings: 6

Ingredients:
- 2 cups of heavy cream
- 1 cup of whole milk
- 3/4 cup of granulated sugar

- 1/2 cup of tahini paste
- 1 tsp vanilla extract
- 1/2 cup of halva, chop-up into chunks (store-bought or homemade)

Instructions:

1. Heat the heavy cream, whole milk, and granulated sugar in a saucepan over medium heat. Stir up to the sugar is dissolved and the sauce is warm but not hot.
2. Take out the saucepan from the heat and set it aside to cool.
3. Combine in the tahini paste and vanilla extract up to thoroughly combined.
4. Cover the pot and place it in the refrigerator for at least 4 hrs or overnight to cold completely.
5. Pour the cold ice cream base into an ice cream machine and churn according to the manufacturer's directions.
6. Add the chop-up halva bits during the last few mins of churning and combine them into the ice cream.
7. Transfer the tahini ice cream with halva chunks to a freezer-safe container and freeze for at least 4 hrs, or up to the desired consistency is reveryed.
8. Tahini ice cream can be served in bowls or cones for a creamy and nutty treat.

Nutrition (per serving):
Cals: 400 kcal, Fat: 30g, Carbs: 30g, Fiber: 1g, Protein: 4g

50.Falafel Pita Bowl with Hummus and Tabouli:

Prep Time: 20 mins

Cook Time: 20 mins

Total Time: 40 mins

Servings: 4

Ingredients:

- 8 falafel patties (store-bought or homemade)
- 4 whole wheat pita bread, slice into wedges
- 1 cup of hummus (store-bought or homemade)
- 1 cup of tabouli salad (chop-up parsley, tomatoes, onions, and bulgur)
- Split cucumbers and radishes
- Lemon wedges for serving

Instructions:

1. Prepare the falafel patties as directed in the recipe above, or use store-bought falafel.
2. Toaster or bake the whole wheat pita bread.
3. Arrange the falafel patties, pita bread wedges, hummus, and tabouli salad on a wide serving dish in separate bowls or sections.

4. In a bowl, combine split cucumbers and radishes for added crunch and freshness.
5. Serve the falafel pita bowl with lemon wedges on the side to squeeze over the falafel and tabouli.

Nutrition (per serving):
Cals: 450 kcal, Fat: 20g, Carbs: 55g, Fiber: 8g, Protein: 15g

51.Israeli Cauliflower Rice with Pine Nuts and Currants:

Prep Time: 10 mins

Cook Time: 15 mins

Total Time: 25 mins

Servings: 4

Ingredients:

- 1 Big cauliflower head, riced (or use store-bought cauliflower rice)
- 1/4 cup of pine nuts
- 1/4 cup of currants
- 2 tbsp olive oil
- 2 cloves garlic, chop-up
- 1 tsp ground cumin
- Salt and pepper as needed
- Fresh parsley, chop-up, for garnish

Instructions:

1. Warm the olive oil in a Big skillet over medium heat.
2. Sauté the chop-up garlic up to fragrant.
3. Cook the cauliflower rice in the skillet for 5-7 mins, or up to it softens slightly.
4. Cook for an additional 3-4 mins, or up to the pine nuts and currants are lightly browned.
5. Season the cauliflower rice with cumin, salt, and pepper as needed.
6. Before serving, garnish with fresh parsley.

Nutrition (per serving):
Cals: 150 kcal, Fat: 10g, Carbs: 12g, Fiber: 4g, Protein: 3g

52.Stuffed Bell Peppers with Rice and Beef:

Prep Time: 20 mins

Cook Time: 1 hr

Total Time: 1 hr 20 mins

Servings: 6

Ingredients:

- 6 bell peppers (any color), tops take outd, and seeds take outd
- 1 cup of cooked rice (white or brown)
- 500g ground beef
- 1 onion, lightly chop-up

- 2 cloves garlic, chop-up
- 1 can (400g) diced tomatoes
- 1 tsp ground cumin
- 1 tsp ground paprika
- Salt and pepper as needed
- Fresh parsley, chop-up, for garnish

Instructions:

1. Preheat the oven to 180 Ds Celsius (350 Ds Fahrenheit) and butter a baking dish.
2. Cook the ground beef in a Big skillet over medium heat up to browned. Take out any extra fat.
3. Cook up to the onion is melted and the garlic is chop-up in the skillet.
4. Add the cooked rice, diced tomatoes, cumin, paprika, salt, and pepper as needed. Combine up to everything is well blended.
5. Fill every bell pepper halfway with the rice and meat Mixture.
6. Place the stuffed bell peppers in the baking dish that has been prepared.
7. Cover the dish with foil and bake for 40 mins in a preheated oven.
8. Bake for another 10-15 mins, or up to the bell peppers are soft and slightly browned on the edges.
9. Before serving, garnish with fresh parsley.

Nutrition (per serving):
Cals: 350 kcal, Fat: 15g, Carbs: 25g, Fiber: 4g, Protein: 25g

53. Shakshuka with Smoked Salmon and Dill:

Prep Time: 10 mins

Cook Time: 25 mins

Total Time: 35 mins

Servings: 4

Ingredients:

- 2 tbsp olive oil
- 1 onion, thinly split
- 2 cloves garlic, chop-up
- 2 bell peppers (any color), thinly split
- 1 tsp ground cumin
- 1 tsp ground paprika
- 1 can (400g) diced tomatoes
- 100g smoked salmon, torn into pieces
- 4-6 Big eggs
- Fresh dill, chop-up, for garnish
- Salt and pepper as needed

Instructions:

1. Heat the olive oil in a big skillet or frying pan over medium heat.

2. Cook up to the onions are transparent, about 5 mins.
3. Combine the chop-up garlic and thinly split bell peppers in a combining bowl. Cook for a few mins, or up to the peppers begin to soften.
4. Combine in the cumin and paprika powders. Cook for another min, or up to the Mixture is aromatic.
5. Pour in the diced tomatoes and cook for about 10-15 mins to enable the flavors to blend and the sauce to thicken slightly.
6. Gently fold in the smoked salmon chunks and combine to incorporate.
7. Make mini wells in the sauce and delicately place the eggs inside.
8. Cover the skillet and cook the shakshuka for 5-7 mins, or up to the eggs are cooked to your liking.
9. Before serving, garnish the shakshuka with chop-up fresh dill.

Nutrition (per serving):
Cals: 250 kcal, Fat: 15g, Carbs: 15g, Fiber: 4g, Protein: 15g

54. Challah French Toast with Maple Syrup:

Prep Time: 10 mins

Cook Time: 10 mins

Total Time: 20 mins

Servings: 4

Ingredients:

- 8 slices of challah bread
- 4 Big eggs
- 1 cup of milk (dairy or plant-based)
- 1 tsp ground cinnamon
- 1 tsp vanilla extract
- Butter or oil for cooking
- Maple syrup for serving

Instructions:

1. Whisk together the eggs, milk, ground cinnamon, and vanilla essence in a mini bowl.
2. Heat a little amount of butter or oil in a Big skillet or griddle over medium heat.
3. Dip every slice of challah bread into the egg Mixture, coating both sides thoroughly.
4. Cook the coated challah slices for 2-3 mins per side on a heated skillet or griddle, or up to golden brown and cooked through.
5. Serve the challah French toast warm, drizzled with maple syrup.

Nutrition (per serving):
Cals: 300 kcal, Fat: 10g, Carbs: 40g, Fiber: 2g, Protein: 10g

55. Kibbeh Soup with Lemon and Mint:

Prep Time: 20 mins

Cook Time: 30 mins

Total Time: 50 mins

Servings: 6

Ingredients:

- 500g ground beef or lamb
- 1 cup of fine bulgur
- 1 onion, lightly chop-up
- 2 tbsp olive oil
- 2 tsp ground cumin
- 1 tsp ground cinnamon
- 1/2 tsp ground allspice
- 2 liters beef or vegetable broth
- Juice of 1 lemon
- Fresh mint leaves, chop-up, for garnish
- Salt and pepper as needed

Instructions:

1. Combine the ground beef or lamb, fine bulgur, lightly diced onion, ground cumin, ground cinnamon, ground allspice, salt, and pepper in a Big combining bowl.
2. Knead the dough with your hands up to it is smooth and homogeneous.
3. Make little walnut-sized balls or ovals out of the kibbeh dough.
4. Warm the olive oil in a big pot over medium heat.
5. Sauté the kibbeh balls in the pot up to they are browned on all sides.
6. Bring the beef or vegetable broth to a simmer in the pot.
7. Let the kibbeh soup to boil for 20-25 mins, or up to the kibbeh balls are cooked through and the flavors have combined.
8. Season with salt and pepper as needed after adding the lemon juice.
9. Before serving, garnish the kibbeh soup with chop-up fresh mint.

Nutrition (per serving):
Cals: 350 kcal, Fat: 15g, Carbs: 25g, Fiber: 4g, Protein: 25g

56.Israeli Shakshuka Bagel Sandwich:

Prep Time: 10 mins

Cook Time: 20 mins

Total Time: 30 mins

Servings: 4

Ingredients:

- 4 bagels, split in half
- 1 batch of shakshuka (use the Shakshuka with Smoked Salmon and Dill recipe above)
- 4 slices of smoked salmon

- Fresh dill, for garnish

Instructions:

1. Follow the directions in the recipe above to make the shakshuka.
2. Toast the bagel slices till golden brown and crispy.
3. Scoop shakshuka onto the bottom half of every bagel.
4. Garnish with fresh dill and a sliver of smoked salmon.
5. Cover the sandwich with the bagel's top half.
6. Serve the Israeli shakshuka bagel sandwich as a filling and satisfying supper.

Nutrition (per serving):
Cals: 400 kcal, Fat: 15g

Carbs: 45g, Fiber: 4g, Protein: 20g

57.Bourekas with Sweet Potato and Caramelized Onions:

Prep Time: 30 mins

Cook Time: 30 mins

Total Time: 1 hr

Servings: 8

Ingredients:

- 1 box/pkg puff pastry sheets (store-bought or homemade)
- 2 cups of cooked sweet potatoes, mashed
- 1 Big onion, thinly split
- 2 tbsp olive oil
- 1 tbsp balsamic vinegar
- Salt and pepper as needed
- 1 egg, beaten (for egg wash)

Instructions:

1. Preheat the oven to 200 Ds Celsius (400 Ds Fahrenheit) and line a baking sheet with parchment paper.
2. Warm the olive oil in a Big skillet over medium heat.
3. Cook the thinly split onions up to they are caramelized and golden brown.
4. Season with salt and pepper after adding the balsamic vinegar. Cook for 1 min more.

5. On a floured board, roll out the puff pastry sheets and slice them into squares or rectangles, depending on your preference.
6. Fill every pastry square with a dollop of mashed sweet potatoes and caramelized onions.
7. Fold the pastry over the filling to make a triangle

or rectangle shape, then seal the edges with a fork.

8. Place the bourekas on the baking sheet that has been prepared.
9. For a golden finish, brush the tops of the bourekas with beaten egg.
10. Bake for 20-25 mins, or up to the bourekas are puffy and golden brown in a preheated oven.

Nutrition (per serving):
Cals: 250 kcal, Fat: 10g, Carbs: 35g, Fiber: 2g, Protein: 5g

58.Israeli Tomato Salad with Fresh Herbs:

Prep Time: 10 mins

Cook Time: None

Total Time: 10 mins

Servings: 4

Ingredients:
- 4 Big tomatoes, diced
- 1 cucumber, diced
- 1/2 red onion, thinly split
- 1/4 cup of fresh parsley, chop-up
- 1/4 cup of fresh mint, chop-up
- 2 tbsp olive oil
- 1 tbsp lemon juice
- Salt and pepper as needed

Instructions:
1. Combine the diced tomatoes, diced cucumber, thinly split red onion, chop-up fresh parsley, and chop-up fresh mint in a Big combining dish.
2. Drizzle the salad with olive oil and lemon juice.
3. Season as needed with salt and pepper.
4. Toss the salad with the dressing up to it is equally distributed.
5. As a pleasant and tasty side dish, serve the Israeli tomato salad.

Nutrition (per serving):
Cals: 100 kcal, Fat: 7g, Carbs: 10g, Fiber: 3g, Protein: 2g

59.Rugelach with Raspberry Jam and Almonds:

Prep Time: 20 mins

Cook Time: 25 mins

Total Time: 45 mins

Servings: 12

Ingredients:
- 2 cups of all-purpose flour
- 1/4 cup of granulated sugar
- 1 cup of unsalted butter, chilled and cubed
- 1 tsp vanilla extract

- 1/2 cup of raspberry jam
- 1/2 cup of chop-up almonds
- Powdered sugar for dusting

Instructions:
1. In a Big combining bowl, combine the all-purpose flour and granulated sugar.
2. To the flour Mixture, add the cold and diced butter.
3. Work the butter into the flour with your hands or a pastry sliceter up to the Mixture resembles coarse crumbs.
4. Knead the dough up to it comes together after adding the vanilla essence.
5. Divide the dough into two equal parts and roll every into a ball.
6. Refrigerate for at least 30 mins after flattening every dough ball into a disc and wrapping it in plastic wrap.
7. Preheat the oven to 180 Ds Celsius (350 Ds Fahrenheit) and line a baking sheet with parchment paper.
8. Roll out one of the cold dough discs into a circle approximately 1/8 inch thick on a floured surface.
9. Half of the raspberry jam Must be equally distributed over the rolled-out dough.
10. Half of the chop-up almonds Must be sprinkled on top of the raspberry jam.
11. Slice the dough circle into 6-8 triangular wedges with a pizza sliceter or knife.
12. Roll up every wedge to form a rugelach shape, beginning at the widest end.
13. Place the rugelach on the baking sheet that has been prepared.
14. Steps 8–13 are repeated with the second cold dough disc, remaining raspberry jam, and chop-up almonds.
15. Rugelach Must be baked in a preheated oven for 20-25 mins, or up to golden brown.
16. Let the rugelach to cool on a wire rack before dusting with powdered sugar and serving.

Nutrition (per serving):
Cals: 300 kcal, Fat: 20g, Carbs: 25g, Fiber: 1g, Protein: 4g

60.Knafeh with Ricotta and Pistachio Topping:

Prep Time: 30 mins

Cook Time: 30 mins

Total Time: 1 hr

Servings: 8

- 1 box/pkg of kataifi dough (shredded phyllo dough, thawed)
- 1 cup of unsalted butter, dilute
- 2 cups of ricotta cheese
- 1 cup of granulated sugar
- 1 tsp orange blossom water
- 1 cup of pistachios, chop-up
- 1/2 cup of simple syrup (combine equal parts water and sugar, bring to a boil up to sugar dissolves)

Instructions:

1. Preheat the oven to 180°C (350°F) and coat a 9x13-inch baking dish with cooking spray.
2. Separate the strands of kataifi dough with your fingertips.
3. Half of the kataifi dough Must be placed in the greased baking dish and pressed down to produce a uniform layer.
4. Pour the dilute butter over the kataifi dough to fully coat it.
5. In a combining bowl, combine the ricotta cheese, granulated sugar, and orange blossom water.
6. Over the buttered kataifi dough layer, spread the ricotta Mixture.
7. Sprinkle the chop-up pistachios over the ricotta layer evenly.
8. Gently press the remaining half of the kataifi dough over the ricotta and pistachio layer.
9. Drizzle the remaining dilute butter over the kataifi dough layer.
10. Bake for approximately 30 mins, or up to the knafeh is golden brown and crispy.
11. Take out the knafeh from the oven and drizzle with the simple syrup while it is still warm.
12. Let the knafeh to cool for a few mins before Cuttingit into squares or diamonds.
13. Top the knafeh with a sprinkle of chop-up pistachios.

Nutrition (per serving):
Cals: 400 kcal, Fat: 25g, Carbs: 35g, Fiber: 2g, Protein: 10g

61.Hummus Bowl with Roasted Vegetables and Quinoa:

Prep Time: 15 mins

Cook Time: 30 mins

Total Time: 45 mins

Servings: 4

Ingredients:

- 1 cup of cooked quinoa
- 2 cups of cooked chickpeas (canned or homemade)
- 1/4 cup of tahini paste
- 2 cloves garlic, chop-up
- Juice of 1 lemon
- 1/4 cup of water (or more for desired consistency)
- Salt and pepper as needed
- 2 cups of combined roasted vegetables (such as bell peppers, zucchini, and eggplant)
- Fresh parsley, chop-up, for garnish
- Olive oil for drizzling

Instructions:

1. Combine the cooked chickpeas, tahini paste, chop-up garlic, lemon juice, water, salt, and pepper in a blender or mixer.
2. Blend up to the Mixture is smooth and creamy. If necessary, adjust the consistency by adding more water.
3. Arrange a bed of cooked quinoa in a serving bowl.
4. Spread the quinoa with the creamy hummus.
5. Add the roasted vegetables to the hummus bowl.
6. Before serving, garnish with chop-up fresh parsley and drizzle with olive oil.

Nutrition (per serving):
Cals: 400 kcal, Fat: 15g, Carbs: 50g, Fiber: 10g, Protein: 15g

62.Sabich Bagel with Eggplant and Pickled Vegetables:

Prep Time: 20 mins

Cook Time: 20 mins

Total Time: 40 mins

Servings: 4

Ingredients:

- 4 bagels, split in half
- 2 Big eggplants, split
- 1 cup of hummus (store-bought or homemade)
- 1 cup of Israeli salad (diced cucumbers, tomatoes, and onions)
- 1/2 cup of pickled vegetables (such as pickles or pickled turnips)
- Tahini sauce for drizzling
- Fresh parsley, chop-up, for garnish

Instructions:

1. Preheat the oven to 200 Ds Celsius (400 Ds Fahrenheit) and line a baking sheet with parchment paper.
2. Drizzle olive oil over the split eggplants on the

baking sheet. Season with salt and pepper as needed.

3. Cook the eggplants in a warm oven for 15-20 mins, or up to tender and slightly browned.
4. Toast the bagel slices till golden brown and crispy.
5. Spread hummus generously over the bottom half of every bagel.
6. Add the roasted eggplant slices, Israeli salad, and pickled vegetables on the top.
7. Drizzle the tahini sauce over the toppings and top with fresh parsley.
8. Cover the sandwich with the bagel's top half.
9. As a delectable and savory meal, serve the Sabich bagel.

Nutrition (per serving):
Cals: 450 kcal, Fat: 15g, Carbs: 65g, Fiber: 8g, Protein: 12g

63.Lachuch with Labneh and Za'atar:

Prep Time: 10 mins

Cook Time: 20 mins

Total Time: 30 mins

Servings: 4

Ingredients:
- 2 cups of all-purpose flour
- 1 packet (7g) active dry yeast
- 1 tsp sugar
- 1 tsp salt
- 1 1/2 cups of warm water
- 1/4 cup of vegetable oil
- Labneh (strained yogurt) for serving
- Za'atar seasoning for sprinkling

Instructions:
1. Combine the all-purpose flour, active dry yeast, sugar, and salt in a Big combining basin.
2. Add the warm water and vegetable oil to the dry ingredients gradually, kneading the dough up to smooth and elastic.
3. Cover the basin with a moist cloth and set aside for 1 hr, or up to the dough has doubled in size.
4. Preheat a griddle or nonstick skillet over medium heat.
5. On a floured surface, flatten a part of the dough into a round pancake form.
6. Cook for about 2-3 mins on every side, or up to the lachuch puffs up and has golden brown spots, in a hot skillet.
7. Steps 5 and 6 Must be repeated with the remaining dough halves.
8. Serve the lachuch warm, topped with a big dollop of labneh.

9. To add flavor, sprinkle Za'atar seasoning over the labneh.

Nutrition (per serving):
Cals: 300 kcal, Fat: 10g, Carbs: 45g, Fiber: 2g, Protein: 8g

64.Israeli Rice Pudding with Cinnamon and Raisins:

Prep Time: 5 mins

Cook Time: 25 mins

Total Time: 30 mins

Servings: 6

Ingredients:
- 1 cup of Arborio rice
- 4 cups of whole milk
- 1/2 cup of granulated sugar
- 1 tsp ground cinnamon
- 1/2 cup of raisins
- 1 tsp vanilla extract
- Ground cinnamon for garnish

Instructions:
1. Combine the Arborio rice, whole milk, granulated sugar, and ground cinnamon in a Big pot.
2. Bring the Mixture to a boil over medium heat while constantly stirring.
3. Reduce the heat to low and continue to cook the rice pudding for 20-25 mins, or up to the rice is soft and the pudding thickens.
4. Cook for another 2-3 mins after adding the raisins and vanilla extract.
5. Take out the rice pudding from the heat and set aside to cool.
6. Serve the Israeli rice pudding warm or chilled, topped with ground cinnamon.

Nutrition (per serving):
Cals: 300 kcal, Fat: 6g, Carbs: 55g, Fiber: 1g, Protein: 8g

65.Falafel Plate with Israeli Salad and Tahini Sauce:

- Prep Time: 20 mins
- Cook Time: 20 mins
- Total Time: 40 mins
- Servings: 4

Ingredients:
- 16 falafel patties (store-bought or homemade)
- 2 cups of cooked quinoa or rice
- 2 cups of Israeli salad (diced cucumbers, tomatoes, and onions)
- 1/2 cup of hummus (store-bought or homemade)

- Tahini sauce for drizzling
- Fresh parsley, chop-up, for garnish

Instructions:

1. Prepare the falafel patties as directed in the recipe above, or use store-bought falafel.
2. Follow the box/pkg directions for cooking the quinoa or rice.
3. On a Big serving tray, arrange the cooked quinoa or rice, falafel patties, and Israeli salad.
4. Serve the falafel plate with hummus and tahini sauce on the side.
5. Before serving, garnish with fresh parsley.

Nutrition (per serving):

Cals: 400 kcal, Fat: 15g, Carbs: 55g, Fiber: 8g, Protein: 15g

66.Shakshuka with Chard and Goat Cheese:

Prep Time: 10 mins

Cook Time: 30 mins

Total Time: 40 mins

Servings: 4

Ingredients:

- 2 tbsp olive oil
- 1 onion, thinly split
- 2 cloves garlic, chop-up
- 1 red bell pepper, thinly split
- 1 yellow bell pepper, thinly split
- 1 bunch Swiss chard, chop-up (take out tough stems)
- 1 can (400g) diced tomatoes
- 1 tsp ground cumin
- 1 tsp ground paprika
- Salt and pepper as needed
- 100g goat cheese, cut up
- Fresh parsley, chop-up, for garnish

Instructions:

1. Heat the olive oil in a big skillet or frying pan over medium heat.
2. Cook up to the onions are transparent, about 5 mins.
3. Combine the chop-up garlic and split bell peppers in a combining bowl. Cook for a few mins, or up to the peppers begin to soften.
4. Cook the chop-up Swiss chard in the skillet up to it wilts.
5. Pour in the diced tomatoes and cook for about 10-15 mins to enable the flavors to blend and the sauce to thicken slightly.
6. Shakshuka Must be seasoned with cumin, paprika, salt, and pepper.
7. Make mini wells in the sauce and delicately place the eggs inside.

8. Cover the skillet and cook the shakshuka for 5-7 mins, or up to the eggs are cooked to your liking.
9. Before serving, top the shakshuka with cut up goat cheese and sprinkle with chop-up fresh parsley.

Nutrition (per serving):

Cals: 300 kcal, Fat: 15g, Carbs: 25g, Fiber: 6g, Protein: 12g

67.Bourekas with Mushroom and Onion Filling:

Prep Time: 30 mins

Cook Time: 25 mins

Total Time: 55 mins

Servings: 8

Ingredients:

- 1 box/pkg puff pastry sheets (store-bought or homemade)
- 2 cups of split mushrooms
- 1 Big onion, lightly chop-up
- 2 tbsp olive oil
- 1 tsp dried thyme
- Salt and pepper as needed
- 1 egg, beaten (for egg wash)

Instructions:

1. Preheat the oven to 180 Ds Celsius (350 Ds Fahrenheit) and line a baking sheet with parchment paper.
2. Warm the olive oil in a Big skillet over medium heat.
3. Cook up to the onion is transparent, about 5 mins.
4. Incorporate the split mushrooms and dried thyme. Cook, stirring occasionally, up to the mushrooms are cooked and any excess moisture has gone.
5. Season the mushroom and onion filling as needed with salt and pepper.
6. On a floured board, roll out the puff pastry sheets and slice them into squares or rectangles, depending on your preference.
7. Fill every pastry square with a dollop of the mushroom and onion filling.
8. Fold the pastry over the filling to make a triangle or rectangle shape, then seal the edges with a fork.
9. Place the bourekas on the baking sheet that has been prepared.
10. For a golden finish, brush the tops of the bourekas with beaten egg.
11. Bake for 20-25 mins, or up to puffed and golden brown, in a preheated oven.

Nutrition (per serving):
Cals: 250 kcal, Fat: 15g, Carbs: 25g, Fiber: 2g, Protein: 5g

68.Israeli Shakshuka Omelette:

Prep Time: 10 mins

Cook Time: 15 mins

Total Time: 25 mins

Servings: 2

Ingredients:

- 4 Big eggs
- 1 tbsp olive oil
- 1/2 onion, lightly chop-up
- 1 red bell pepper, diced
- 1 can (400g) diced tomatoes
- 1 tsp ground cumin
- 1 tsp ground paprika
- Salt and pepper as needed
- Fresh parsley, chop-up, for garnish

Instructions:

1. In a combining basin, blend the eggs up to well incorporated.
2. Heat the olive oil in a nonstick skillet or frying pan over medium heat.
3. Cook the lightly chop-up onions up to they are transparent.
4. Cook up to the red bell peppers soften, about 5 mins.
5. Pour the beaten eggs over the veggies and simmer for a few mins, stirring occasionally, up to the edges set.
6. Cover one side of the omelette with diced tomatoes.
7. Sprinkle the tomatoes with cumin, paprika, salt, and pepper.
8. To cover the tomatoes and seasonings, fold the omelette in half.
9. Cook for 1 min more, or up to the omelette is thoroughly cooked and the flavors have melded.
10. Before serving, garnish with fresh parsley.

Nutrition (per serving):
Cals: 300 kcal, Fat: 20g, Carbs: 10g, Fiber: 2g, Protein: 15g

69.Tahini Energy Bites with Dates and Almonds:

Prep Time: 15 mins

Cook Time: None

Total Time: 15 mins

Servings: 12

Ingredients:

- 1 cup of dates, pitted
- 1/2 cup of tahini paste
- 1/2 cup of almond meal
- 1/4 cup of shredded coconut (non-compulsory)
- 1 tsp vanilla extract
- Pinch of salt
- Additional shredded coconut for coating

Instructions:

1. Blend the pitted dates, tahini paste, almond meal, shredded coconut (if using), vanilla essence, and a pinch of salt in a mixer up to the Mixture resembles a sticky dough.
2. Roll out mini amounts of the dough into bite-sized balls.
3. To coat the energy bites, roll them in shredded coconut.
4. Refrigerate the tahini energy bites for at least 30 mins in an airtight container to firm up.

Nutrition (per serving - 1 energy bite):
Cals: 100 kcal, Fat: 6g, Carbs: 10g, Fiber: 2g, Protein: 3g

70.Israeli Stuffed Cabbage Rolls with Beef and Rice:

Prep Time: 30 mins

Cook Time: 1 hr

Total Time: 1 hr and 30 mins

Servings: 6

Ingredients:

- 12 Big cabbage leaves
- 500g ground beef
- 1 cup of cooked rice
- 1 onion, lightly chop-up
- 2 cloves garlic, chop-up
- 1 tsp ground cumin
- 1 tsp ground paprika
- 1 can (400g) diced tomatoes
- 1 cup of beef or vegetable broth
- Salt and pepper as needed
- Fresh parsley, chop-up, for garnish

Instructions:

1. Bring a Big pot of water to a boil and blanch the cabbage leaves for a few mins, or up to they soften. Set aside after draining.
2. Combine the ground beef, cooked rice, lightly diced onion, chop-up garlic, ground cumin, ground paprika, salt, and pepper in a combining bowl.
3. Place a spoonful of the beef and rice Mixture in the center of every cabbage leaf.

4. Tuck the sides of the cabbage leaf in to contain the filling.
5. Steps 3 and 4 Must be repeated with the remaining cabbage leaves and filling.
6. Place the stuffed cabbage rolls in a single layer in a big saucepan.
7. Over the cabbage rolls, pour the diced tomatoes and beef or vegetable broth.
8. Cover the pot and cook the cabbage rolls for 45 mins to an hr, or up to tender and the flavors have melded together.
9. Before serving, garnish with fresh parsley.

Nutrition (per serving - 2 cabbage rolls):
Cals: 350 kcal, Fat: 15g, Carbs: 25g, Fiber: 4g, Protein: 25g

71.Kibbeh Kofta with Yogurt Sauce:

Prep Time: 30 mins

Cook Time: 25 mins

Total Time: 55 mins

Servings: 6

Ingredients:

- 500g ground lamb or beef
- 1 cup of fine bulgur
- 1 onion, lightly chop-up
- 2 tbsp pine nuts
- 2 tbsp olive oil
- 1 tsp ground allspice
- 1 tsp ground cinnamon
- Salt and pepper as needed
- Fresh mint leaves, chop-up, for garnish
- For the yogurt sauce:
- 1 cup of Greek yogurt
- 2 tbsp fresh lemon juice
- 1 clove garlic, chop-up
- Salt and pepper as needed

Instructions:

1. Combine the ground lamb or beef, fine bulgur, lightly diced onion, ground allspice, ground cinnamon, salt, and pepper in a Big combining bowl.
2. Knead the dough with your hands up to it is smooth and homogeneous.
3. Shape a part of the kibbeh kofta dough into a tiny oval or torpedo shape.
4. Warm the olive oil in a pan over medium heat.
5. Cook up to the kibbeh kofta is browned on both sides and cooked thoroughly in the skillet.
6. Lightly roast the pine nuts in a separate pan up to golden brown.

7. To make the yogurt sauce, combine the Greek yogurt, fresh lemon juice, chop-up garlic, salt, and pepper in a mini bowl.
8. Arrange the kibbeh kofta on a serving plate and top with toasted pine nuts and chop-up fresh mint.
9. Serve the kibbeh kofta with the yogurt sauce for a delicious and filling meal.

Nutrition (per serving - 3 kofta):
Cals: 400 kcal, Fat: 25g, Carbs: 15g, Fiber: 2g, Protein: 30g

72.Israeli Breakfast Burrito with Eggs and Hummus:

Prep Time: 10 mins

Cook Time: 10 mins

Total Time: 20 mins

Servings: 2

Ingredients:

- 4 Big eggs
- 2 Big tortillas or wraps
- 1/2 cup of hummus (store-bought or homemade)
- 1 cup of baby spinach leaves
- 1/2 cup of diced tomatoes
- 1/4 cup of diced cucumbers
- Salt and pepper as needed
- Hot sauce or sriracha (non-compulsory, for added spice)

Instructions:

1. Whisk the eggs in a combining dish and season with salt and pepper.
2. Scramble the eggs in a nonstick skillet over medium heat up to they are done to your liking.
3. Microwave or cook the tortillas or wraps on a skillet.
4. Spread hummus generously on every tortilla.
5. Scrambled eggs, baby spinach, chop-up tomatoes, and diced cucumbers Must be layered on top of the hummus.
6. If you like it hot, add some hot sauce or sriracha.
7. Roll the tortillas into burritos, tucking in the sides to keep the filling within.
8. Serve the Israeli breakfast burritos as a filling and nutritious breakfast.

Nutrition (per serving):
Cals: 400 kcal, Fat: 20g, Carbs: 30g, Fiber: 5g, Protein: 22g

73.Rugelach with Poppy Seed Filling:

Prep Time: 30 mins

Cook Time: 20 mins

Total Time: 50 mins

Servings: 16

Ingredients:

- 2 cups of all-purpose flour
- 1/4 cup of granulated sugar
- 1/2 tsp salt
- 1 cup of unsalted butter, chilled and cubed
- 1 cup of cream cheese, chilled and cubed
- 1 tsp vanilla extract
- 1/2 cup of poppy seed filling (store-bought or homemade)
- 1/4 cup of apricot jam (or any jam of your choice)
- Powdered sugar for dusting

Instructions:

1. In a Big combining basin, combine the all-purpose flour, granulated sugar, and salt.
2. To the flour Mixture, add the cooled and diced butter and cream cheese.
3. Work the butter and cream cheese into the flour with your hands or a pastry sliceter up to the Mixture resembles coarse crumbs.
4. Knead the dough up to it comes together after adding the vanilla essence.
5. Divide the dough into two equal parts and roll every into a ball.
6. Refrigerate for at least 30 mins after flattening every dough ball into a disc and wrapping it in plastic wrap.
7. Preheat the oven to 180 Ds Celsius (350 Ds Fahrenheit) and line a baking sheet with parchment paper.
8. Roll out one of the cold dough discs into a circle approximately 1/8 inch thick on a floured surface.
9. Half of the poppy seed filling Must be equally distributed over the rolled-out dough.
10. Slice the dough circle into 8 triangular wedges with a knife or pizza sliceter.
11. Roll up every wedge to form a rugelach shape, beginning at the widest end.
12. Place the rugelach on the baking sheet that has been prepared.
13. Steps 8–12 are repeated with the second cold dough disc and the leftover poppy seed filling.
14. Rugelach Must be baked in a preheated oven for about 20 mins, or up to golden brown.
15. Brush the rugelach with apricot jam to glaze while they are still warm.
16. Let the rugelach to cool on a wire rack before dusting with powdered sugar and serving.

Nutrition (per serving):

Cals: 250 kcal, mFat: 15g, Carbs: 25g, Fiber: 1g, Protein: 3g

74.Bamba Cheesecake with Peanut Butter Crust:

Prep Time: 20 mins

Cook Time: 50 mins

Total Time: 1 hr and 10 mins

Servings: 8

Ingredients:

- For the crust:
- 1 1/2 cups of crushed Bamba peanut snacks
- 1/4 cup of unsalted butter, dilute
- 2 tbsp granulated sugar
- For the cheesecake filling:
- 500g cream cheese, melted
- 1/2 cup of granulated sugar
- 2 Big eggs
- 1 tsp vanilla extract
- 1/2 cup of smooth peanut butter
- 1/4 cup of heavy cream
- 1/4 cup of all-purpose flour

Instructions:

1. Preheat the oven to 160°C (325°F) and oil a 9-inch springform pan with cooking spray.
2. For the crust, combine the crushed Bamba peanut snacks, dilute unsalted butter, and granulated sugar in a combining dish.
3. To get a uniform layer, press the crust Mixture into the bottom of an oiled springform pan.
4. Separately, in a Big combining basin, combine the melted cream cheese and granulated sugar up to smooth and creamy.
5. Add the eggs one at a time, beating thoroughly after every addition.
6. Combine the vanilla extract, smooth peanut butter, heavy cream, and all-purpose flour.
7. Pour the cheesecake filling into the springform pan over the crust.
8. Using a spatula, smooth the top of the cheesecake.
9. Bake the Bamba cheesecake for 50 mins, or up to the sides are set and the center is slightly jiggly, in a warmed oven.
10. Turn off the oven and leave the cheesecake in there for about 1 hr, with the door slightly ajar.
11. Take out the cheesecake from the oven and place it in the refrigerator to chill and set for at least 4 hrs or overnight.
12. Serve the Bamba cheesecake split with whipped cream or drizzled with chocolate sauce.

Nutrition (per serving):

Cals: 500 kcal. Fat: 35g. Carbs: 35g, Fiber: 2g, Protein: 10g

75. Sabich Bowl with Quinoa and Tahini Dressing:

Prep Time: 15 mins

Cook Time: 20 mins

Total Time: 35 mins

Servings: 4

Ingredients:

- 1 cup of quinoa
- 2 cups of water
- 2 cups of cooked chickpeas (canned or homemade)
- 2 Big eggplants, split
- 2 tbsp olive oil
- 1 tsp ground cumin
- 1 tsp ground paprika
- Salt and pepper as needed
- 1 cup of Israeli salad (diced cucumbers, tomatoes, and onions)
- 1/2 cup of pickled vegetables (such as pickles or pickled turnips)
- Tahini dressing (see below)
- Fresh parsley, chop-up, for garnish
- Tahini Dressing:
- 1/4 cup of tahini paste
- Juice of 1 lemon
- 1 clove garlic, chop-up
- 1/4 cup of water (or more for desired consistency)
- Salt and pepper as needed

Instructions:

1. In a fine-mesh strainer, rinse the quinoa under cold water.
2. Bring the quinoa and water to a boil in a saucepan. Reduce the heat to low, cover, and cook for 15-20 mins, or up to the quinoa is tender and the water has been absorbed.
3. Preheat the oven to 200°C (400°F) and line a baking sheet with parchment paper in the meantime.
4. Drizzle olive oil over the split eggplants on the baking sheet. Season with cumin, paprika, salt, and pepper as needed.
5. Cook the eggplants in a warm oven for 15-20 mins, or up to tender and slightly browned.
6. To create the tahini dressing, combine the tahini paste, lemon juice, chop-up garlic, water, salt, and pepper in a combining bowl and whisk up to smooth and creamy. If necessary, adjust the consistency by adding more water.
7. Layer the cooked quinoa, cooked chickpeas, roasted eggplants, Israeli salad, and pickled vegetables in the Sabich bowls.
8. Drizzle the tahini dressing over the tops of the bowls.
9. Before serving, garnish the Sabich dishes with chop-up fresh parsley.

Nutrition (per serving):

Cals: 400 kcal, Fat: 15g, Carbs: 50g, Fiber: 10g, Protein: 15g

76. Lachuch with Honey and Butter:

Prep Time: 10 mins

Cook Time: 15 mins

Total Time: 25 mins

Servings: 4

Ingredients:

- 2 cups of all-purpose flour
- 1 packet (7g) active dry yeast
- 1 tsp sugar
- 1 tsp salt
- 1 1/2 cups of warm water
- 2 tbsp unsalted butter, dilute
- 2 tbsp honey
- Powdered sugar for dusting

Instructions:

1. Combine the all-purpose flour, active dry yeast, sugar, and salt in a Big combining basin.
2. Add the warm water gradually to the dry ingredients and knead the dough up to smooth and elastic.
3. Cover the basin with a moist cloth and set aside for 1 hr, or up to the dough has doubled in size.
4. Melt 1 tbsp unsalted butter in a nonstick skillet or griddle over medium heat.
5. On a floured surface, flatten a part of the dough into a round pancake form.
6. Cook for about 2-3 mins on every side, or up to the lachuch puffs up and has golden brown spots, in a hot skillet.
7. Steps 5 and 6 Must be repeated with the remaining dough halves.
8. Brush the lachuch with dilute butter and drizzle with honey while it is still warm.
9. Before serving, dust the lachuch with powdered sugar.

Nutrition (per serving):

Cals: 300 kcal, Fat: 6g, Carbs: 55g, Fiber: 2g, Protein: 6g

77. Malabi with Mango and Coconut Flakes:

Prep Time: 10 mins

Cook Time: 10 mins

Total Time: 20 mins

Servings: 4

Ingredients:

- 1/2 cup of cornstarch
- 3 cups of coconut milk
- 1/4 cup of granulated sugar
- 1 tsp rosewater (non-compulsory)
- 1 ripe mango, diced
- 1/4 cup of coconut flakes

Instructions:

1. To make a smooth paste, combine the cornstarch and 1/2 cup of coconut milk in a mini bowl. Place aside.
2. Heat the remaining coconut milk in a saucepan over medium heat. Stir in the granulated sugar up to it melts.
3. Stir in the cornstarch paste and simmer, stirring constantly, up to the sauce thickens and boils.
4. Take out the saucepan from the heat and, if using, whisk in the rosewater.
5. Let the malabi Mixture to cool to room temperature in individual serving bowls or glasses.
6. Refrigerate the malabi for at least 2 hrs, or up to it hardens and sets.
7. Before serving, top the malabi with diced mango and sprinkle with coconut flakes.

Nutrition (per serving):
Cals: 250 kcal, Fat: 15g, Carbs: 25g, Fiber: 2g, Protein: 2g

78.Israeli Shakshuka Frittata:

Prep Time: 15 mins

Cook Time: 25 mins

Total Time: 40 mins

Servings: 4

Ingredients:

- 8 Big eggs
- 1 tbsp olive oil
- 1 onion, lightly chop-up
- 1 red bell pepper, diced
- 2 cloves garlic, chop-up
- 1 can (400g) diced tomatoes
- 1 tsp ground cumin
- 1 tsp ground paprika
- Salt and pepper as needed
- Fresh parsley, chop-up, for garnish

Instructions:

1. Preheat the oven to 180 Ds Celsius (350 Ds Fahrenheit).
2. Warm the olive oil in a Big oven-safe skillet or frying pan over medium heat.
3. Cook the lightly chop-up onions up to they are transparent.
4. Cook up to the red bell peppers soften, about 5 mins.
5. Cook for another min after adding the chop-up garlic.
6. Pour in the diced tomatoes and cook for about 10 mins to enable the flavors to blend and the sauce to thicken slightly.
7. Season the shakshuka with cumin, paprika, salt, and pepper as needed.
8. In a separate dish, whisk together the eggs up to well blended.
9. Make sure the beaten eggs are properly distributed over the shakshuka Mixture in the skillet.
10. Bake for about 15 mins, or up to the frittata is set and slightly brown on top, in a preheated oven.
11. Before serving, garnish the Israeli shakshuka frittata with chop-up fresh parsley.

Nutrition (per serving):
Cals: 250 kcal, Fat: 15g, Carbs: 10g, Fiber: 2g, Protein: 18g

79.Tahini Glazed Carrots with Sesame Seeds:

Prep Time: 10 mins

Cook Time: 15 mins

Total Time: 25 mins

Servings: 4

Ingredients:

- 8 Big carrots, peel off and split into thin sticks
- 2 tbsp tahini paste
- 2 tbsp honey
- 1 tbsp lemon juice
- 2 tbsp water
- 1 tbsp olive oil
- 2 tbsp sesame seeds
- Salt and pepper as needed
- Fresh parsley, chop-up, for garnish

Instructions:

1. Steam the split carrots in a steamer or a saucepan with a steamer basket up to cooked but still somewhat crunchy.
2. To make a smooth glaze, whisk together the tahini paste, honey, lemon juice, and water in a mini bowl.

3. Heat the olive oil in a separate nonstick skillet over medium heat.
4. Add the steamed carrots to the skillet and cook for a few mins, or up to they begin to brown.
5. Toss the carrots in the tahini glaze to coat them evenly.
6. Cook for another min, stirring constantly, up to the sauce thickens slightly and coats the carrots.
7. Season as needed with salt and pepper.
8. Before serving, garnish the tahini-glazed carrots with chop-up fresh parsley.

Nutrition (per serving):
Cals: 150 kcal, Fat: 8g, Carbs: 18g, Fiber: 5g, Protein: 3g

80.Falafel Wraps with Hummus and Tahini Sauce:

Prep Time: 30 mins

Cook Time: 15 mins

Total Time: 45 mins

Servings: 4

Ingredients:
- 8 falafel patties (store-bought or homemade)
- 4 Big tortillas or wraps
- 1 cup of hummus (store-bought or homemade)
- 1/2 cup of tahini sauce (store-bought or homemade)
- 1 cup of shredded lettuce
- 1/2 cup of diced tomatoes
- 1/4 cup of diced cucumbers
- Fresh parsley, chop-up, for garnish

Instructions:
1. If using store-bought falafel patties, warm them according to box/pkg directions.
2. Microwave or cook the tortillas or wraps on a skillet.
3. Spread hummus and tahini sauce generously on every tortilla or wrap.
4. On every tortilla, place two falafel patties.
5. On top of the falafel, layer shredded lettuce, split tomatoes, and diced cucumbers.
6. Wrap the tortillas, tucking in the sides to surround the filling.
7. Before serving, garnish the falafel wrappers with chop-up fresh parsley.

Nutrition (per serving):
Cals: 400 kcal, Fat: 20g, Carbs: 40g, Fiber: 6g, Protein: 15g

81.Bourekas with Cheese and Dill Filling:

Prep Time: 30 mins

Cook Time: 20 mins

Total Time: 50 mins

Servings: 16

Ingredients:
- 1 box/pkg (400g) puff pastry, thawed if refrigerate
- 1 cup of feta cheese, cut up
- 1 cup of ricotta cheese
- 1/4 cup of chop-up fresh dill
- 1 Big egg, beaten (for egg wash)
- Sesame seeds for sprinkling

Instructions:
1. Preheat the oven to 200 Ds Celsius (400 Ds Fahrenheit) and line a baking sheet with parchment paper.
2. To make the filling, combine the cut up feta cheese, ricotta cheese, and chop-up fresh dill in a combining dish.
3. On a floured surface, unroll the thawed puff pastry and slice it into 16 equal squares.
4. Fill every puff pastry square with a tbsp of the cheese and dill filling.
5. Fold the puff pastry pieces diagonally to make triangles, then seal the edges with a fork.
6. For a golden finish, brush the tops of the bourekas with the beaten egg.
7. Sesame seeds can be sprinkled on top of the bourekas.
8. Place the bourekas on the prepared baking sheet and bake for about 20 mins, or up to they are puffed up and golden brown.
9. Warm bourekas make an excellent snack or appetizer.

Nutrition (per serving - 1 boureka):
Cals: 150 kcal, Fat: 10g, Carbs: 10g, Fiber: 1g, Protein: 4g

82.Israeli Shakshuka Shakelish:

Prep Time: 10 mins

Cook Time: 25 mins

Total Time: 35 mins

Servings: 4

Ingredients:
- 2 tbsp olive oil
- 1 onion, lightly chop-up
- 2 cloves garlic, chop-up
- 1 red bell pepper, diced
- 1 yellow bell pepper, diced
- 2 cups of diced tomatoes (canned or fresh)
- 1 tsp ground cumin
- 1 tsp ground paprika

- 1/2 tsp ground turmeric
- Salt and pepper as needed
- 4 Big eggs
- Fresh parsley, chop-up, for garnish

Instructions:

1. Heat the olive oil in a big skillet or frying pan over medium heat.
2. Sauté the lightly chop-up onions up to they are transparent.
3. Sauté for another min after adding the chop-up garlic.
4. Cook up to the diced red and yellow bell peppers soften in the skillet.
5. Pour in the diced tomatoes and cook for about 10 mins to enable the flavors to combine.
6. Season the shakshuka shakelish with cumin, paprika, turmeric, salt, and pepper as needed.
7. Make wells in the Mixture and place the eggs inside.
8. Let the eggs to cook for about 5-7 mins, or up to the whites are set but the yolks are still runny.
9. Before serving, garnish the Israeli shakshuka shakelish with chop-up fresh parsley.

Nutrition (per serving):
Cals: 250 kcal, Fat: 15g, Carbs: 15g, Fiber: 4g, Protein: 12g,

83. Israeli Harissa Chicken with Couscous:

Prep Time: 15 mins

Cook Time: 30 mins

Total Time: 45 mins

Servings: 4

Ingredients:

- 4 boneless, skinless chicken breasts
- 2 tbsp harissa paste
- 2 tbsp olive oil
- 2 cloves garlic, chop-up
- 1 tsp ground cumin
- 1 tsp ground paprika
- 1/2 tsp ground coriander
- Salt and pepper as needed
- 1 cup of couscous
- 1 1/4 cups of chicken broth
- 1/4 cup of chop-up fresh cilantro

Instructions:

1. To make a marinade, combine the harissa paste, olive oil, chop-up garlic, ground cumin, ground paprika, ground coriander, salt, and pepper in a combining bowl.
2. Coat the chicken breasts evenly with the marinade.
3. Refrigerate the bowl with plastic wrap for at least 1 hr to marinate the chicken.

4. Preheat the oven to 200 Ds Celsius (400 Ds Fahrenheit) and line a baking sheet with parchment paper.
5. Place the marinated chicken breasts on a baking sheet lined with parchment paper and bake for 20-25 mins, or up to the chicken is cooked through and slightly browned.
6. Meanwhile, bring the chicken stock to a boil in a saucepan with the couscous.
7. Stir in the couscous, then cover and take out from the heat.
8. Let the couscous to steam for 5 mins before fluffing with a fork.
9. Serve the harissa chicken over couscous with chop-up fresh cilantro on top.

Nutrition (per serving):
Cals: 400 kcal, Fat: 10g, Carbs: 35g, Fiber: 3g, Protein: 35g

84. Rugelach with Chocolate Chip Filling:

Prep Time: 30 mins

Cook Time: 20 mins

Total Time: 50 mins

Servings: 16

Ingredients:

- 2 cups of all-purpose flour
- 1/4 cup of granulated sugar
- 1/2 tsp salt
- 1 cup of unsalted butter, chilled and cubed
- 1 cup of cream cheese, chilled and cubed
- 1 tsp vanilla extract
- 1/2 cup of chocolate chips
- 1/4 cup of chop-up nuts (such as walnuts or almonds)
- Powdered sugar for dusting

Instructions:

1. In a Big combining basin, combine the all-purpose flour, granulated sugar, and salt.
2. To the flour Mixture, add the cooled and diced butter and cream cheese.
3. Work the butter and cream cheese into the flour with your hands or a pastry sliceter up to the Mixture resembles coarse crumbs.
4. Knead the dough up to it comes together after adding the vanilla essence.
5. Divide the dough into two equal parts and roll every into a ball.
6. Refrigerate for at least 30 mins after flattening every dough ball into a disc and wrapping it in plastic wrap.
7. Preheat the oven to 180 Ds Celsius (350 Ds

Fahrenheit) and line a baking sheet with parchment paper.

8. Roll out one of the cold dough discs into a circle approximately 1/8 inch thick on a floured surface.

9. Half of the chocolate chips and chop-up almonds Must be evenly distributed over the rolled-out dough.

10. Slice the dough circle into 8 triangular wedges with a knife or pizza sliceter.

11. Roll up every wedge to form a rugelach shape, beginning at the widest end.

12. Place the rugelach on the baking sheet that has been prepared.

13. Steps 8 to 12 Must be repeated with the second refrigerated dough disc and the remaining chocolate chips and chop-up nuts.

14. Rugelach Must be baked in a preheated oven for about 20 mins, or up to golden brown.

15. Let the rugelach to cool on a wire rack before dusting with powdered sugar and serving.

Nutrition (per serving):
Cals: 200 kcal, Fat: 12g, Carbs: 18g, Fiber: 1g, Protein: 3g

85. Halva Ice Cream with Tahini Swirls:

Prep Time: 15 mins

Cook Time: 20 mins (+ freezing time)

Total Time: 35 mins (+ freezing time)

Servings: 6

Ingredients:
- 2 cups of heavy cream
- 1 cup of whole milk
- 3/4 cup of granulated sugar
- 1 tsp vanilla extract
- 1/2 cup of halva, cut up
- 1/4 cup of tahini paste

Instructions:
1. Warm the heavy cream, whole milk, and granulated sugar in a saucepan over medium heat up to the sugar dissolves and the Mixture is warm but not boiling.

2. Take the pot off the heat and add the vanilla extract.

3. Let the ice cream base to cool to room temperature before covering and chilling it for at least 4 hrs or overnight.

4. Pour the cold ice cream base into an ice cream machine and churn according to the manufacturer's directions.

5. To make a swirl, combine the cut up halva and tahini paste in a separate bowl.

6. Layer the churned ice cream and swirl Mixture in a freezer-safe container, beginning and finishing with the ice cream.

7. Make swirls in the ice cream using a knife or skewer.

8. Cover the container and place the halva ice cream in the freezer for at least 4 hrs, or up to hard.

9. In bowls or cones, serve the halva ice cream with tahini swirls.

Nutrition (per serving):
Cals: 400 kcal, Fat: 30g, Carbs: 30g, Fiber: 1g, Protein: 4g

86. Sabich Toast with Labneh and Za'atar:

Prep Time: 15 mins

Cook Time: 5 mins

Total Time: 20 mins

Servings: 2

Ingredients:
- 4 slices of bread (such as pita or sourdough)
- 1 cup of labneh (strained yogurt)
- 1 Big eggplant, split
- Olive oil for drizzling
- 1 tbsp za'atar spice blend
- Salt and pepper as needed
- 1/4 cup of pickled vegetables (such as pickles or pickled turnips)
- Fresh parsley, chop-up, for garnish

Instructions:
1. Preheat the oven to 200 Ds Celsius (400 Ds Fahrenheit).

2. Drizzle olive oil over the slice eggplant on a baking sheet. Season with salt and pepper as needed.

3. Roast the eggplant for 10-15 mins, or up to soft and slightly browned, in a preheated oven.

4. While the eggplant roasts, toast the bread pieces in a toaster or on a skillet up to golden.

5. Spread a liberal amount of labneh on every slice of toast.

6. Serve the labneh with the roasted eggplant slices on top.

7. To give a savory and aromatic touch, sprinkle the eggplant with the za'atar spice combination.

8. Garnish the sabich toast with chop-up fresh parsley and serve with pickled veggies on the side.

Nutrition (per serving):
Cals: 300 kcal, Fat: 15g, Carbs: 30g, Fiber: 5g, Protein: 10g

87. Lachuch Sandwich with Falafel and Pickles:

Prep Time: 20 mins

Cook Time: 15 mins

Total Time: 35 mins

Servings: 4

Ingredients:

- 8 lachuch pancakes (store-bought or homemade, see previous recipes for lachuch)
- 16 falafel patties (store-bought or homemade)
- 1/2 cup of tahini sauce (store-bought or homemade)
- 1 cup of shredded lettuce
- 1/2 cup of split tomatoes
- 1/4 cup of split cucumbers
- 1/4 cup of pickles
- Fresh parsley, chop-up, for garnish

Instructions:

1. If using store-bought lachuch pancakes, heat them according to box/pkg directions.
2. Warm the falafel patties in the oven or in a skillet up to thoroughly cooked.
3. Spread tahini sauce generously on every lachuch pancake.
4. On every pancake, place two falafel patties.
5. On top of the falafel, layer shredded lettuce, split tomatoes, split cucumbers, and pickles.
6. To make sandwiches, roll up the lachuch pancakes.
7. Before serving, garnish the lachuch sandwiches with chop-up fresh parsley.

Nutrition (per serving):

Cals: 400 kcal, Fat: 20g, Carbs: 40g, Fiber: 4g, Protein: 15g

88. Kibbeh Nayyeh with Lamb and Bulgar:

Prep Time: 20 mins

Cook Time: 0 mins

Total Time: 20 mins

Servings: 4

Ingredients:

- 1 lb fresh lamb, lightly ground
- 1/2 cup of fine bulgar wheat
- 1/4 cup of chop-up fresh mint leaves
- 1/4 cup of chop-up fresh parsley leaves
- 1/4 cup of chop-up green onions
- 1/4 cup of chop-up white onions
- 2 tbsp extra-virgin olive oil
- 1 tbsp ground cumin
- Salt and pepper as needed

- Pita bread or crackers for serving

Instructions:

1. Drain the bulgar wheat after rinsing it in a fine-mesh strainer with cold water.
2. Combine the lightly ground lamb, drained bulgar wheat, chop-up fresh mint, chop-up fresh parsley, chop-up green onions, chop-up white onions, olive oil, ground cumin, salt, and pepper in a Big combining bowl.
3. Knead the Mixture with your hands up to it is thoroughly incorporated.
4. Individually portion the kibbeh nayyeh Mixture and form it into patties or balls.
5. Serve with pita bread or crackers to accompany the kibbeh nayyeh.

Nutrition (per serving):

Cals: 300 kcal, Fat: 20g, Carbs: 10g, Fiber: 3g, Protein: 20g

89. Israeli Green Shakshuka with Spinach and Zucchini:

Prep Time: 10 mins

Cook Time: 20 mins

Total Time: 30 mins

Servings: 4

Ingredients:

- 2 tbsp olive oil
- 1 onion, lightly chop-up
- 2 cloves garlic, chop-up
- 2 cups of baby spinach
- 2 cups of diced zucchini
- 1 tsp ground cumin
- 1 tsp ground coriander
- 1/2 tsp ground turmeric
- 1/4 tsp cayenne pepper (non-compulsory, for heat)
- Salt and pepper as needed
- 4 Big eggs
- Fresh cilantro, chop-up, for garnish

Instructions:

1. Heat the olive oil in a big skillet or frying pan over medium heat.
2. Sauté the lightly chop-up onions up to they are transparent.
3. Sauté for another min after adding the chop-up garlic.
4. Cook up to the baby spinach and diced zucchini wilt and soften in the skillet.
5. Season the green shakshuka with cumin, coriander, turmeric, cayenne pepper (if using), salt, and pepper as needed.

6. Make wells in the Mixture and place the eggs inside.
7. Let the eggs to cook for about 5-7 mins, or up to the whites are set but the yolks are still runny.
8. Before serving, garnish the Israeli green shakshuka with chop-up fresh cilantro.

Nutrition (per serving):
Cals: 200 kcal, Fat: 12g, Carbs: 10g, Fiber: 3g, Protein: 10g

90.Bamba Brownies with Chocolate Chips:

Prep Time: 15 mins

Cook Time: 25 mins

Total Time: 40 mins

Servings: 16

Ingredients:

- 1 cup of unsalted butter, dilute
- 1 1/2 cups of granulated sugar
- 2 tsp vanilla extract
- 4 Big eggs
- 1 cup of all-purpose flour
- 1/2 cup of cocoa powder
- 1/2 tsp baking powder
- 1/4 tsp salt
- 1 cup of Bamba peanut snacks, crushed
- 1/2 cup of chocolate chips

Instructions:

1. Preheat the oven to 180°C (350°F) and coat a 9x13-inch baking dish with cooking spray.
2. Whisk together the dilute butter, granulated sugar, and vanilla extract in a Big combining basin.
3. Whisk in the eggs one at a time, after every addition.
4. Sift together the all-purpose flour, cocoa powder, baking powder, and salt in a separate bowl.
5. Add the dry ingredients to the liquid components gradually, stirring up to just blended.
6. Combine the smashed Bamba peanut snacks and chocolate chips in a combining bowl.
7. Spread out the brownie batter evenly in the prepared baking dish.
8. Bake the Bamba brownies for about 25 mins, or up to a toothpick inserted into the center emerges with a few wet crumbs.
9. Let the brownies to cool completely in the pan before slicing and serving.

Nutrition (per serving):
Cals: 250 kcal, Fat: 15g, Carbs: 25g, Fiber: 2g, Protein: 5g

91.Tahini Chickpea Salad with Cumin Dressing:

Prep Time: 15 mins

Cook Time: 0 mins

Total Time: 15 mins

Servings: 4

Ingredients:

- 2 cans (15 oz every) chickpeas, drained and rinsed
- 1/2 cup of diced cucumbers
- 1/2 cup of diced tomatoes
- 1/4 cup of chop-up fresh parsley
- 1/4 cup of chop-up fresh mint
- 1/4 cup of chop-up red onions
- 1/4 cup of cut up feta cheese (non-compulsory)
- 1/4 cup of tahini paste
- 3 tbsp lemon juice
- 2 tbsp olive oil
- 1 tsp ground cumin
- Salt and pepper as needed

Instructions:

1. Combine the chickpeas, diced cucumbers, diced tomatoes, chop-up fresh parsley, chop-up fresh mint, chop-up red onions, and cut up feta cheese (if using) in a Big combining dish.
2. To make the dressing, combine together the tahini paste, lemon juice, olive oil, ground cumin, salt, and pepper in a separate mini bowl.
3. Toss the chickpea salad with the dressing up to everything is fully coated.
4. Serve the tahini chickpea salad as a light side dish or as a light main.

Nutrition (per serving):
Cals: 350 kcal, Fat: 20g, Carbs: 30g, Fiber: 8g, Protein: 10g

92.Israeli Roasted Eggplant Dip with Garlic and Lemon:

Prep Time: 15 mins

Cook Time: 25 mins

Total Time: 40 mins

Servings: 6

Ingredients:

- 2 Big eggplants
- 3 cloves garlic, chop-up
- 1/4 cup of tahini paste
- 1/4 cup of lemon juice
- 2 tbsp extra-virgin olive oil
- 1/2 tsp ground cumin
- Salt and pepper as needed

- Fresh parsley, chop-up, for garnish

Instructions:

1. Preheat the oven to 200 Ds Celsius (400 Ds Fahrenheit).
2. Pierce the eggplants several times with a fork to enable steam to escape during roasting.
3. Place the eggplants on a baking sheet and roast for approximately 25 mins, or up to tender and browned on the outside.
4. Let the roasted eggplants to cool slightly before Cuttingthem in half and scooping out the flesh.
5. Combine the roasted eggplant flesh, chop-up garlic, tahini paste, lemon juice, extra-virgin olive oil, ground cumin, salt, and pepper in a blender or mixer.
6. Blend up to the Mixture is smooth and creamy.
7. Before serving, transfer the roasted eggplant dip to a serving bowl and top with chop-up fresh parsley.

Nutrition (per serving):
Cals: 150 kcal, Fat: 10g, Carbs: 15g, Fiber: 6g, Protein: 3g

93.Falafel Burger Bowl with Quinoa and Avocado:

Prep Time: 20 mins

Cook Time: 20 mins

Total Time: 40 mins

Servings: 4

Ingredients:

- 16 falafel patties (store-bought or homemade)
- 1 cup of cooked quinoa
- 1 cup of cherry tomatoes, halved
- 1 cucumber, diced
- 1 avocado, split
- 1/4 cup of pickled red onions (non-compulsory)
- 1/4 cup of chop-up fresh parsley
- 1/4 cup of tahini sauce (store-bought or homemade)
- Lemon wedges for serving

Instructions:

1. Warm the falafel patties in the oven or in a skillet up to thoroughly cooked.
2. Assemble the falafel burger bowls in four serving bowls by layering cooked quinoa, split cherry tomatoes, diced cucumber, split avocado, pickled red onions (if using), and chop-up fresh parsley.
3. Add four falafel patties to every bowl.
4. Drizzle the falafel burger bowls with tahini sauce.
5. Serve the falafel burger bowls with lemon wedges on the side.

Nutrition (per serving):
Cals: 400 kcal, Fat: 20g, Carbs: 40g, Fiber: 10g, Protein: 15g

94.Bourekas with Potato and Cheese Filling:

Prep Time: 30 mins

Cook Time: 25 mins

Total Time: 55 mins

Servings: 16

Ingredients:

- 2 sheets puff pastry (store-bought or homemade)
- 2 Big potatoes, peel off, boiled, and mashed
- 1 cup of shredded mozzarella cheese
- 1/4 cup of chop-up fresh parsley
- 1/4 cup of chop-up green onions
- 1/2 tsp garlic powder
- Salt and pepper as needed
- 1 Big egg, beaten (for egg wash)
- Sesame seeds for sprinkling

Instructions:

1. Preheat the oven to 200 Ds Celsius (400 Ds Fahrenheit) and line a baking sheet with parchment paper.
2. To make the filling, combine the mashed potatoes, shredded mozzarella cheese, chop-up fresh parsley, chop-up green onions, garlic powder, salt, and pepper in a combining bowl.
3. On a floured surface, unroll the puff pastry sheets and slice every sheet into 8 equal squares.
4. Fill every puff pastry square with a tbsp of the potato and cheese filling.
5. Fold the puff pastry pieces diagonally to make triangles, then seal the edges with a fork.
6. For a golden finish, brush the tops of the bourekas with the beaten egg.
7. Sesame seeds can be sprinkled on top of the bourekas.
8. Place the bourekas on the prepared baking sheet and bake for 20-25 mins, or up to they are puffed up and golden brown.
9. Warm bourekas with potato and cheese filling make a tasty snack or appetizer.

Nutrition (per serving - 1 boureka):
Cals: 200 kcal, Fat: 12g, Carbs: 18g, Fiber: 1g, Protein: 5g

95.Israeli Shakshuka with Artichokes and Olives:

Prep Time: 10 mins

Cook Time: 25 mins

Total Time: 35 mins

Servings: 4

Ingredients:

- 2 tbsp olive oil
- 1 onion, lightly chop-up
- 2 cloves garlic, chop-up
- 1 red bell pepper, diced
- 1 yellow bell pepper, diced
- 1 can (14 oz) diced tomatoes
- 1 can (14 oz) artichoke hearts, drained and chop-up
- 1/2 cup of pitted green olives, halved
- 1 tsp ground cumin
- 1 tsp ground paprika
- 1/2 tsp ground cayenne pepper (non-compulsory, for heat)
- Salt and pepper as needed
- 4 Big eggs
- Fresh parsley, chop-up, for garnish

Instructions:

1. Heat the olive oil in a big skillet or frying pan over medium heat.
2. Sauté the lightly chop-up onions up to they are transparent.
3. Sauté for another min after adding the chop-up garlic.
4. Cook up to the diced red and yellow bell peppers soften in the skillet.
5. Pour in the diced tomatoes, artichoke hearts, and green olives, halved.
6. enable the Mixture to boil for about 10 mins to enable the flavors to blend.
7. Season the shakshuka with artichokes and olives with ground cumin, paprika, cayenne pepper (if using), salt, and pepper.
8. Make wells in the Mixture and place the eggs inside.
9. Let the eggs to cook for about 5-7 mins, or up to the whites are set but the yolks are still runny.
10. Before serving, garnish the Israeli shakshuka with artichokes and olives and fresh parsley.

Nutrition (per serving):

Cals: 250 kcal, Fat: 15g, Carbs: 15g, Fiber: 5g, Protein: 10g

96.Malabi with Cardamom and Rose Petals:

Prep Time: 5 mins

Cook Time: 10 mins (+ chilling time)

Total Time: 15 mins (+ chilling time)

Servings: 4

Ingredients:

- 4 cups of milk (dairy or plant-based)
- 1/2 cup of cornstarch
- 1/2 cup of granulated sugar
- 1 tsp ground cardamom
- 1 tsp rose water
- Crushed pistachios for garnish
- Dried rose petals for garnish

Instructions:

1. Whisk together the milk, cornstarch, granulated sugar, and ground cardamom in a saucepan.
2. Cook, stirring constantly, over medium heat up to the Mixture thickens and revereyes a custard-like consistency.
3. Take the saucepan off the heat and add the rose water.
4. Fill individual serving dishes or glasses with the malabi Mixture.
5. Let the malabi to chill in the refrigerator for at least 2 hrs, or up to totally set.
6. For a beautiful touch, sprinkle the malabi with crushed pistachios and dried rose petals before serving.

Nutrition (per serving):

Cals: 200 kcal, Fat: 5g, Carbs: 35g, Fiber: 0g, Protein: 3g

97.Rugelach with Nutella and Hazelnuts:

Prep Time: 30 mins

Cook Time: 20 mins

Total Time: 50 mins

Servings: 24

Ingredients:

- 2 cups of all-purpose flour
- 1 cup of unsalted butter, melted
- 1/2 cup of granulated sugar
- 1 tsp vanilla extract
- 1/4 tsp salt
- 3/4 cup of Nutella (or other chocolate spread)
- 1/2 cup of chop-up hazelnuts
- 1/4 cup of powdered sugar for dusting

Instructions:

1. In a Big combining basin, beat the melted butter and granulated sugar together up to light and fluffy.
2. Combine the vanilla extract and salt in a combining bowl.
3. Add the all-purpose flour gradually to the butter Mixture and stir up to a soft dough forms.
4. Divide the dough into two equal parts and form every into a disc.

5. Wrap the dough discs in plastic wrap and place them in the refrigerator for at least 30 mins to firm up.
6. Preheat the oven to 180 Ds Celsius (350 Ds Fahrenheit) and line a baking sheet with parchment paper.
7. Roll out one cold dough disc into a circle approximately 1/8-inch thick on a floured surface.
8. Spread half of the Nutella evenly over the rolled-out dough, followed by half of the chop-up hazelnuts.
9. Slice the dough circle into 12 equal triangles with a knife or pizza sliceter.
10. Roll up every triangle to form rugelach, beginning with the wider end, and set them on the prepared baking sheet.
11. Steps 7–10 are repeated with the second cold dough disc and the leftover Nutella and hazelnuts.
12. Rugelach Must be baked in a preheated oven for about 20 mins, or up to golden brown.
13. Let the rugelach to cool on a wire rack before dusting with powdered sugar and serving.

Nutrition (per serving - 1 rugelach):
Cals: 150 kcal, Fat: 10g, Carbs: 15g, Fiber: 1g, Protein: 2g

98.Halva Cookies with Sesame Seeds:

Prep Time: 15 mins

Cook Time: 12 mins

Total Time: 27 mins

Servings: 18

Ingredients:
- 1/2 cup of unsalted butter, melted
- 1/2 cup of granulated sugar
- 1/2 cup of light brown sugar, packed
- 1 Big egg
- 1 tsp vanilla extract
- 1 3/4 cups of all-purpose flour
- 1/2 tsp baking soda
- 1/4 tsp salt
- 1/2 cup of cut up halva
- 2 tbsp sesame seeds

Instructions:
1. Whisk together the all-purpose flour, granulated sugar, active dry yeast, baking powder, and salt in a Big combining basin.
2. Add the heated water and vegetable oil to the dry ingredients in a slow, steady stream up to a smooth batter develops.

3. Cover the bowl with a clean kitchen towel and set aside for 30 mins in a warm location.
4. Preheat a nonstick skillet or griddle over medium heat and gently coat with cooking spray or oil.
5. Spread about 1/4 cup of the lachuch batter onto the skillet in a circular shape.
6. Cook the lachuch for 2-3 mins per side, or up to gently browned and fluffy.
7. Before serving, drizzle the cooked lachuch with maple syrup and top with fresh berries.

Nutrition (per serving - 1 cookie):
Cals: 150 kcal, Fat: 8g, Carbs: 18g,Fiber: 1g, Protein: 2g

99.Lachuch with Maple Syrup and Fresh Berries:

Prep Time: 10 mins

Cook Time: 10 mins

Total Time: 20 mins

Servings: 4

Ingredients:
- 2 cups of all-purpose flour
- 1 tbsp granulated sugar
- 1 packet active dry yeast (about 2 1/4 tsp)
- 1 tsp baking powder
- 1/2 tsp salt
- 1 1/4 cups of warm water
- 1 tbsp vegetable oil
- Maple syrup for drizzling
- Fresh berries (such as strawberries, blueberries, or raspberries) for topping

Instructions:
1. Whisk together the all-purpose flour, granulated sugar, active dry yeast, baking powder, and salt in a Big combining basin.
2. Add the heated water and vegetable oil to the dry ingredients in a slow, steady stream up to a smooth batter develops.
3. Cover the bowl with a clean kitchen towel and set aside for 30 mins in a warm location.
4. Preheat a nonstick skillet or griddle over medium heat and gently coat with cooking spray or oil.
5. Spread about 1/4 cup of the lachuch batter onto the skillet in a circular shape.
6. Cook the lachuch for 2-3 mins per side, or up to gently browned and fluffy.
7. Before serving, drizzle the cooked lachuch with maple syrup and top with fresh berries.

Nutrition (per serving):
Cals: 200 kcal, Fat: 3g, Carbs: 38g, Fiber: 2g, Protein: 4g

100. Tahini Truffles with Pistachio Coating:

Prep Time: 15 mins

Cook Time: 0 mins

Total Time: 15 mins

Servings: 12

Ingredients:

- 1 cup of tahini paste
- 1/4 cup of honey or maple syrup
- 1/4 cup of coconut flour
- 1/4 tsp vanilla extract
- Pinch of salt
- Crushed pistachios for coating

Instructions:

1. In a combining dish, combine the tahini paste, honey or maple syrup, coconut flour, vanilla essence, and a pinch of salt.
2. Refrigerate the tahini Mixture, covered, for about 30 mins to firm up.
3. When the Mixture is solid enough to handle, roll it into little truffle-sized balls using your palms.
4. To coat the tahini truffles, roll them in crushed pistachios.
5. Refrigerate the tahini truffles in an airtight jar up to ready to serve.

Nutrition (per serving - 1 truffle):

Cals: 150 kcal, Fat: 12g, Carbs: 8g, Fiber: 2g, Protein: 3g

101. Israeli Vegetable Shakshuka with Eggplant and Bell Peppers:

Prep Time: 10 mins

Cook Time: 25 mins

Total Time: 35 mins

Servings: 4

Ingredients:

- 2 tbsp olive oil
- 1 onion, lightly chop-up
- 2 cloves garlic, chop-up
- 1 eggplant, diced
- 1 red bell pepper, diced
- 1 yellow bell pepper, diced
- 1 can (14 oz) diced tomatoes
- 1 tsp ground cumin
- 1 tsp ground paprika
- 1/2 tsp ground cayenne pepper (non-compulsory, for heat)
- Salt and pepper as needed
- 4 Big eggs
- Fresh cilantro, chop-up, for garnish

Instructions:

1. Heat the olive oil in a big skillet or frying pan over medium heat.
2. Sauté the lightly chop-up onions up to they are transparent.
3. Sauté for another min after adding the chop-up garlic.
4. Cook up to the diced eggplant, red bell pepper, and yellow bell pepper melt in the skillet.
5. Add the diced tomatoes with their juices.
6. Season the veggie shakshuka with cumin, paprika, cayenne pepper (if using), salt, and pepper as needed.
7. enable the Mixture to boil for about 10 mins to enable the flavors to blend.
8. Make wells in the Mixture and place the eggs inside.
9. Let the eggs to cook for about 5-7 mins, or up to the whites are set but the yolks are still runny.
10. Before serving, garnish the Israeli veggie shakshuka with chop-up fresh cilantro.

Nutrition (per serving):

Cals: 200 kcal, Fat: 12g, Carbs: 15g Fiber: 5g, Protein: 10g

102. Sabich Burrito with Egg and Pita Bread:

Prep Time: 15 mins

Cook Time: 15 mins

Total Time: 30 mins

Servings: 4

Ingredients:

- 4 Big eggs
- 4 pita bread
- 1 cup of hummus
- 1 cup of Israeli salad (diced tomatoes, cucumbers, and onions)
- 1 cup of shredded lettuce
- 1/2 cup of pickled eggplant
- 1/4 cup of tahini sauce
- Hot sauce (non-compulsory, for added spice)

Instructions:

1. Fry the eggs in a skillet up to they are done to your liking.
2. Microwave or bake the pita bread up to warm.
3. On every pita bread, spread a dollop of hummus.
4. Add Israeli salad, shredded lettuce, pickled eggplant, and a fried egg on the top.
5. Drizzle the filling with tahini sauce and spicy sauce (if using).
6. Serve the pita bread folded into a burrito.

Nutrition (per serving):
Cals: 400 kcal, Fat: 20g, Carbs: 40g, Fiber: 5g, Protein: 15g

103. Bourekas with Spinach and Ricotta Filling:

Prep Time: 30 mins

Cook Time: 25 mins

Total Time: 55 mins

Servings: 16

Ingredients:
- 2 sheets puff pastry (store-bought or homemade)
- 1 cup of refrigerate spinach, thawed and drained
- 1 cup of ricotta cheese
- 1/2 cup of feta cheese, cut up
- 1/4 cup of chop-up fresh dill
- 1/4 cup of chop-up green onions
- Salt and pepper as needed
- 1 Big egg, beaten (for egg wash)
- Sesame seeds for sprinkling

Instructions:
1. Preheat the oven to 200 Ds Celsius (400 Ds Fahrenheit) and line a baking sheet with parchment paper.
2. To make the filling, combine the refrigerate and drained spinach, ricotta cheese, cut up feta cheese, chop-up fresh dill, chop-up green onions, salt, and pepper in a combining dish.
3. On a floured surface, unroll the puff pastry sheets and slice every sheet into 8 equal squares.
4. Fill every puff pastry square with a tbsp of the spinach and ricotta filling.
5. Fold the puff pastry pieces diagonally to make triangles, then seal the edges with a fork.
6. For a golden finish, brush the tops of the bourekas with the beaten egg.
7. Sesame seeds can be sprinkled on top of the bourekas.
8. Place the bourekas on the prepared baking sheet and bake for 20-25 mins, or up to they are puffed up and golden brown.
9. Warm bourekas with spinach and ricotta filling make an excellent snack or appetizer.

Nutrition (per serving - 1 boureka):
Cals: 150 kcal, Fat: 10g, Carbs: 12g, Fiber: 1g, Protein: 5g

104. Israeli Lemon Herb Chicken with Potatoes:

Prep Time: 10 mins

Cook Time: 40 mins

Total Time: 50 mins

Servings: 4

Ingredients:
- 4 bone-in, skin-on chicken thighs
- 1 lb baby potatoes, halved
- 2 lemons, juiced and zested
- 3 tbsp olive oil
- 4 cloves garlic, chop-up
- 1 tbsp fresh thyme leaves
- 1 tbsp fresh rosemary leaves
- Salt and pepper as needed

Instructions:
1. Preheat the oven to 200 Ds Celsius (400 Ds Fahrenheit) and line a baking sheet with parchment paper.
2. To make the marinade, combine the lemon juice, lemon zest, olive oil, chop-up garlic, fresh thyme, fresh rosemary, salt, and pepper in a Big combining bowl.
3. Place the chicken thighs in the marinade, making sure they are uniformly coated. Let them to marinade for 20 mins.
4. Place the marinated chicken thighs and slice up baby potatoes on the baking sheet that has been prepared.
5. Bake for 35-40 mins, or up to the chicken is cooked through and the potatoes are soft, in a preheated oven.
6. Serve the Israeli lemon herb chicken with potatoes hot, topped with fresh herbs if desired.

Nutrition (per serving):
Cals: 400 kcal, Fat: 20g, Carbs: 20g, Fiber: 3g, Protein: 30g

105. Rugelach with Cherry Jam and Coconut:

Prep Time: 20 mins

Cook Time: 20 mins

Total Time: 40 mins

Servings: 24

Ingredients:
- 2 cups of all-purpose flour
- 1 cup of unsalted butter, melted
- 1/2 cup of granulated sugar
- 1 tsp vanilla extract
- 1/4 tsp salt
- 3/4 cup of cherry jam (or any fruit jam of your choice)
- 1/2 cup of shredded coconut
- 1/4 cup of powdered sugar for dusting

1. Cream together the melted butter, granulated sugar, and vanilla extract in a Big combining bowl up to smooth.
2. Combine in the salt.
3. Add the all-purpose flour gradually to the butter Mixture and stir up to a soft dough forms.
4. Divide the dough into two equal parts and form every into a disc.
5. Wrap the dough discs in plastic wrap and place them in the refrigerator for at least 30 mins to firm up.
6. Preheat the oven to 180 Ds Celsius (350 Ds Fahrenheit) and line a baking sheet with parchment paper.
7. Roll out one cold dough disc into a circle approximately 1/8-inch thick on a floured surface.
8. Spread half of the cherry jam evenly over the rolled-out dough, followed by half of the shredded coconut.
9. Slice the dough circle into 12 equal triangles with a knife or pizza sliceter.
10. Roll up every triangle to form rugelach, beginning with the wider end, and set them on the prepared baking sheet.
11. Steps 7–10 are repeated with the second cold dough disc, remaining cherry jam, and crushed coconut.
12. Rugelach Must be baked in a preheated oven for 18-20 mins, or up to lightly golden.
13. Let the rugelach to cool on a wire rack before dusting with powdered sugar and serving.

Nutrition (per serving - 1 rugelach):
Cals: 150 kcal, Fat: 8g, Carbs: 18g, Fiber: 1g, Protein: 2g

106.Halva Cheesecake with Caramel Swirls:

Prep Time: 20 mins

Cook Time: 1 hr

Total Time: 1 hr 20 mins

Servings: 12

Ingredients:

- 2 cups of graham cracker crumbs
- 1/2 cup of unsalted butter, dilute
- 4 box/pkgs (8 oz every) cream cheese, melted
- 1 cup of granulated sugar
- 4 Big eggs
- 1 tsp vanilla extract
- 1 cup of cut up halva
- 1/2 cup of caramel sauce

Instructions:

1. Preheat the oven to 160°C (325°F) and oil a 9-inch springform pan with cooking spray.
2. In a combining dish, combine the graham cracker crumbs and dilute butter up to equally coated.
3. To make the crust, press the crumb Mixture into the bottom of the prepared springform pan.
4. In a Big combining bowl, combine the melted cream cheese and the granulated sugar and beat up to smooth and creamy.
5. Add the eggs one at a time, followed by the vanilla essence.
6. Fold the cut up halva into the cheesecake batter gently.
7. Pour the cheesecake batter into the springform pan over the crust.
8. Drizzle the caramel sauce over the top of the cheesecake and swirl it into the batter with a toothpick for a marbled look.
9. Bake the halva cheesecake for 55-60 mins, or up to the middle is almost set, in a preheated oven.
10. Let the cheesecake to cool in the pan for approximately an hr before refrigerating it for at least 4 hrs, or up to completely cooled and set.
11. Take out the edges of the springform pan and slice the halva cheesecake before serving.

Nutrition (per serving):
Cals: 450 kcal, Fat: 30g, Carbs: 35g, Fiber: 1g, Protein: 8g

107.Lachuch Sandwich with Labneh and Olives:

Prep Time: 15 mins

Cook Time: 10 mins

Total Time: 25 mins

Servings: 4

Ingredients:

- 8 lachuch (Yemeni flatbread) or pita bread
- 1 cup of labneh (strained yogurt)
- 1/2 cup of black olives, pitted and split
- 1/4 cup of chop-up fresh mint
- 1/4 cup of chop-up fresh parsley
- 2 tbsp olive oil
- 1 tbsp lemon juice
- Salt and pepper as needed

Instructions:

1. Warm the lachuch in a skillet or microwave up to soft and malleable.
2. To create the filling, combine the labneh, split black olives, chop-up fresh mint, chop-up fresh parsley, olive oil, lemon juice, salt, and pepper in a combining dish.

3. Fill every lachuch or pita bread with a heaping tbsp of the labneh and olive filling.
4. Make a sandwich with the lachuch or pita bread and serve.

Nutrition (per serving):

Cals: 300 kcal, Fat: 15g, Carbs: 30g, Fiber: 3g, Protein: 10g

108. Tahini Oatmeal with Honey and Almonds:

Prep Time: 5 mins

Cook Time: 10 mins

Total Time: 15 mins

Servings: 2

Ingredients:

- 1 cup of rolled oats
- 2 cups of milk (dairy or plant-based)
- 2 tbsp tahini
- 2 tbsp honey
- 1/4 cup of split almonds
- Pinch of salt
- Fresh fruit for topping (such as bananas or berries)

Instructions:

1. Combine the rolled oats, milk, tahini, honey, chop-up almonds, and a bit of salt in a saucepan.
2. Cook the oats, stirring periodically, over medium heat up to it reveryes the desired consistency.
3. Serve the tahini oatmeal in individual dishes.
4. To add sweetness and taste, top with fresh fruit, such as split bananas or berries.

Nutrition (per serving):

Cals: 400 kcal, Fat: 15g, Carbs: 55g, Fiber: 8g, Protein: 12g

109. Malabi with Pistachio and Orange Blossom Syrup:

Prep Time: 5 mins

Cook Time: 10 mins (+ chilling time)

Total Time: 15 mins (+ chilling time)

Servings: 4

Ingredients:

- 4 cups of milk (dairy or plant-based)
- 1/2 cup of cornstarch
- 1/2 cup of granulated sugar
- 1 tsp vanilla extract
- 1 tbsp orange blossom water
- Crushed pistachios for garnish

Instructions:

1. Whisk together the milk, cornstarch, granulated sugar, and vanilla extract in a saucepan.
2. Cook, stirring constantly, over medium heat up to the Mixture thickens and reveryes a custard-like consistency.
3. Incorporate the orange blossom water.
4. Fill individual serving dishes or glasses with the malabi Mixture.
5. Let the malabi to chill in the refrigerator for at least 2 hrs, or up to totally set.
6. Garnish the malabi with crushed pistachios before serving for a wonderful crunch.

Nutrition (per serving):

Cals: 250 kcal, Fat: 5g, Carbs: 40g, Fiber: 0g, Protein: 6g

110. Shakshuka Stuffed Peppers with Feta Cheese:

Prep Time: 15 mins

Cook Time: 30 mins

Total Time: 45 mins

Servings: 4

Ingredients:

- 4 Big bell peppers (any color), halved and seeds take outd
- 1 tbsp olive oil
- 1 onion, chop-up
- 2 cloves garlic, chop-up
- 1 can (14 oz) diced tomatoes
- 1 tsp ground cumin
- 1 tsp ground paprika
- 1/2 tsp ground cayenne pepper (non-compulsory, for heat)
- Salt and pepper as needed
- 4 Big eggs
- 1/2 cup of cut up feta cheese
- Fresh parsley for garnish

Instructions:

1. Preheat the oven to 200°C (400°F) and line a baking dish with parchment paper.
2. Warm the olive oil in a Big skillet over medium heat.
3. Sauté the chop-up onion up to it gets translucent.
4. Sauté for another min after adding the chop-up garlic.
5. To the skillet, add the diced tomatoes and their liquids.
6. Season the tomato Mixture with cumin, paprika, cayenne pepper (if using), salt, and pepper as needed.

7. Let the tomato Mixture to boil for about 10 mins to let the flavors to blend.
8. Fill the baking dish halfway with halved bell peppers.
9. Shakshuka Mixture Must be spooned into every pepper half.
10. Make wells in the shakshuka Mixture, then crack the eggs into them.
11. Cut up the feta cheese over the filled peppers.
12. Bake the stuffed peppers with shakshuka in a preheated oven for 15-20 mins, or up to the eggs are cooked to your preference.
13. Before serving, garnish the filled peppers with fresh parsley.

Nutrition (per serving):
Cals: 250 kcal, Fat: 10g, Carbs: 25g, Fiber: 6g, Protein: 15g

111.Bourekas with Feta and Herb Filling:

Prep Time: 25 mins

Cook Time: 20 mins

Total Time: 45 mins

Servings: 16

Ingredients:

- 2 sheets puff pastry (store-bought or homemade)
- 1 cup of cut up feta cheese
- 1/4 cup of chop-up fresh parsley
- 1/4 cup of chop-up fresh dill
- 1/4 cup of chop-up fresh mint
- 1/4 cup of chop-up green onions
- 1/4 cup of unsalted butter, dilute
- Sesame seeds for sprinkling

Instructions:

1. Preheat the oven to 200 Ds Celsius (400 Ds Fahrenheit) and line a baking sheet with parchment paper.
2. To make the filling, combine the cut up feta cheese, chop-up fresh parsley, chop-up fresh dill, chop-up fresh mint, and chop-up green onions in a combining bowl.
3. On a floured surface, unroll the puff pastry sheets and slice every sheet into 8 equal squares.
4. Fill every puff pastry square with a tbsp of the feta and herb filling.
5. Fold the puff pastry pieces diagonally to make triangles, then seal the edges with a fork.
6. Brush the bourekas' tops with dilute butter for a golden finish.
7. Sesame seeds can be sprinkled on top of the bourekas.
8. Place the bourekas on the prepared baking sheet and bake for 15-20 mins, or up to they are puffed up and golden brown.
9. Warm bourekas with feta and herb filling make an excellent appetizer or snack.

Nutrition (per serving - 1 boureka):
Cals: 150 kcal, Fat: 10g, Carbs: 12g, Fiber: 1g, Protein: 3g

112.Israeli Shakshuka with Swiss Chard and Feta:

Prep Time: 10 mins

Cook Time: 25 mins

Total Time: 35 mins

Servings: 4

Ingredients:

- 2 tbsp olive oil
- 1 onion, thinly split
- 2 cloves garlic, chop-up
- 1 bunch Swiss chard, chop-up
- 1 can (14 oz) diced tomatoes
- 1 tsp ground cumin
- 1 tsp ground paprika
- Salt and pepper as needed
- 4-6 Big eggs
- 1/2 cup of cut up feta cheese
- Fresh parsley for garnish

Instructions:

1. Heat the olive oil in a big skillet or frying pan over medium heat.
2. Sauté the thinly split onions up to they become transparent.
3. Sauté for another min after adding the chop-up garlic.
4. Cook the chop-up Swiss chard in the skillet up to it wilts.
5. Add the diced tomatoes with their juices.
6. Season the shakshuka with cumin, paprika, salt, and pepper as needed.
7. enable the Mixture to boil for about 10 mins to enable the flavors to blend.
8. Make wells in the Mixture and place the eggs inside.
9. Let the eggs to cook for about 5-7 mins, or up to the whites are set but the yolks are still runny.
10. Before serving, top the shakshuka with cut up feta cheese and sprinkle with fresh parsley.

Nutrition (per serving):
Cals: 250 kcal, Fat: 17g, Carbs: 15g, Fiber: 4g, Protein: 10g

113. Rugelach with Blueberry Jam and Lemon Zest:

Prep Time: 30 mins

Cook Time: 20 mins

Total Time: 50 mins

Servings: 24

Ingredients:

- 2 cups of all-purpose flour
- 1 cup of unsalted butter, melted
- 1 cup of cream cheese, melted
- 1/4 cup of granulated sugar
- 1 tsp vanilla extract
- 1/4 tsp salt
- 1 cup of blueberry jam
- Zest of 1 lemon
- 1/4 cup of powdered sugar for dusting

Instructions:

1. Cream together the melted butter, cream cheese, granulated sugar, and vanilla extract in a Big combining bowl up to smooth.
2. Combine in the salt.
3. Add the all-purpose flour gradually to the butter Mixture and stir up to a soft dough forms.
4. Divide the dough into two equal parts and form every into a disc.
5. Wrap the dough discs in plastic wrap and place them in the refrigerator for at least 30 mins to firm up.
6. Preheat the oven to 180 Ds Celsius (350 Ds Fahrenheit) and line a baking sheet with parchment paper.
7. Roll out one cold dough disc into a circle approximately 1/8-inch thick on a floured surface.
8. Spread half of the blueberry jam over the rolled-out dough and equally sprinkle with lemon zest.
9. Slice the dough circle into 12 equal triangles with a knife or pizza sliceter.
10. Roll up every triangle to form rugelach, beginning with the wider end, and set them on the prepared baking sheet.
11. Steps 7–10 are repeated with the second cold dough disc, remaining blueberry jam, and lemon zest.
12. Rugelach Must be baked in a preheated oven for 18-20 mins, or up to lightly golden.
13. Let the rugelach to cool on a wire rack before dusting with powdered sugar and serving.

Nutrition (per serving - 1 rugelach):
Cals: 150 kcal, Fat: 10g, Carbs: 14g, Fiber: 1g, Protein: 2g

114. Tahini Energy Bars with Dates and Cashews:

Prep Time: 15 mins

No Cook Time

Total Time: 15 mins

Servings: 12

Ingredients:

- 1 cup of pitted dates
- 1 cup of cashews
- 1/2 cup of tahini
- 1/4 cup of honey
- 1 tsp vanilla extract
- Pinch of salt

Instructions:

1. Blend the pitted dates and cashews in a mixer up to lightly chop-up and combined.
2. In a mixer, combine the tahini, honey, vanilla essence, and a pinch of salt.
3. Continue blending up to all of the ingredients are fully incorporated and the Mixture is sticky.
4. Line a baking dish with parchment paper, either square or rectangular.
5. Fill the prepared baking dish halfway with the tahini energy bar Mixture.
6. Refrigerate the Mixture for at least one hr to let it to firm up.
7. When the Mixture has cold, slice it into bars and serve.

Nutrition (per serving - 1 energy bar):
Cals: 200 kcal, Fat: 12g, Carbs: 20g, Fiber: 2g, Protein: 4g

115. Falafel Stuffed Pita with Hummus and Tabouli:

Prep Time: 30 mins

Cook Time: 15 mins

Total Time: 45 mins

Servings: 4

Ingredients:

- 8 falafel patties (store-bought or homemade)
- 4 pita bread
- 1 cup of hummus
- 1 cup of tabouli salad (chop-up fresh parsley, tomatoes, onions, mint, and bulgur wheat)
- 1/2 cup of cucumber, split
- 1/4 cup of tahini sauce

Instructions:

1. If you're using store-bought falafel patties, cook them according to the box/pkg directions. Cook

or bake homemade falafel till crispy and golden brown.
2. Microwave or bake the pita bread up to warm.
3. Fill every pita bread with a Big scoop of hummus.
4. Stuff two falafel patties inside every pita.
5. Fill every pita with a dollop of tabouli salad and slices of cucumber.
6. Drizzle the tahini sauce on top of the falafel and tabouli filling.
7. As a wonderful and filling meal, serve the falafel stuffed pita with hummus and tabouli.

Nutrition (per serving):
Cals: 500 kcal, Fat: 20g, Carbs: 60g, Fiber: 8g, Protein: 18g

116. Lachuch Sandwich with Za'atar and Labneh:

Prep Time: 10 mins
Cook Time: 10 mins
Total Time: 20 mins
Servings: 4

Ingredients:
- 4 lachuch (Yemeni flatbread) or pita bread
- 1 cup of labneh (strained yogurt)
- 2 tbsp za'atar spice blend
- 1/4 cup of chop-up fresh mint
- 1/4 cup of chop-up fresh parsley
- 2 tbsp olive oil
- Salt and pepper as needed

Instructions:
1. Warm the lachuch in a skillet or microwave up to soft and malleable. Warm up the pita bread in the oven or toaster.
2. To make the spread, combine the labneh, za'atar spice blend, chop-up fresh mint, chop-up fresh parsley, olive oil, salt, and pepper in a combining dish.
3. Spread a heaping spoonful of za'atar labneh spread onto every lachuch or pita bread.
4. Make a sandwich with the lachuch or pita bread and serve.

Nutrition (per serving):
Cals: 300 kcal, Fat: 15g, Carbs: 30g, Fiber: 2g, Protein: 10g

117. Israeli Roasted Red Pepper Dip with Walnuts:

Prep Time: 10 mins
Cook Time: 25 mins
Total Time: 35 mins

Servings: 8

Ingredients:
- 3 Big red bell peppers
- 1/2 cup of walnuts
- 2 cloves garlic
- 2 tbsp olive oil
- 2 tbsp lemon juice
- 1 tsp ground cumin
- Salt and pepper as needed
- Fresh parsley for garnish

Instructions:
1. Preheat the oven to 200 Ds Celsius (400 Ds Fahrenheit) and line a baking sheet with parchment paper.
2. Take out the seeds and membranes from the red bell peppers by Cuttingthem in half.
3. Place the red bell pepper halves, skin side up, on the prepared baking sheet.
4. Roast the red bell peppers for 20-25 mins, or up to the skins are roasted and blistered, in a preheated oven.
5. Let the roasted red bell peppers to cool slightly once they have been take outd from the oven.
6. Take out the red bell peppers' burnt skins.
7. Combine the roasted red bell peppers, walnuts, garlic, olive oil, lemon juice, ground cumin, salt, and pepper in a mixer.
8. Pulse the ingredients up to they form a smooth and creamy dip.
9. Before serving, transfer the roasted red pepper dip to a serving bowl and top with fresh parsley.

Nutrition (per serving):
Cals: 120 kcal, Fat: 10g, Carbs: 6g, Fiber: 2g, Protein: 2g

118. Shakshuka with Eggplant and Chickpeas:

Prep Time: 15 mins
Cook Time: 30 mins
Total Time: 45 mins
Servings: 4

Ingredients:
- 2 tbsp olive oil
- 1 onion, thinly split
- 1 eggplant, diced
- 2 cloves garlic, chop-up
- 1 tsp ground cumin
- 1 tsp ground paprika
- 1/2 tsp ground cayenne pepper (non-compulsory, for heat)
- 1 can (14 oz) diced tomatoes

- 1 can (14 oz) chickpeas, drained and rinsed
- Salt and pepper as needed
- 4-6 Big eggs
- Fresh parsley for garnish

Instructions:

1. Heat the olive oil in a big skillet or frying pan over medium heat.
2. Sauté the thinly split onions up to they become transparent.
3. Add the diced eggplant and cook up to tender.
4. Cook for another min after adding the chop-up garlic to the skillet.
5. Season the eggplant Mixture with cumin, paprika, cayenne pepper (if using), salt, and pepper as needed.
6. Add the diced tomatoes with their juices.
7. Stir in the drained and rinsed chickpeas to combine all of the ingredients.
8. Let the shakshuka Mixture to simmer for 10 mins to let the flavors to blend.
9. Make wells in the Mixture and place the eggs inside.
10. Let the eggs to cook for about 5-7 mins, or up to the whites are set but the yolks are still runny.
11. Before serving, garnish the shakshuka with eggplant and chickpeas and fresh parsley.

Nutrition (per serving):
Cals: 300 kcal, Fat: 15g, Carbs: 30g, Fiber: 8g, Protein: 12g

119.Malabi with Almond Milk and Raspberry Sauce:

Prep Time: 5 mins

Cook Time: 10 mins (+ chilling time)

Total Time: 15 mins (+ chilling time)

Servings: 4

Ingredients:

- 2 cups of almond milk
- 1/4 cup of cornstarch
- 1/4 cup of granulated sugar
- 1 tsp rosewater (non-compulsory)
- Fresh raspberries for garnish

Instructions:

1. Whisk together the almond milk, cornstarch, granulated sugar, and rosewater (if using) in a saucepan.
2. Cook, stirring constantly, over medium heat up to the Mixture thickens and reveryes a custard-like consistency.
3. Fill serving cups of or glasses halfway with the malabi Mixture.

4. Let the malabi to chill in the refrigerator for at least 2 hrs, or up to totally set.
5. Garnish the malabi with fresh raspberries before serving for a pop of color and taste.

Nutrition (per serving):
Cals: 120 kcal, Fat: 3g, Carbs: 22g, Fiber: 2g, Protein: 2g

120.Rugelach with Apple Cinnamon Filling:

Prep Time: 30 mins

Cook Time: 20 mins

Total Time: 50 mins

Servings: 24

Ingredients:

- 2 cups of all-purpose flour
- 1 cup of unsalted butter, melted
- 1 cup of cream cheese, melted
- 1/4 cup of granulated sugar
- 1 tsp vanilla extract
- 1/4 tsp salt
- 2 cups of apple, peel off and lightly chop-up
- 1/4 cup of brown sugar
- 1 tsp ground cinnamon
- 1/4 cup of powdered sugar for dusting

Instructions:

1. Cream together the melted butter, cream cheese, granulated sugar, and vanilla extract in a Big combining bowl up to smooth.
2. Combine in the salt.
3. Add the all-purpose flour gradually to the butter Mixture and stir up to a soft dough forms.
4. Divide the dough into two equal parts and form every into a disc.
5. Wrap the dough discs in plastic wrap and place them in the refrigerator for at least 30 mins to firm up.
6. Preheat the oven to 180 Ds Celsius (350 Ds Fahrenheit) and line a baking sheet with parchment paper.
7. To make the filling, combine the lightly diced apples, brown sugar, and ground cinnamon in a separate bowl.
8. Roll out one cold dough disc into a circle approximately 1/8-inch thick on a floured surface.
9. Half of the apple cinnamon filling Must be spread over the rolled-out dough.
10. Slice the dough circle into 12 equal triangles with a knife or pizza sliceter.
11. Roll up every triangle to form rugelach, beginning with the wider end, and set them on the prepared baking sheet.

12. Steps 7–11 Must be repeated with the second cold dough disc and the remaining apple cinnamon filling.
13. Rugelach Must be baked in a preheated oven for 18-20 mins, or up to lightly golden.
14. Let the rugelach to cool on a wire rack before dusting with powdered sugar and serving.

Cals: 150 kcal, Fat: 10g, Carbs: 14g, Fiber: 1g, Protein: 2g

121.Tahini Yogurt Parfait with Honey and Granola:

Prep Time: 10 mins

No Cook Time

Total Time: 10 mins

Servings: 2

Ingredients:
- 1 cup of Greek yogurt
- 2 tbsp tahini
- 2 tbsp honey
- 1/2 cup of granola
- Fresh berries for topping (such as strawberries or blueberries)

Instructions:
1. In a combining bowl, blend the Greek yogurt and tahini up to well incorporated.
2. Layer the tahini yogurt, honey, and granola in serving glasses or bowls.
3. For extra sweetness and freshness, top the parfait with fresh berries.

Nutrition (per serving):
Cals: 300 kcal, Fat: 15g, Carbs: 30g, Fiber: 2g, Protein: 15g

122.Bourekas with Mushroom and Cheese Filling:

Prep Time: 20 mins

Cook Time: 25 mins

Total Time: 45 mins

Servings: 12

Ingredients:
- 2 sheets puff pastry (store-bought or homemade)
- 1 cup of mushrooms, lightly chop-up
- 1 cup of shredded cheese (such as mozzarella or cheddar)
- 1/4 cup of chop-up fresh parsley
- 1/4 cup of chop-up green onions
- 1/2 tsp garlic powder
- Salt and pepper as needed

- 1 egg, beaten (for egg wash)
- Sesame seeds for sprinkling

Instructions:
1. Preheat the oven to 200 Ds Celsius (400 Ds Fahrenheit) and line a baking sheet with parchment paper.
2. To make the filling, combine the lightly chop-up mushrooms, shredded cheese, chop-up fresh parsley, chop-up green onions, garlic powder, salt, and pepper in a combining dish.
3. On a floured surface, unroll the puff pastry sheets and slice every sheet into 6 equal squares.
4. Fill every puff pastry square with a dollop of the mushroom and cheese filling.
5. Fold the puff pastry squares into triangles and press the edges with a fork to seal.
6. For a golden finish, brush the tops of the bourekas with beaten egg.
7. Sesame seeds can be sprinkled on top of the bourekas.
8. Place the bourekas on the prepared baking sheet and bake for 20-25 mins, or up to they are puffed up and golden brown.
9. Warm bourekas with mushroom and cheese filling make an excellent appetizer or snack.

Nutrition (per serving - 1 boureka):
Cals: 180 kcal, Fat: 10g, Carbs: 15g, Fiber: 1g, Protein: 6g

123.Falafel Pita Bowl with Quinoa and Hummus:

Prep Time: 30 mins

Cook Time: 20 mins

Total Time: 50 mins

Servings: 4

Ingredients:
- 16 falafel patties (store-bought or homemade)
- 1 cup of quinoa, cooked according to box/pkg instructions
- 1 cup of cherry tomatoes, halved
- 1 cucumber, diced
- 1/2 cup of red onion, thinly split
- 1/4 cup of chop-up fresh parsley
- 1/4 cup of chop-up fresh mint
- 1/4 cup of hummus
- Juice of 1 lemon
- Salt and pepper as needed

Instructions:
1. If you're using store-bought falafel patties, cook them according to the box/pkg directions. Cook

or bake homemade falafel till crispy and golden brown.

2. Combine cooked quinoa, halved cherry tomatoes, diced cucumber, thinly split red onion, chop-up fresh parsley, and chop-up fresh mint in a combining bowl.
3. Drizzle the lemon juice over the quinoa salad and season as needed with salt and pepper.
4. Begin by making a bed of quinoa salad for the falafel pita bowls.
5. Fill every bowl with 4 falafel patties.
6. Dollop hummus on top of the falafel.
7. If preferred, garnish the falafel pita bowls with fresh parsley and mint.

Nutrition (per serving):

Cals: 400 kcal, Fat: 15g, Carbs: 50g, Fiber: 10g, Protein: 20g

124.Lachuch with Nutella and Split Bananas:

Prep Time: 10 mins

Cook Time: 10 mins

Total Time: 20 mins

Servings: 4

Ingredients:

- 2 cups of all-purpose flour
- 1 packet active dry yeast (about 2 1/4 tsp)
- 1 tsp sugar
- 1 tsp salt
- 1 cup of warm water
- 1/4 cup of vegetable oil
- Nutella for spreading
- 2 ripe bananas, split
- Powdered sugar for dusting

Instructions:

1. Combine the all-purpose flour, active dry yeast, sugar, and salt in a Big combining basin.
2. To the flour Mixture, add the warm water and vegetable oil.
3. Stir constantly up to a smooth, sticky dough develops.
4. Cover the bowl with a clean dish towel and set aside for 1 hr to rest and rise.
5. Preheat a griddle or nonstick skillet over medium heat.
6. Spread 1/4 cup of the lachuch batter into a circular shape on the skillet.
7. Cook the lachuch for 2-3 mins per side, or up to gently browned and heated through.
8. Steps 6 and 7 Must be repeated with the leftover lachuch batter.
9. Top every lachuch with Nutella and split bananas.

10. Before serving, dust the lachuch with powdered sugar.

Nutrition (per serving - 1 lachuch):

Cals: 350 kcal, Fat: 15g, Carbs: 50g, Fiber: 3g, Protein: 5g

125.Israeli Shakshuka with Swiss Chard and Olives:

Prep Time: 10 mins

Cook Time: 25 mins

Total Time: 35 mins

Servings: 4

Ingredients:

- 2 tbsp olive oil
- 1 onion, thinly split
- 2 cloves garlic, chop-up
- 1 bunch Swiss chard, chop-up
- 1 can (14 oz) diced tomatoes
- 1 tsp ground cumin
- 1 tsp ground paprika
- Salt and pepper as needed
- 4-6 Big eggs
- 1/4 cup of pitted green olives, split
- Fresh parsley for garnish

Instructions:

1. Heat the olive oil in a big skillet or frying pan over medium heat.
2. Sauté the thinly split onions up to they become transparent.
3. Sauté for another min after adding the chop-up garlic.
4. Cook the chop-up Swiss chard in the skillet up to it wilts.
5. Add the diced tomatoes with their juices.
6. Season the shakshuka with cumin, paprika, salt, and pepper as needed.
7. Let the shakshuka Mixture to simmer for 10 mins to let the flavors to blend.
8. Make wells in the Mixture and place the eggs inside.
9. Scatter the shakshuka with the slice green olives.
10. Let the eggs to cook for about 5-7 mins, or up to the whites are set but the yolks are still runny.
11. Before serving, garnish the Israeli shakshuka with Swiss chard and olives and fresh parsley.

Nutrition (per serving):

Cals: 250 kcal, Fat: 15g, Carbs: 20g, Fiber: 5g, Protein: 12g

126.Rugelach with Fig Jam and Pistachios:

Prep Time: 30 mins

Cook Time: 20 mins

Total Time: 50 mins

Servings: 24

Ingredients:

- 2 cups of all-purpose flour
- 1 cup of unsalted butter, melted
- 1 cup of cream cheese, melted
- 1/4 cup of granulated sugar
- 1 tsp vanilla extract
- 1/4 tsp salt
- 1 cup of fig jam
- 1/2 cup of chop-up pistachios
- 1/4 cup of powdered sugar for dusting

Instructions:

1. Cream together the melted butter, cream cheese, granulated sugar, and vanilla extract in a Big combining bowl up to smooth.
2. Combine in the salt.
3. Add the all-purpose flour gradually to the butter Mixture and stir up to a soft dough forms.
4. Divide the dough into two equal parts and form every into a disc.
5. Wrap the dough discs in plastic wrap and place them in the refrigerator for at least 30 mins to firm up.
6. Preheat the oven to 180 Ds Celsius (350 Ds Fahrenheit) and line a baking sheet with parchment paper.
7. Roll out one cold dough disc into a circle approximately 1/8-inch thick on a floured surface.
8. Half of the fig jam Must be spread over the rolled-out dough.
9. Pistachios, chop-up, Must be sprinkled over the fig jam.
10. Slice the dough circle into 12 equal triangles with a knife or pizza sliceter.
11. Roll up every triangle to form rugelach, beginning with the wider end, and set them on the prepared baking sheet.
12. Steps 7–11 Must be repeated with the second cold dough disc and the leftover fig jam and pistachios.
13. Rugelach Must be baked in a preheated oven for 18-20 mins, or up to lightly golden.
14. Let the rugelach to cool on a wire rack before dusting with powdered sugar and serving.

Nutrition (per serving - 1 rugelach):
Cals: 150 kcal, Fat: 10g, Carbs: 14g, Fiber: 1g, Protein: 2g

127.Bourekas with Sweet Potato and Caramelized Onions:

Prep Time: 30 mins

Cook Time: 45 mins

Total Time: 1 hr 15 mins

Servings: 12

Ingredients:

- 2 sheets puff pastry (store-bought or homemade)
- 2 Big sweet potatoes, peel off and diced
- 2 tbsp olive oil
- 1 Big onion, thinly split
- 1 tsp ground cumin
- Salt and pepper as needed
- 1 egg, beaten (for egg wash)

Instructions:

1. Preheat the oven to 200 Ds Celsius (400 Ds Fahrenheit) and line a baking sheet with parchment paper.
2. Cook the diced sweet potatoes in a pot of boiling water up to cooked. Set aside after draining.
3. Warm the olive oil in a pan over medium heat. Sauté the thinly split onions up to they caramelize and become golden brown.
4. Season the cooked sweet potatoes with ground cumin, salt, and pepper before adding them to the caramelized onions. Combine thoroughly and set aside to cool slightly.
5. On a floured surface, unroll the puff pastry sheets and slice every sheet into 6 equal squares.
6. Fill every puff pastry square with a tbsp of the sweet potato and caramelized onion Mixture.
7. Fold the puff pastry squares into triangles and press the edges with a fork to seal.
8. For a golden finish, brush the tops of the bourekas with beaten egg.
9. Place the bourekas on the prepared baking sheet and bake for 20-25 mins, or up to they are puffed up and golden brown.
10. Warm bourekas with sweet potato and caramelized onion filling make a tasty appetizer or snack.

Nutrition (per serving - 1 boureka):
Cals: 200 kcal, Fat: 10g, Carbs: 20g, Fiber: 2g, Protein: 3g

128.Shakshuka with Kale and Feta:

Prep Time: 10 mins

Cook Time: 25 mins

Total Time: 35 mins

Servings: 4

- 2 tbsp olive oil
- 1 onion, thinly split
- 2 cloves garlic, chop-up
- 1 bunch kale, stems take outd and chop-up
- 1 can (14 oz) diced tomatoes
- 1 tsp ground cumin
- 1 tsp ground paprika
- Salt and pepper as needed
- 4-6 Big eggs
- 1/2 cup of cut up feta cheese
- Fresh parsley for garnish

Instructions:

1. Heat the olive oil in a big skillet or frying pan over medium heat.
2. Sauté the thinly split onions up to they become transparent.
3. Sauté for another min after adding the chop-up garlic.
4. Cook the chop-up kale in the skillet up to it wilts.
5. Add the diced tomatoes with their juices.
6. Season the shakshuka with cumin, paprika, salt, and pepper as needed.
7. Let the shakshuka Mixture to simmer for 10 mins to let the flavors to blend.
8. Make wells in the Mixture and place the eggs inside.
9. Cut up the feta cheese over the shakshuka.
10. Let the eggs to cook for about 5-7 mins, or up to the whites are set but the yolks are still runny.
11. Before serving, garnish the shakshuka with kale and feta and fresh parsley.

Nutrition (per serving):
Cals: 250 kcal, Fat: 15g, Carbs: 20g, Fiber: 5g, Protein: 12g

129.Israeli Halva Pancakes with Maple Syrup:

Prep Time: 15 mins

Cook Time: 15 mins

Total Time: 30 mins

Servings: 4

Ingredients:

- 1 cup of all-purpose flour
- 2 tbsp granulated sugar
- 1 tsp baking powder
- 1/2 tsp baking soda
- 1/4 tsp salt
- 1 cup of buttermilk
- 1 Big egg
- 2 tbsp vegetable oil
- 1/4 cup of cut up halva (sesame candy)
- Maple syrup for serving

Instructions:

1. Whisk together the all-purpose flour, granulated sugar, baking powder, baking soda, and salt in a Big combining basin.
2. Whisk together the buttermilk, egg, and vegetable oil in a separate basin.
3. Combine the wet and dry materials together up to they are barely blended.
4. Fold in the cut up halva up to it is equally distributed throughout the pancake batter.
5. Preheat a griddle or nonstick skillet over medium heat.
6. Spread 1/4 cup of the pancake batter into a circular shape on the skillet.
7. Cook the pancake for 2-3 mins per side, or up to golden brown and cooked through.
8. Steps 6 and 7 Must be repeated with the leftover pancake batter.
9. For a sweet and nutty treat, serve the Israeli halva pancakes with maple syrup.

Nutrition (per serving - 2 pancakes):
Cals: 400 kcal, Fat: 15g, Carbs: 55g, Fiber: 2g, Protein: 10g

130.Lachuch Sandwich with Falafel and Hummus:

Prep Time: 15 mins

Cook Time: 15 mins

Total Time: 30 mins

Servings: 4

Ingredients:

- 2 cups of all-purpose flour
- 1 packet active dry yeast (about 2 1/4 tsp)
- 1 tsp sugar
- 1 tsp salt
- 1 cup of warm water
- 1/4 cup of vegetable oil
- 8 falafel patties (store-bought or homemade)
- 1/2 cup of hummus
- Split tomatoes
- Split cucumbers
- Split red onion
- Fresh parsley for garnish

Instructions:

1. Combine the all-purpose flour, active dry yeast, sugar, and salt in a Big combining basin.
2. To the flour Mixture, add the warm water and vegetable oil.

3. Stir constantly up to a smooth, sticky dough develops.
4. Cover the bowl with a clean dish towel and set aside for 1 hr to rest and rise.
5. Preheat a griddle or nonstick skillet over medium heat.
6. Spread 1/4 cup of the lachuch batter into a circular shape on the skillet.
7. Cook the lachuch for 2-3 mins per side, or up to gently browned and heated through.
8. Steps 6 and 7 Must be repeated with the leftover lachuch batter.
9. Spread hummus on top of every lachuch.
10. Place two falafel patties on top of every lachuch.
11. Serve with split tomatoes, cucumbers, and red onion on top of the falafel.
12. Before serving, garnish the lachuch sandwich with falafel and hummus with fresh parsley.

Nutrition (per serving - 1 sandwich):
Cals: 400 kcal, Fat: 20g, Carbs: 45g, Fiber: 5g, Protein: 10g

131. Tahini Chocolate Chip Cookies:

Prep Time: 15 mins

Cook Time: 12 mins

Total Time: 27 mins

Servings: 24 cookies

Ingredients:
- 1 cup of all-purpose flour
- 1/2 tsp baking soda
- 1/4 tsp salt
- 1/2 cup of unsalted butter, melted
- 1/2 cup of granulated sugar
- 1/2 cup of packed brown sugar
- 1/4 cup of tahini
- 1 Big egg
- 1 tsp vanilla extract
- 1 cup of chocolate chips

Instructions:
1. Preheat the oven to 180 Ds Celsius (350 Ds Fahrenheit) and line a baking sheet with parchment paper.
2. In a medium combining bowl, combine the all-purpose flour, baking soda, and salt.
3. Cream together the melted butter, granulated sugar, and brown sugar in a separate Big combining basin up to light and fluffy.
4. Combine in the tahini, egg, and vanilla essence up to smooth.
5. Combine the dry ingredients into the wet components up to just combined.
6. Add the chocolate chips and combine well.

7. Drop spoonfuls of cookie dough onto the prepared baking sheet, giving enough space for spreading.
8. Bake for 10-12 mins, or up to the edges are lightly golden, in a preheated oven.
9. Let the tahini chocolate chip cookies to cool for a few mins on the baking sheet before moving them to a wire rack to cool fully.

Nutrition (per cookie):
Cals: 150 kcal, Fat: 8g, Carbs: 18g, Fiber: 1g, Protein: 2g

132. Malabi with Mango and Passionfruit Sauce:

Prep Time: 10 mins

Cook Time: 10 mins

Total Time: 20 mins

Servings: 4

Ingredients:
- 4 cups of coconut milk
- 1/2 cup of cornstarch
- 1/2 cup of sugar
- 1 tsp rose water
- Fresh mango slices
- Fresh passionfruit pulp

Instructions:
1. Whisk together the coconut milk, cornstarch, sugar, and rose water in a saucepan up to well blended.
2. Cook, stirring constantly, over medium heat up to the Mixture thickens and reveryes a custard-like consistency.
3. Let the malabi Mixture to cool slightly after removing it from the heat.
4. Distribute the malabi among serving basins or glasses.
5. Refrigerate the malabi for at least 2 hrs to let it to solidify.
6. Top every malabi with fresh mango slices and a dollop of passionfruit pulp before serving.

Nutrition (per serving):
Cals: 300 kcal, Fat: 15g, Carbs: 35g, Fiber: 1g, Protein: 2g

133. Rugelach with Raspberry Preserves and White Chocolate:

Prep Time: 30 mins

Cook Time: 20 mins

Total Time: 50 mins

Servings: 24

- 2 cups of all-purpose flour
- 1/2 cup of granulated sugar
- 1/4 tsp salt
- 1 cup of unsalted butter, melted
- 8 ozs cream cheese, melted
- 1 tsp vanilla extract
- 1 cup of raspberry preserves
- 1 cup of white chocolate chips
- Powdered sugar for dusting

Instructions:

1. In a Big combining basin, combine the all-purpose flour, granulated sugar, and salt.
2. In a separate combining bowl, combine the melted butter, melted cream cheese, and vanilla extract up to smooth.
3. Combine in the dry ingredients gradually with the wet components up to a soft dough forms.
4. Divide the dough into two equal parts and form every into a disc.
5. Wrap the dough discs in plastic wrap and place them in the refrigerator for at least 1 hr to firm up.
6. Preheat the oven to 180 Ds Celsius (350 Ds Fahrenheit) and line a baking sheet with parchment paper.
7. Roll out one cold dough disc into a circle approximately 1/8-inch thick on a floured surface.
8. Half of the raspberry preserves Must be spread over the rolled-out dough.
9. Half of the white chocolate chips Must be sprinkled over the raspberry preserves.
10. Slice the dough circle into 12 equal triangles with a knife or pizza sliceter.
11. Roll up every triangle to form rugelach, beginning with the wider end, and set them on the prepared baking sheet.
12. Steps 7–11 are repeated with the second cold dough disc, leftover raspberry preserves, and white chocolate chips.
13. Rugelach Must be baked in a preheated oven for 18-20 mins, or up to lightly golden.
14. Let the rugelach to cool on a wire rack before dusting with powdered sugar and serving.

Nutrition (per serving - 1 rugelach):
Cals: 180 kcal, Fat: 10g, Carbs: 20g, Fiber: 1g, Protein: 2g

134.Israeli Spinach and Feta Quiche:

Prep Time: 20 mins
Cook Time: 40 mins

Total Time: 1 hr
Servings: 6

Ingredients:

- 1 pre-made pie crust or homemade pie crust
- 1 tbsp olive oil
- 1 mini onion, lightly chop-up
- 2 cups of fresh spinach, chop-up
- 1 cup of cut up feta cheese
- 4 Big eggs
- 1 cup of heavy cream
- Salt and pepper as needed
- Pinch of nutmeg

Instructions:

1. Preheat the oven to 180 Ds Celsius (350 Ds Fahrenheit).
2. Use a 9-inch pie plate if using a pre-made pie crust. Roll out the pie crust and set it in the pie dish if using handmade pie crust.
3. Warm the olive oil in a pan over medium heat. Sauté the lightly chop-up onion up to it gets translucent.
4. Cook the chop-up fresh spinach in the skillet up to it wilts.
5. Whisk together the eggs, heavy cream, cut up feta cheese, salt, pepper, and nutmeg in a combining bowl.
6. Evenly distribute the sautéed spinach and onion Mixture over the pie crust.
7. Pour the spinach Mixture over the egg and feta Mixture.
8. Bake for 35-40 mins, or up to the quiche is set and faintly browned on top, in a preheated oven.
9. Let the quiche to cool slightly before slicing and serving.

Nutrition (per serving):
Cals: 350 kcal, Fat: 25g, Carbs: 15g, Fiber: 1g, Protein: 15g

135.Bourekas with Potato and Spinach Filling:

Prep Time: 30 mins
Cook Time: 25 mins
Total Time: 55 mins
Servings: 12

Ingredients:

- 2 sheets puff pastry (store-bought or homemade)
- 2 Big potatoes, peel off and diced
- 2 cups of fresh spinach, chop-up
- 1 mini onion, lightly chop-up
- 2 tbsp olive oil
- 1 tsp ground cumin

- 1/2 tsp garlic powder
- Salt and pepper as needed
- 1 egg, beaten (for egg wash)
- Sesame seeds for sprinkling

Instructions:

1. Preheat the oven to 200 Ds Celsius (400 Ds Fahrenheit) and line a baking sheet with parchment paper.
2. Cook the cubed potatoes in a pot of boiling water up to cooked. Set aside after draining.
3. Warm the olive oil in a pan over medium heat. Sauté the lightly chop-up onion up to it gets translucent.
4. Cook the chop-up fresh spinach in the skillet up to it wilts.
5. Add the cooked diced potatoes, cumin, garlic powder, salt, and pepper as needed. Combine thoroughly and set aside to cool slightly.
6. On a floured surface, unroll the puff pastry sheets and slice every sheet into 6 equal squares.
7. Fill every puff pastry square with a tbsp of the potato and spinach filling.
8. Fold the puff pastry squares into triangles and press the edges with a fork to seal.
9. For a golden finish, brush the tops of the bourekas with beaten egg and sprinkle with sesame seeds.
10. Place the bourekas on the prepared baking sheet and bake for 20-25 mins, or up to they are puffed up and golden brown.
11. Warm bourekas with potato and spinach filling make an excellent appetizer or snack.

Nutrition (per serving - 1 boureka):
Cals: 200 kcal, Fat: 10g, Carbs: 20g, Fiber: 2g, Protein: 3g

136.Falafel Platter with Tahini and Pickles:

Prep Time: 20 mins

Cook Time: 20 mins

Total Time: 40 mins

Servings: 4

Ingredients:

- 16 falafel patties (store-bought or homemade)
- 1 cup of tahini sauce
- 1 cup of pickles (cucumber, turnips, or combined)
- 1 cup of cherry tomatoes, halved
- 1 cup of shredded lettuce or cabbage
- 1/2 cup of chop-up fresh parsley
- 4 pita bread or flatbreads

Instructions:

1. Preheat the oven to 180 Ds Celsius (350 Ds Fahrenheit) and line a baking sheet with parchment paper.
2. Arrange the falafel patties on the baking sheet that has been prepared.
3. Bake the falafel for 15-20 mins, or up to heated through and crispy on the outside, in a preheated oven.
4. Prepare the tahini sauce and slice the pickles, cherry tomatoes, lettuce, and parsley while the falafel bakes.
5. Warm the pita bread or flatbreads for a few mins in the oven, or up to soft and flexible.
6. Place the warm pita bread or flatbreads on a serving tray to make the falafel platter.
7. Every bread Must be topped with falafel patties, tahini sauce, pickles, cherry tomatoes, shredded lettuce or cabbage, and fresh parsley.
8. As a tasty and filling supper, serve the falafel plate with tahini and pickles.

Nutrition (per serving - 4 falafel patties with toppings):
Cals: 500 kcal, Fat: 25g, Carbs: 45g, Fiber: 5g, Protein: 20g

137.Shakshuka with Pumpkin and Sage:

Prep Time: 15 mins

Cook Time: 30 mins

Total Time: 45 mins

Servings: 4

Ingredients:

- 2 tbsp olive oil
- 1 mini onion, lightly chop-up
- 2 cloves garlic, chop-up
- 2 cups of diced pumpkin or butternut squash
- 1 can (14 oz) diced tomatoes
- 1 tbsp tomato paste
- 1 tsp ground cumin
- 1/2 tsp ground paprika
- Salt and pepper as needed
- 4-6 Big eggs
- Fresh sage leaves for garnish

Instructions:

1. Heat the olive oil in a big skillet or frying pan over medium heat.
2. Sauté the lightly chop-up onion up to it gets translucent.
3. Sauté for another min after adding the chop-up garlic.
4. Cook up to the cubed pumpkin or butternut squash melts slightly in the skillet.

5. Add the diced tomatoes with their juices.
6. Add the tomato paste, cumin, paprika, salt, and pepper as needed.
7. Let the shakshuka Mixture to boil for 20-25 mins, or up to the pumpkin is thoroughly cooked and the flavors have combined.
8. Make wells in the Mixture and place the eggs inside.
9. Let the eggs to cook for about 5-7 mins, or up to the whites are set but the yolks are still runny.
10. Before serving, garnish the shakshuka with pumpkin and sage leaves.

Nutrition (per serving):
Cals: 250 kcal, Fat: 15g, Carbs: 20g, Fiber: 5g, Protein: 12g

138.Malabi with Pomegranate and Mint:

Prep Time: 10 mins

Cook Time: 10 mins

Total Time: 20 mins

Servings: 4

Ingredients:
- 4 cups of whole milk
- 1/2 cup of cornstarch
- 1/2 cup of sugar
- 1 tsp rose water
- Pomegranate arils
- Fresh mint leaves

Instructions:
1. Whisk together the whole milk, cornstarch, sugar, and rose water in a saucepan up to well blended.
2. Cook, stirring constantly, over medium heat up to the Mixture thickens and reveryes a custard-like consistency.
3. Let the malabi Mixture to cool slightly after removing it from the heat.
4. Distribute the malabi among serving basins or glasses.
5. Refrigerate the malabi for at least 2 hrs to let it to solidify.
6. Top every malabi with pomegranate arils and fresh mint leaves before serving.

Nutrition (per serving):
Cals: 300 kcal, Fat: 15g, Carbs: 35g, Fiber: 1g, Protein: 2g

139.Rugelach with Apricot Jam and Coconut:

Prep Time: 30 mins

Cook Time: 20 mins

Total Time: 50 mins

Servings: 24

Ingredients:
- 2 cups of all-purpose flour
- 1/2 cup of granulated sugar
- 1/4 tsp salt
- 1 cup of unsalted butter, melted
- 8 ozs cream cheese, melted
- 1 tsp vanilla extract
- 1 cup of apricot jam
- 1/2 cup of shredded coconut
- Powdered sugar for dusting

Instructions:
1. In a Big combining basin, combine the all-purpose flour, granulated sugar, and salt.
2. In a separate combining bowl, combine the melted butter, melted cream cheese, and vanilla extract up to smooth.
3. Combine in the dry ingredients gradually with the wet components up to a soft dough forms.
4. Divide the dough into two equal parts and form every into a disc.
5. Wrap the dough discs in plastic wrap and place them in the refrigerator for at least 1 hr to firm up.
6. Preheat the oven to 180 Ds Celsius (350 Ds Fahrenheit) and line a baking sheet with parchment paper.
7. Roll out one cold dough disc into a circle approximately 1/8-inch thick on a floured surface.
8. Half of the apricot jam Must be spread over the rolled-out dough.
9. Half of the shredded coconut Must be sprinkled over the apricot jam.
10. Slice the dough circle into 12 equal triangles with a knife or pizza sliceter.
11. Roll up every triangle to form rugelach, beginning with the wider end, and set them on the prepared baking sheet.
12. Steps 7 to 11 Must be repeated with the second refrigerated dough disc and the leftover apricot jam and crushed coconut.
13. Rugelach Must be baked in a preheated oven for 18-20 mins, or up to lightly golden.
14. Let the rugelach to cool on a wire rack before dusting with powdered sugar and serving.

Nutrition (per serving - 1 rugelach):
Cals: 180 kcal, Fat: 10g, Carbs: 20g, Fiber: 1g, Protein: 2g

140.Tahini Brownie Bites:

Prep Time: 15 mins

Cook Time: 20 mins

Total Time: 35 mins

Servings: 24

Ingredients:

- 1/2 cup of unsalted butter, dilute
- 1 cup of granulated sugar
- 2 Big eggs
- 1 tsp vanilla extract
- 1/2 cup of all-purpose flour
- 1/3 cup of unsweetened cocoa powder
- 1/4 tsp baking powder
- 1/4 tsp salt
- 1/2 cup of tahini paste
- 1/2 cup of chocolate chips

Instructions:

1. Preheat oven to 180°C (350°F) and line a mini muffin pan with paper liners.
2. In a Big combining basin, thoroughly incorporate the dilute butter and granulated sugar.
3. Add the eggs and vanilla essence and stir up to smooth.
4. Whisk together the all-purpose flour, cocoa powder, baking powder, and salt in a separate basin.
5. Combine the dry ingredients into the wet components up to just combined.
6. Stir in the tahini paste and chocolate chips up to equally distributed throughout the brownie batter.
7. Divide the brownie batter among the mini muffin cups of with a cookie scoop or spoon.
8. Bake the tahini brownie pieces for 12-15 mins, or up to firm and a toothpick inserted into the center comes out with a few moist crumbs.
9. Let the brownie bites to cool for a few mins in the muffin tray before transferring them to a wire rack to cool completely.

Nutrition (per serving - 1 brownie bite):
Cals: 100 kcal, Fat: 6g, Carbs: 11g, Fiber: 1g, Protein: 2g

141.Israeli Roasted Garlic Hummus:

Prep Time: 10 mins

Cook Time: 45 mins (for roasting garlic)

Total Time: 55 mins

Servings: 8

Ingredients:

- 2 cans (15 oz every) chickpeas, drained and rinsed
- 1/3 cup of tahini
- 1/4 cup of freshly squeezed lemon juice
- 1/4 cup of water
- 3 tbsp extra-virgin olive oil
- 1 head of garlic
- 1/2 tsp ground cumin
- Salt and pepper as needed
- Fresh parsley and olive oil for garnish

Instructions:

1. Preheat the oven to 200 Ds Celsius (400 Ds Fahrenheit).
2. Take out the top of the garlic head to expose the cloves.
3. Wrap the head of garlic in aluminum foil and drizzle olive oil over the exposed garlic cloves.
4. Roast the garlic cloves in a warm oven for 45 mins, or up to tender and golden brown.
5. Combine the roasted garlic cloves (squeeze the melted cloves from the head), drained and rinsed chickpeas, tahini, lemon juice, water, extra-virgin olive oil, ground cumin, salt, and pepper in a mixer.
6. Blend the ingredients up to smooth and creamy, adding more water if necessary to obtain the required consistency.
7. Season with salt and pepper as needed.
8. Place the Israeli roasted garlic hummus in a serving bowl and top with fresh parsley and olive oil.
9. Serve with pita bread, fresh vegetables, or as a sandwich spread.

Nutrition (per serving - 1/4 cup of):
Cals: 180 kcal, Fat: 12g, Carbs: 14g, Fiber: 4g, Protein: 5g

142.Falafel Sliders with Tahini Mayo:

Prep Time: 20 mins

Cook Time: 15 mins

Total Time: 35 mins

Servings: 4

Ingredients:

- 16 mini falafel patties (store-bought or homemade)
- 8 slider buns
- 1/2 cup of tahini sauce
- Lettuce leaves
- Split tomatoes
- Split red onions
- Pickles

Instructions:

1. Preheat the oven to 180°C (350°F) and warm the falafel patties according to the box/pkg directions if using store-bought falafel patties.

2. Slice the slider buns in half and sprinkle the tahini sauce on the bottom half of every.
3. On the bottom bread, place a lettuce leaf, then two falafel patties.
4. Garnish the falafel with split tomatoes, red onions, and pickles.
5. To finish the sliders, place the top half of the slider bread on top of the toppings.
6. As a delectable and pleasant supper, serve the falafel sliders with tahini mayo.

Nutrition (per serving - 1 slider):
Cals: 300 kcal, Fat: 12g, Carbs: 35g, Fiber: 5g, Protein: 15g

143.Shakshuka with Mushroom and Swiss Chard:

Prep Time: 10 mins
Cook Time: 25 mins
Total Time: 35 mins
Servings: 4

Ingredients:
- 2 tbsp olive oil
- 1 onion, lightly chop-up
- 2 cloves garlic, chop-up
- 1 cup of split mushrooms
- 2 cups of chop-up Swiss chard leaves
- 1 can (14 oz) diced tomatoes
- 1 tbsp tomato paste
- 1 tsp ground cumin
- 1/2 tsp ground paprika
- Salt and pepper as needed
- 4-6 Big eggs
- Fresh parsley for garnish

Instructions:
1. Heat the olive oil in a big skillet or frying pan over medium heat.
2. Sauté the lightly chop-up onion up to it gets translucent.
3. Sauté for another min after adding the chop-up garlic.
4. Cook up to the split mushrooms shed their moisture and begin to brown in the skillet.
5. Cook, stirring constantly, up to the Swiss chard leaves wilt.
6. Add the diced tomatoes with their juices.
7. Add the tomato paste, cumin, paprika, salt, and pepper as needed.
8. enable the shakshuka Mixture to simmer for 10-15 mins to enable the flavors to mingle.
9. Make wells in the Mixture and place the eggs inside.

10. Let the eggs to cook for about 5-7 mins, or up to the whites are set but the yolks are still runny.
11. Before serving, garnish the shakshuka with mushrooms and Swiss chard and fresh parsley.

Nutrition (per serving):
Cals: 250 kcal, Fat: 15g, Carbs: 15g, Fiber: 5g, Protein: 12g

144.Malabi with Strawberry and Pistachio Topping:

Prep Time: 10 mins
Cook Time: 10 mins
Total Time: 20 mins
Servings: 4

Ingredients:
- 4 cups of coconut milk
- 1/2 cup of cornstarch
- 1/2 cup of sugar
- 1 tsp rose water
- Fresh strawberries, split
- Chop-up pistachios

Instructions:
1. Whisk together the coconut milk, cornstarch, sugar, and rose water in a saucepan up to well blended.
2. Cook, stirring constantly, over medium heat up to the Mixture thickens and reveryes a custard-like consistency.
3. Let the malabi Mixture to cool slightly after removing it from the heat.
4. Distribute the malabi among serving basins or glasses.
5. Refrigerate the malabi for at least 2 hrs to let it to solidify.
6. Top every malabi with split strawberries and chop-up pistachios before serving.

Nutrition (per serving):
Cals: 300 kcal, Fat: 15g, Carbs: 35g, Fiber: 1g, Protein: 2g

145.Rugelach with Nutella and Hazelnuts:

Prep Time: 30 mins
Cook Time: 20 mins
Total Time: 50 mins
Servings: 24

Ingredients:
- 2 cups of all-purpose flour
- 1/2 cup of granulated sugar
- 1/4 tsp salt
- 1 cup of unsalted butter, melted

- 8 ozs cream cheese, melted
- 1 tsp vanilla extract
- 1/2 cup of Nutella
- 1/2 cup of chop-up hazelnuts
- Powdered sugar for dusting

1. Instructions:
2. In a Big combining basin, combine the all-purpose flour, granulated sugar, and salt.
3. In a separate combining bowl, combine the melted butter, melted cream cheese, and vanilla extract up to smooth.
4. Combine in the dry ingredients gradually with the wet components up to a soft dough forms.
5. Divide the dough into two equal parts and form every into a disc.
6. Wrap the dough discs in plastic wrap and place them in the refrigerator for at least 1 hr to firm up.
7. Preheat the oven to 180 Ds Celsius (350 Ds Fahrenheit) and line a baking sheet with parchment paper.
8. Roll out one cold dough disc into a circle approximately 1/8-inch thick on a floured surface.
9. Half of the Nutella Must be spread over the rolled-out dough.
10. Half of the chop-up hazelnuts Must be sprinkled over the Nutella.
11. Slice the dough circle into 12 equal triangles with a knife or pizza sliceter.
12. Roll up every triangle to form rugelach, beginning with the wider end, and set them on the prepared baking sheet.
13. Steps 7–11 Must be repeated with the second cold dough disc and the leftover Nutella and chop-up hazelnuts.
14. Rugelach Must be baked in a preheated oven for 18-20 mins, or up to lightly golden.
15. Let the rugelach to cool on a wire rack before dusting with powdered sugar and serving.

Nutrition (per serving - 1 rugelach):
Cals: 180 kcal, Fat: 10g, Carbs: 20g, Fiber: 1g, Protein: 2g

146.Tahini Energy Balls with Oats and Chocolate Chips:

Prep Time: 15 mins

Cook Time: No cook time

Total Time: 15 mins

Servings: 12

Ingredients:
- 1 cup of rolled oats

- 1/2 cup of tahini
- 1/4 cup of honey or maple syrup
- 1/4 cup of chocolate chips
- 1 tsp vanilla extract
- Pinch of salt
- Non-compulsory: shredded coconut, chop-up nuts, or chia seeds for coating

Instructions:
1. Combine the rolled oats, tahini, honey or maple syrup, chocolate chips, vanilla essence, and a pinch of salt in a Big combining basin.
2. Combine all of the ingredients in a combining bowl.
3. Roll little amounts of the Mixture into bite-sized balls.
4. Non-compulsory: To add texture and taste, roll the energy balls in shredded coconut, chop-up almonds, or chia seeds.
5. Place the tahini energy balls on a parchment-lined tray or baking sheet.
6. Refrigerate the energy balls for around 30 mins before serving to firm up.
7. Any leftovers Must be refrigerated in an airtight container.

Nutrition (per serving - 1 energy ball):
Cals: 120 kcal, Fat: 6g, Carbs: 12g, Fiber: 2g, Protein: 3g

147.Bourekas with Spinach and Feta Filling:

Prep Time: 30 mins

Cook Time: 20 mins

Total Time: 50 mins

Servings: 12

Ingredients:
- 1 box/pkg (17.3 oz) puff pastry sheets (2 sheets)
- 1 cup of refrigerate chop-up spinach, thawed and drained
- 1 cup of cut up feta cheese
- 1 egg, beaten (for egg wash)
- Sesame seeds (non-compulsory, for topping)

Instructions:
1. Preheat the oven to 200 Ds Celsius (400 Ds Fahrenheit) and line a baking sheet with parchment paper.
2. Combine the chop-up spinach and cut up feta cheese in a combining bowl up to well combined.
3. On a floured board, roll out one sheet of puff pastry and slice it into six equal squares.
4. Fill every puff pastry square with a tbsp of the spinach and feta filling.
5. Fold the puff pastry squares into triangles and press the edges with a fork to seal.

6. Steps 3–5 are repeated with the second sheet of puff pastry and the remaining filling.
7. Place the bourekas on the baking sheet that has been prepared.
8. For a golden finish, brush the tops of the bourekas with beaten egg and sprinkle with sesame seeds.
9. Bake the bourekas in a preheated oven for 15-20 mins, or up to puffy and golden brown.
10. Warm bourekas with spinach and feta filling make an excellent appetizer or snack.

Nutrition (per serving - 1 boureka):
Cals: 200 kcal, Fat: 12g, Carbs: 18g, Fiber: 1g, Protein: 5g

148.Israeli Stuffed Bell Peppers with Quinoa and Vegetables:

Prep Time: 20 mins

Cook Time: 30 mins

Total Time: 50 mins

Servings: 4

Ingredients:
- 4 Big bell peppers (any color)
- 1 cup of cooked quinoa
- 1 cup of diced combined vegetables (carrots, zucchini, corn, peas, etc.)
- 1/2 cup of diced onion
- 2 cloves garlic, chop-up
- 1 tbsp olive oil
- 1 tsp ground cumin
- 1/2 tsp ground paprika
- Salt and pepper as needed
- 1/2 cup of shredded cheese (non-compulsory, for topping)

Instructions:
1. Preheat the oven to 200°C (400°F) and butter a baking dish lightly.
2. Take out the tops of the bell peppers and the seeds and membranes.
3. Warm the olive oil in a Big skillet over medium heat.
4. Cook up to the onion is transparent and the garlic is chop-up.
5. Cook up to the diced combined vegetables are soft in the skillet.
6. Stir in the cooked quinoa, cumin, paprika, salt, and pepper up to thoroughly incorporated.
7. Fill every bell pepper halfway with the quinoa-vegetable Mixture.
8. If using cheese, top the stuffed bell peppers with shredded cheese.

9. Cover the stuffed bell peppers with aluminum foil in the prepared baking dish.
10. Bake the stuffed bell peppers for about 20-25 mins, or up to the peppers are soft.
11. Take out the foil and bake for 5 mins more to melt the cheese (if using).
12. As a filling and savory main course, serve the Israeli stuffed bell peppers with quinoa and veggies.

Nutrition (per serving - 1 stuffed bell pepper):
Cals: 250 kcal, Fat: 8g, Carbs: 35g, Fiber: 6g, Protein: 10g

149.Falafel Tacos with Avocado-Tahini Sauce:

Prep Time: 20 mins

Cook Time: 15 mins

Total Time: 35 mins

Servings: 4

Ingredients:
- 16 mini falafel patties (store-bought or homemade)
- 8 mini soft tortillas or taco shells
- 1 cup of shredded lettuce
- 1 cup of diced tomatoes
- 1/2 cup of diced red onions
- 1/4 cup of chop-up fresh parsley
- 1 ripe avocado, split
- 1/4 cup of tahini sauce
- 2 tbsp lemon juice
- Salt and pepper as needed

Instructions:
1. Preheat the oven to 180°C (350°F) and warm the falafel patties according to the box/pkg directions if using store-bought falafel patties.
2. To make the avocado-tahini sauce, combine the tahini sauce, lemon juice, salt, and pepper in a mini bowl.
3. Warm the tortillas or taco shells as directed on the box/pkg.
4. Place 2 falafel patties in the center of every tortilla or taco shell to make the falafel tacos.
5. Add shredded lettuce, diced tomatoes, diced red onions, chop-up fresh parsley, and split avocado to the falafel.
6. Drizzle the avocado-tahini sauce over the salad ingredients.
7. Fold the tortillas or taco shells around the ingredients and serve right away.

Cals: 400 kcal, Fat: 18g, Carbs: 48g, Fiber: 8g, Protein: 15g

150.Shakshuka with Feta and Olives:

Prep Time: 10 mins

Cook Time: 25 mins

Total Time: 35 mins

Servings: 4

Ingredients:

- 2 tbsp olive oil
- 1 onion, lightly chop-up
- 2 cloves garlic, chop-up
- 1 red bell pepper, diced
- 1 yellow bell pepper, diced
- 1 can (14 oz) diced tomatoes
- 1 tbsp tomato paste
- 1 tsp ground cumin
- 1/2 tsp ground paprika
- 1/4 tsp red pepper flakes (non-compulsory, for heat)
- Salt and pepper as needed
- 4-6 Big eggs
- 1/2 cup of cut up feta cheese
- 1/4 cup of pitted Kalamata olives
- Fresh parsley for garnish

Instructions:

1. Heat the olive oil in a big skillet or frying pan over medium heat.
2. Sauté the lightly chop-up onion up to it gets translucent.
3. Sauté for another min after adding the chop-up garlic.
4. Cook the diced red and yellow bell peppers in the skillet up to soft.
5. Add the diced tomatoes with their juices.
6. Add the tomato paste, cumin, paprika, red pepper flakes (if using), salt, and pepper as needed.
7. enable the shakshuka Mixture to simmer for 10-15 mins to enable the flavors to mingle.
8. Make wells in the Mixture and place the eggs inside.
9. Let the eggs to cook for about 5-7 mins, or up to the whites are set but the yolks are still runny.
10. Over the shakshuka, top with cut up feta cheese and pitted Kalamata olives.
11. Before serving, garnish the shakshuka with feta and olives and fresh parsley.

Nutrition (per serving):
Cals: 250 kcal, Fat: 15g, Carbs: 18g, Fiber: 5g, Protein: 12g

151.Malabi with Cardamom and Rosewater Syrup:

Prep Time: 10 mins

Cook Time: 10 mins

Total Time: 20 mins

Servings: 4

Ingredients:

- 4 cups of coconut milk
- 1/2 cup of cornstarch
- 1/4 cup of sugar
- 1 tsp ground cardamom
- 1 tsp rose water
- Crushed pistachios for garnish

Instructions:

1. In a mini saucepan, combine the coconut milk, cornstarch, sugar, and ground cardamom.
2. Cook, stirring constantly, over medium heat up to the Mixture thickens and reveryes a custard-like consistency.
3. Take the malabi Mixture off the stove and add the rose water.
4. Distribute the malabi among serving basins or glasses.
5. Refrigerate the malabi for at least 2 hrs to let it to solidify.
6. Garnish the malabi with cardamom and rosewater syrup and cut up pistachios before serving.

Nutrition (per serving):
Cals: 200 kcal, Fat: 10g, Carbs: 25g, Fiber: 1g, Protein: 2g

152.Rugelach with Raspberry and White Chocolate Filling:

Prep Time: 30 mins

Cook Time: 20 mins

Total Time: 50 mins

Servings: 24

Ingredients:

- 2 cups of all-purpose flour
- 1/2 cup of granulated sugar
- 1/4 tsp salt
- 1 cup of unsalted butter, melted
- 8 ozs cream cheese, melted
- 1 tsp vanilla extract
- 1/2 cup of raspberry jam
- 1/2 cup of white chocolate chips
- 1 egg, beaten (for egg wash)
- Powdered sugar for dusting

1. In a Big combining basin, combine the all-purpose flour, granulated sugar, and salt.
2. In a separate combining bowl, combine the melted butter, melted cream cheese, and vanilla extract up to smooth.
3. Combine in the dry ingredients gradually with the wet components up to a soft dough forms.
4. Divide the dough into two equal parts and form every into a disc.
5. Wrap the dough discs in plastic wrap and place them in the refrigerator for at least 1 hr to firm up.
6. Preheat the oven to 180 Ds Celsius (350 Ds Fahrenheit) and line a baking sheet with parchment paper.
7. Roll out one cold dough disc into a circle approximately 1/8-inch thick on a floured surface.
8. Half of the raspberry jam Must be spread over the rolled-out dough, leaving a little border around the edges.
9. Half of the white chocolate chips Must be sprinkled over the raspberry jam.
10. Slice the dough circle into 12 equal triangles with a knife or pizza sliceter.
11. Roll up every triangle to form rugelach, beginning with the wider end, and set them on the prepared baking sheet.
12. Steps 7–11 are repeated with the second cold dough disc, leftover raspberry jam, and white chocolate chips.
13. Brush the rugelach tops with beaten egg.
14. Rugelach Must be baked in a preheated oven for 18-20 mins, or up to lightly golden.
15. Let the rugelach to cool on a wire rack before dusting with powdered sugar and serving.

Nutrition (per serving - 1 rugelach):
Cals: 150 kcal, Fat: 9g, Carbs: 15g, Fiber: 1g, Protein: 2g

153. Tahini Cheesecake with Almond Crust:

Prep Time: 25 mins

Cook Time: 1 hr

Total Time: 1 hr 25 mins

Servings: 12

Ingredients:

- For the Crust:
- 1 1/2 cups of almond flour
- 1/4 cup of granulated sugar
- 1/4 cup of unsalted butter, dilute
- For the Filling:
- 24 ozs cream cheese, melted
- 1 cup of granulated sugar
- 1 cup of tahini
- 4 Big eggs
- 1 tsp vanilla extract
- For the Topping:
- 1/4 cup of tahini
- 2 tbsp honey
- Crushed almonds for garnish

Instructions:

1. Preheat the oven to 160°C (325°F) and oil a 9-inch springform pan with cooking spray.
2. To make the crust, combine the almond flour, granulated sugar, and dilute butter in a medium combining bowl.
3. To get a uniform layer, press the crust Mixture into the bottom of the greased springform pan.
4. In a Big combining bowl, combine the melted cream cheese and granulated sugar.
5. Continue combining the cream cheese Mixture with the tahini, eggs, and vanilla extract up to fully combined.
6. Pour the tahini cheesecake Mixture into the springform pan over the almond crust.
7. Bake the cheesecake for 55-60 mins, or up to the middle is set, in a preheated oven.
8. Let the cheesecake to cool to room temperature after removing it from the oven.
9. To make the topping, combine the tahini and honey in a mini bowl.
10. Drizzle the chilled cheesecake with the tahini-honey Mixture.
11. Before serving, sprinkle the tahini cheesecake with almond flakes.

Nutrition (per serving - 1 slice):
Cals: 450 kcal, Fat: 35g, Carbs: 28g, Fiber: 2g, Protein: 10g

154. Israeli Cauliflower Rice with Chickpeas and Turmeric:

Prep Time: 10 mins

Cook Time: 20 mins

Total Time: 30 mins

Servings: 4

Ingredients:

- 1 Big cauliflower head, slice into florets
- 2 tbsp olive oil
- 1 onion, lightly chop-up
- 2 cloves garlic, chop-up
- 1 can (15 oz) chickpeas, drained and rinsed
- 1 tsp ground turmeric
- 1/2 tsp ground cumin

- Salt and pepper as needed
- Fresh parsley for garnish

Instructions:

1. In a mixer, pulse the cauliflower florets up to they resemble rice grains.
2. Heat the olive oil in a big skillet or frying pan over medium heat.
3. Sauté the lightly chop-up onion up to it gets translucent.
4. Sauté for another min after adding the chop-up garlic.
5. Cook the riced cauliflower in the skillet for 5-7 mins, or up to soft.
6. Combine in the drained chickpeas, turmeric, cumin, salt, and pepper.
7. Cook the cauliflower rice with chickpeas and turmeric for 5 mins more to let the flavors to blend.
8. Before serving, garnish with fresh parsley.

Nutrition (per serving):

Cals: 200 kcal, Fat: 10g, Carbs: 20g, Fiber: 7g, Protein: 8g

155. Bourekas with Mushroom and Onion Filling:

Prep Time: 30 mins

Cook Time: 25 mins

Total Time: 55 mins

Servings: 12

Ingredients:

- 1 box/pkg (17.3 oz) puff pastry sheets (2 sheets)
- 2 cups of split mushrooms
- 1 Big onion, lightly chop-up
- 2 tbsp olive oil
- 1 tsp dried thyme
- 1/2 tsp garlic powder
- Salt and pepper as needed
- 1 egg, beaten (for egg wash)
- Sesame seeds (non-compulsory, for topping)

Instructions:

1. Preheat the oven to 200 Ds Celsius (400 Ds Fahrenheit) and line a baking sheet with parchment paper.
2. Warm the olive oil in a pan over medium heat.
3. Sauté the lightly chop-up onion up to it gets translucent.
4. Cook up to the split mushrooms are soft, about 10 mins.
5. Dry thyme, garlic powder, salt, and pepper season the mushroom and onion filling. Combine thoroughly.
6. On a floured board, roll out one sheet of puff pastry and slice it into six equal squares.
7. Fill every puff pastry square with a tbsp of the mushroom and onion filling.
8. Fold the puff pastry squares into triangles and press the edges with a fork to seal.
9. Steps 6–8 are repeated with the second sheet of puff pastry and the remaining filling.
10. Place the bourekas on the baking sheet that has been prepared.
11. For a golden finish, brush the tops of the bourekas with beaten egg and sprinkle with sesame seeds.
12. Bake the bourekas in a preheated oven for 20-25 mins, or up to puffy and golden brown.
13. Warm bourekas with mushroom and onion filling make an excellent appetizer or snack.

Nutrition (per serving - 1 boureka):

Cals: 180 kcal, Fat: 10g, Carbs: 15g, Fiber: 1g, Protein: 5g

156. Falafel Bowl with Quinoa and Lemon-Tahini Dressing:

Prep Time: 30 mins

Cook Time: 20 mins

Total Time: 50 mins

Servings: 4

Ingredients:

- For the Falafel:
- 1 can (15 oz) chickpeas, drained and rinsed
- 1/2 cup of chop-up fresh parsley
- 1/2 cup of chop-up fresh cilantro
- 2 cloves garlic, chop-up
- 1 tsp ground cumin
- 1 tsp ground coriander
- 1/2 tsp baking soda
- Salt and pepper as needed
- 2 tbsp all-purpose flour
- 2 tbsp olive oil (for frying)
- For the Quinoa:
- 1 cup of quinoa
- 2 cups of water
- Salt as needed
- For the Lemon-Tahini Dressing:
- 1/4 cup of tahini
- 2 tbsp lemon juice
- 1 tbsp water
- 1 clove garlic, chop-up
- Salt and pepper as needed
- For the Bowl Toppings:
- Split cucumbers
- Cherry tomatoes, halved

- Split red onion
- Fresh parsley and cilantro
- Lemon wedges

Instructions:

1. Combine the drained and rinsed chickpeas, chop-up fresh parsley, chop-up fresh cilantro, chop-up garlic, ground cumin, ground coriander, baking soda, salt, and pepper in a mixer.
2. Pulse the Mixture up to it is coarsely chop-up.
3. To bind the falafel Mixture, transfer it to a bowl and toss in the all-purpose flour.
4. Make tiny patties with the falafel Mixture and lay them on a baking sheet coated with parchment paper.
5. In a pan over medium heat, heat the olive oil and fry the falafel patties up to golden brown on both sides. To take out excess oil, place them on a platter lined with paper towels.
6. To prepare the Quinoa:
7. Cold water Must be used to rinse the quinoa.
8. Combine the rinsed quinoa, water, and salt in a saucepan.
9. Bring the quinoa to a boil, then decrease the heat to low, cover the pot, and leave it to cook for about 15 mins, or up to the quinoa is tender and the water has been absorbed.
10. To make the Lemon-Tahini Dressing, whisk together the tahini, lemon juice, water, chop-up garlic, salt, and pepper in a mini bowl up to thoroughly blended.
11. Making the Falafel Bowl:
12. Divide the cooked quinoa across four serving bowls.
13. Top the quinoa with the falafel patties, cucumber slices, halved cherry tomatoes, red onion slices, fresh parsley, and cilantro.
14. Drizzle over the falafel bowl the Lemon-Tahini Dressing.
15. Before serving, garnish the bowl with lemon wedges.

Nutrition (per serving):
Cals: 500 kcal, Fat: 25g, Carbs: 55g, Fiber: 12g, Protein: 18g

157.Shakshuka with Spinach and Feta:

Prep Time: 10 mins

Cook Time: 25 mins

Total Time: 35 mins

Servings: 4

Ingredients:

- 2 tbsp olive oil
- 1 onion, lightly chop-up
- 2 cloves garlic, chop-up
- 1 red bell pepper, diced
- 1 yellow bell pepper, diced
- 1 can (14 oz) diced tomatoes
- 1 tbsp tomato paste
- 1 tsp ground cumin
- 1/2 tsp ground paprika
- 1/4 tsp red pepper flakes (non-compulsory, for heat)
- Salt and pepper as needed
- 4 cups of fresh spinach leaves
- 1/2 cup of cut up feta cheese
- Fresh parsley for garnish

Instructions:

1. Heat the olive oil in a big skillet or frying pan over medium heat.
2. Sauté the lightly chop-up onion up to it gets translucent.
3. Sauté for another min after adding the chop-up garlic.
4. Cook up to the diced red and yellow bell peppers are soft in the skillet.
5. Add the diced tomatoes with their juices.
6. Add the tomato paste, cumin, paprika, red pepper flakes (if using), salt, and pepper as needed.
7. Let the shakshuka Mixture to boil for 10 mins.
8. Cook up to the fresh spinach leaves wilt in the skillet.
9. Shakshuka Must be topped with cut up feta cheese.
10. Before serving, garnish the shakshuka with spinach and feta and fresh parsley.

Nutrition (per serving):
Cals: 200 kcal, Fat: 10g, Carbs: 20g, Fiber: 5g, Protein: 8g

158.Malabi with Mango and Coconut:

Prep Time: 10 mins

Cook Time: 10 mins

Total Time: 2 hrs 20 mins (includes chilling time)

Servings: 4

Ingredients:

- 2 cups of coconut milk
- 1/2 cup of cornstarch
- 1/4 cup of granulated sugar
- 1 tsp vanilla extract
- 1/2 cup of diced ripe mango
- 1/4 cup of shredded coconut

Instructions:

1. In a mini saucepan, combine the coconut milk, cornstarch, granulated sugar, and vanilla essence.
2. Cook, stirring constantly, over medium heat up to the Mixture thickens and reveryes a custard-like consistency.
3. Let the malabi Mixture to cool slightly after removing it from the heat.
4. Divide the malabi among the cups of or bowls.
5. Refrigerate the malabi for at least 2 hrs, or up to completely cooled and set.
6. Serve the malabi topped with diced ripe mango and shredded coconut.

Nutrition (per serving):

Cals: 250 kcal, Fat: 15g, Carbs: 30g, Fiber: 2g, Protein: 2g

159. Rugelach with Apple and Cinnamon Filling:

Prep Time: 30 mins

Cook Time: 20 mins

Total Time: 50 mins

Servings: 24

Ingredients:

- 2 cups of all-purpose flour
- 1/2 cup of granulated sugar
- 1/4 tsp salt
- 1 cup of unsalted butter, melted
- 8 ozs cream cheese, melted
- 1 tsp vanilla extract
- 2 medium apples, peel off, cored, and lightly diced
- 1/4 cup of brown sugar
- 1 tsp ground cinnamon
- 1/2 cup of chop-up walnuts or pecans
- 1 egg, beaten (for egg wash)
- Powdered sugar for dusting

Instructions:

1. In a Big combining basin, combine the all-purpose flour, granulated sugar, and salt.
2. In a separate combining bowl, combine the melted butter, melted cream cheese, and vanilla extract up to smooth.
3. Combine in the dry ingredients gradually with the wet components up to a soft dough forms.
4. Divide the dough into two equal parts and form every into a disc.
5. Wrap the dough discs in plastic wrap and place them in the refrigerator for at least 1 hr to firm up.

6. Preheat the oven to 180 Ds Celsius (350 Ds Fahrenheit) and line a baking sheet with parchment paper.
7. For the filling, combine the lightly diced apples, brown sugar, ground cinnamon, and chop-up walnuts or pecans in a combining dish.
8. Roll out one cold dough disc into a circle approximately 1/8-inch thick on a floured surface.
9. Cover the rolled-out dough with half of the apple and cinnamon filling, leaving a little border around the sides.
10. Slice the dough circle into 12 equal triangles with a knife or pizza sliceter.
11. Roll up every triangle to form rugelach, beginning with the wider end, and set them on the prepared baking sheet.
12. Steps 7–11 Must be repeated with the second cold dough disc and the remaining apple and cinnamon filling.
13. Brush the rugelach tops with beaten egg.
14. Rugelach Must be baked in a preheated oven for 18-20 mins, or up to lightly golden.
15. Let the rugelach to cool on a wire rack before dusting with powdered sugar and serving.

Nutrition (per serving - 1 rugelach):

Cals: 150 kcal, Fat: 9g, Carbs: 15g, Fiber: 1g, Protein: 2g

160. Tahini Chocolate Mousse:

Prep Time: 20 mins

Total Time: 2 hrs 20 mins (includes chilling time)

Servings: 6

Ingredients:

- 1/2 cup of tahini
- 1/2 cup of unsweetened cocoa powder
- 1/4 cup of maple syrup or honey
- 1 tsp vanilla extract
- 1 can (14 oz) coconut milk, chilled overnight
- 1 tbsp powdered sugar (non-compulsory, for added sweetness)
- Chocolate shavings for garnish

Instructions:

1. In a combining bowl, combine the tahini, unsweetened cocoa powder, maple syrup or honey, and vanilla extract.
2. Open the cold coconut milk can and carefully scoop out the thick coconut cream from the top.
3. Beat the coconut cream into the tahini-chocolate Mixture up to smooth and creamy.
4. If desired, add powdered sugar to the mousse for

more sweetness and beat up to completely combined.

5. Serve the tahini chocolate mousse in glasses or bowls.

6. Refrigerate the mousse for at least 2 hrs, or up to completely cooled and set.

7. Garnish the tahini chocolate mousse with chocolate shavings before serving.

Nutrition (per serving):
Cals: 300 kcal, Fat: 24g, Carbs: 18g, Fiber: 4g, Protein: 6g

161.Israeli Spinach and Cheese Bourekas:

Prep Time: 30 mins

Cook Time: 25 mins

Total Time: 55 mins

Servings: 12

Ingredients:

- 1 box/pkg (17.3 oz) puff pastry sheets (2 sheets)
- 2 cups of fresh spinach leaves
- 1 cup of cut up feta cheese
- 1 cup of shredded mozzarella cheese
- 1 egg, beaten (for egg wash)
- Sesame seeds (non-compulsory, for topping)

Instructions:

1. Preheat the oven to 200 Ds Celsius (400 Ds Fahrenheit) and line a baking sheet with parchment paper.

2. Wilt the fresh spinach leaves in a pan over medium heat. Squeeze any extra liquid from the spinach and slice it.

3. To make the filling, combine the chop-up spinach, cut up feta cheese, and shredded mozzarella cheese in a combining bowl.

4. On a floured board, roll out one sheet of puff pastry and slice it into six equal squares.

5. Fill every puff pastry square with a tbsp of the spinach and cheese filling.

6. Fold the puff pastry squares into triangles and press the edges with a fork to seal.

7. Steps 4–6 Must be repeated with the second sheet of puff pastry and the remaining filling.

8. Place the bourekas on the baking sheet that has been prepared.

9. For a golden finish, brush the tops of the bourekas with beaten egg and sprinkle with sesame seeds.

10. Bake the bourekas in a preheated oven for 20-25 mins, or up to puffy and golden brown.

11. Warm Israeli spinach and cheese bourekas make an excellent appetizer or snack.

Nutrition (per serving - 1 boureka):
Cals: 180 kcal, Fat: 10g, Carbs: 15g, Fiber: 1g, Protein: 5g

162.Falafel Bites with Tahini Dip:

Prep Time: 20 mins

Cook Time: 15 mins

Total Time: 35 mins

Servings: 4

Ingredients:

- For the Falafel Bites:
- 1 can (15 oz) chickpeas, drained and rinsed
- 1/2 cup of chop-up fresh parsley
- 1/2 cup of chop-up fresh cilantro
- 2 cloves garlic, chop-up
- 1 tsp ground cumin
- 1 tsp ground coriander
- 1/2 tsp baking soda
- Salt and pepper as needed
- 2 tbsp all-purpose flour
- 2 tbsp olive oil (for frying)
- For the Tahini Dip:
- 1/4 cup of tahini
- 2 tbsp lemon juice
- 2 tbsp water
- 1 clove garlic, chop-up
- Salt as needed

Instructions:

1. Combine the drained and rinsed chickpeas, chop-up fresh parsley, chop-up fresh cilantro, chop-up garlic, ground cumin, ground coriander, baking soda, salt, and pepper in a mixer.

2. Pulse the Mixture up to it is coarsely chop-up.

3. To bind the falafel Mixture, transfer it to a bowl and toss in the all-purpose flour.

4. Make mini bite-sized patties out of the falafel Mixture.

5. In a skillet over medium heat, heat the olive oil and cook the falafel bites up to golden brown and crispy on both sides. To take out excess oil, place them on a platter lined with paper towels.

6. To make the Tahini Dip, combine together the tahini, lemon juice, water, chop-up garlic, and salt in a mini bowl up to thoroughly incorporated.

Nutrition (per serving - 1/4 of the recipe):
Cals: 280 kcal, Fat: 16g, Carbs: 28g, Fiber: 7g, Protein: 9g

163.Shakshuka with Roasted Red Peppers and Goat Cheese:

Prep Time: 10 mins

Cook Time: 25 mins

Total Time: 35 mins

Servings: 4

Ingredients:

- 2 tbsp olive oil
- 1 onion, lightly chop-up
- 2 cloves garlic, chop-up
- 2 roasted red peppers, chop-up
- 1 can (14 oz) diced tomatoes
- 1 tbsp tomato paste
- 1 tsp ground cumin
- 1/2 tsp ground paprika
- 1/4 tsp cayenne pepper (non-compulsory, for heat)
- Salt and pepper as needed
- 4-6 Big eggs
- 2 ozs goat cheese, cut up
- Fresh parsley for garnish

Instructions:

1. Heat the olive oil in a big skillet or frying pan over medium heat.
2. Sauté the lightly chop-up onion up to it gets translucent.
3. Sauté for another min after adding the chop-up garlic.
4. Cook for a few mins after adding the chop-up roasted red peppers to the skillet.
5. Add the diced tomatoes with their juices.
6. Add the tomato paste, cumin, paprika, cayenne pepper (if using), salt, and pepper as needed.
7. Let the shakshuka Mixture to boil for 10 mins.
8. Make mini wells in the shakshuka and crack the eggs into them.
9. Cook the eggs in a covered skillet over low heat up to they are done to your liking.
10. Shake the shakshuka with cut up goat cheese.
11. Before serving, garnish the shakshuka with roasted red peppers and goat cheese, as well as fresh parsley.

Nutrition (per serving):
Cals: 240 kcal, Fat: 17g, Carbs: 13g, Fiber: 3g, Protein: 10g

164.Malabi with Raspberry Coulis and Crushed Pistachios:

Prep Time: 10 mins

Cook Time: 10 mins

Total Time: 2 hrs 20 mins (includes chilling time)

Servings: 4

Ingredients:

- 2 cups of whole milk
- 1/4 cup of cornstarch
- 1/4 cup of granulated sugar
- 1 tsp rosewater or vanilla extract
- 1/4 cup of raspberry coulis (store-bought or homemade)
- 1/4 cup of crushed pistachios

Instructions:

1. Whisk together the whole milk, cornstarch, and granulated sugar in a saucepan up to well blended.
2. Cook, stirring constantly, over medium heat up to the Mixture thickens and reveryes a custard-like consistency.
3. Take the malabi Mixture off the heat and add the rosewater or vanilla extract.
4. Divide the malabi among the cups of or bowls.
5. Refrigerate the malabi for at least 2 hrs, or up to completely cooled and set.
6. Drizzle raspberry coulis over the malabi and top with crushed pistachios before serving.

Nutrition (per serving):
Cals: 220 kcal, Fat: 8g, Carbs: 30g, Fiber: 1g, Protein: 6g

165.Rugelach with Chocolate and Peanut Butter Filling:

Prep Time: 30 mins

Cook Time: 20 mins

Total Time: 50 mins

Servings: 24

Ingredients:

- 2 cups of all-purpose flour
- 1/2 cup of granulated sugar
- 1/4 tsp salt
- 1 cup of unsalted butter, melted
- 8 ozs cream cheese, melted
- 1 tsp vanilla extract
- 1/4 cup of cocoa powder
- 1/4 cup of powdered sugar
- 1/2 cup of peanut butter
- 1/2 cup of chocolate chips
- 1 egg, beaten (for egg wash)
- Chocolate shavings for garnish

Instructions:

1. In a Big combining basin, combine the all-purpose flour, granulated sugar, and salt.
2. In a separate combining bowl, combine the melted butter, melted cream cheese, and vanilla extract up to smooth.
3. Combine in the dry ingredients gradually with the wet components up to a soft dough forms.

4. Divide the dough into two equal parts and form every into a disc.
5. Wrap the dough discs in plastic wrap and place them in the refrigerator for at least 1 hr to firm up.
6. Preheat the oven to 180 Ds Celsius (350 Ds Fahrenheit) and line a baking sheet with parchment paper.
7. To make the chocolate filling, combine the cocoa powder and powdered sugar in a mini bowl.
8. Roll out one cold dough disc into a circle approximately 1/8-inch thick on a floured surface.
9. Cover the rolled-out dough with peanut butter, leaving a tiny border around the edges.
10. Over the peanut butter layer, sprinkle the chocolate chips and chocolate filling.
11. Slice the dough circle into 12 equal triangles with a knife or pizza sliceter.
12. Roll up every triangle to form rugelach, beginning with the wider end, and set them on the prepared baking sheet.
13. Steps 7–12 are repeated with the second cold dough disc.
14. Brush the rugelach tops with beaten egg.
15. Rugelach Must be baked in a preheated oven for 18-20 mins, or up to lightly golden.
16. Let the rugelach to cool on a wire rack before garnishing with chocolate shavings.

Nutrition (per serving - 1 rugelach):
Cals: 180 kcal, Fat: 12g, Carbs: 15g, Fiber: 1g, Protein: 3g

166.Tahini Granola with Honey and Dried Fruits:

Prep Time: 10 mins

Cook Time: 25 mins

Total Time: 35 mins

Servings: 10

Ingredients:
- 3 cups of rolled oats
- 1 cup of split almonds
- 1/2 cup of tahini
- 1/4 cup of honey
- 1/2 tsp vanilla extract
- Pinch of salt
- 1/2 cup of dried apricots, chop-up
- 1/2 cup of dried cranberries

Instructions:
1. Preheat the oven to 160 Ds Celsius (325 Ds Fahrenheit) and line a baking sheet with parchment paper.

2. Combine the rolled oats and split almonds in a Big combining basin.
3. Whisk together the tahini, honey, vanilla essence, and a pinch of salt in a separate mini bowl.
4. Combine the tahini Mixture into the oats and almonds up to everything is evenly coated.
5. Spread the granola Mixture equally on the baking sheet that has been prepared.
6. Bake the granola for 20-25 mins in a preheated oven, stirring halfway through, up to golden and crispy.
7. Let the granola to cool completely after removing it from the oven.
8. When the Mixture has cooled, whisk in the chop-up dried apricots and dried cranberries.
9. Tahini granola Must be stored in an airtight container.

Nutrition (per serving - 1/10 of the recipe):
Cals: 270 kcal, Fat: 14g, Carbs: 31g, Fiber: 4g, Protein: 6g

167.Israeli Stuffed Eggplant with Quinoa and Tomato Sauce:

Prep Time: 15 mins

Cook Time: 40 mins

Total Time: 55 mins

Servings: 4

Ingredients:
- 2 Big eggplants
- 1 cup of cooked quinoa
- 1 mini onion, lightly chop-up
- 2 cloves garlic, chop-up
- 1 cup of canned crushed tomatoes
- 1 tsp dried oregano
- 1/2 tsp ground cumin
- 1/2 tsp paprika
- Salt and pepper as needed
- 2 tbsp olive oil
- Fresh parsley for garnish

Instructions:
1. Preheat the oven to 200 Ds Celsius (400 Ds Fahrenheit) and line a baking sheet with parchment paper.
2. Slice the eggplants in half lengthwise and scoop out the flesh, leaving a 1/2-inch border around the edges to make a boat-like shape.
3. Set aside the scooped-out eggplant flesh in mini pieces.
4. Warm the olive oil in a pan over medium heat.
5. Sauté the lightly chop-up onion up to it gets translucent.

6. Sauté for another min after adding the chop-up garlic.
7. Cook the diced eggplant flesh in the skillet up to it softens.
8. Cooked quinoa, canned crushed tomatoes, dried oregano, ground cumin, paprika, salt, and pepper are all good additions.
9. enable the quinoa Mixture to simmer for 5 mins to enable the flavors to mingle.
10. Fill the quinoa Mixture into the hollowed-out eggplant halves.
11. Place the stuffed eggplants on the baking sheet that has been prepared.
12. Bake the stuffed eggplants for about 30 mins, or up to the eggplant is soft, on a baking sheet lined with foil.
13. Take out the foil and bake for 5 mins more to brown the tops.
14. Before serving, garnish the filled eggplants with fresh parsley.

Nutrition (per serving):
Cals: 280 kcal, Fat: 10g, Carbs: 44g, Fiber: 12g, Protein: 8g

168.Bourekas with Cheese and Dill Filling:

Prep Time: 20 mins

Cook Time: 25 mins

Total Time: 45 mins

Servings: 12

Ingredients:

- 1 box/pkg (17.3 oz) puff pastry sheets (2 sheets)
- 1 cup of cut up feta cheese
- 1 cup of shredded mozzarella cheese
- 1/4 cup of chop-up fresh dill
- 1 egg, beaten (for egg wash)
- Sesame seeds (non-compulsory, for topping)

Instructions:

1. Preheat the oven to 200 Ds Celsius (400 Ds Fahrenheit) and line a baking sheet with parchment paper.
2. To make the filling, combine the cut up feta cheese, shredded mozzarella cheese, and chop-up fresh dill in a combining dish.
3. On a floured board, roll out one sheet of puff pastry and slice it into six equal squares.
4. Fill every puff pastry square with a tbsp of the cheese and dill filling.
5. Fold the puff pastry squares into triangles and press the edges with a fork to seal.
6. Steps 3–5 are repeated with the second sheet of puff pastry and the remaining filling.

7. Place the bourekas on the baking sheet that has been prepared.
8. For a golden finish, brush the tops of the bourekas with beaten egg and sprinkle with sesame seeds.
9. Bake the bourekas in a preheated oven for 20-25 mins, or up to puffy and golden brown.
10. Warm bourekas with cheese and dill filling make an excellent appetizer or snack.

Nutrition (per serving - 1 boureka):
Cals: 180 kcal, Fat: 10g, Carbs: 15g, Fiber: 1g, Protein: 5g

169.Falafel Wrap with Hummus and Salad:

Prep Time: 20 mins

Cook Time: 10 mins

Total Time: 30 mins

Servings: 4

Ingredients:

- 8 falafel patties (store-bought or homemade)
- 4 Big whole wheat or corn tortillas
- 1 cup of hummus
- 1 cup of shredded lettuce
- 1 Big tomato, split
- 1 cucumber, split
- 1/4 cup of split red onion
- 1/4 cup of chop-up fresh parsley
- Tahini sauce or dressing (non-compulsory)

Instructions:

1. If using store-bought falafel, fry the falafel patties according to box/pkg directions up to heated through and crispy.
2. If you're making your own falafel, follow the directions on the box/pkg.
3. Warm the whole wheat or corn tortillas for about 10 seconds on every side in a dry skillet over medium heat.
4. Fill every tortilla with 1/4 cup of hummus, leaving a border around the borders.
5. Place 2 falafel patties, slightly off-center, on every tortilla.
6. Garnish the falafel with shredded lettuce, split tomatoes, cucumber slices, red onion slices, and fresh parsley.
7. If desired, drizzle tahini sauce or dressing over the salad.
8. Fold in the sides of the falafel wrap as you roll it up.
9. Serve the falafel wrap immediately with hummus and salad, or wrap it in foil for a portable dinner.

Cals: 400 kcal, Fat: 16g, Carbs: 54g, Fiber: 10g, Protein: 14g

170.Shakshuka with Swiss Chard and Harissa:

Prep Time: 15 mins

Cook Time: 25 mins

Total Time: 40 mins

Servings: 4

Ingredients:

- 2 tbsp olive oil
- 1 Big onion, lightly chop-up
- 2 cloves garlic, chop-up
- 1 bunch Swiss chard, stems take outd and leaves chop-up
- 1 can (14 oz) diced tomatoes
- 2 tbsp harissa paste (adjust to your spice preference)
- 1 tsp ground cumin
- 1 tsp ground paprika
- Salt and pepper as needed
- 4-6 Big eggs
- Fresh cilantro or parsley for garnish

Instructions:

1. Heat the olive oil in a big skillet or frying pan over medium heat.
2. Sauté the lightly chop-up onion up to it gets translucent.
3. Sauté for another min after adding the chop-up garlic.
4. Cook up to the chop-up Swiss chard leaves wilt in the skillet.
5. Add the diced tomatoes with their juices.
6. Add the harissa paste, ground cumin, ground paprika, salt, and pepper as needed.
7. Let the shakshuka Mixture to boil for 10 mins.
8. Make mini wells in the shakshuka and crack the eggs into them.
9. Cook the eggs in a covered skillet over low heat up to they are done to your liking.
10. Before serving, garnish the shakshuka with fresh cilantro or parsley.

Nutrition (per serving):

Cals: 230 kcal, Fat: 14g, Carbs: 17g, Fiber: 5g, Protein: 10g

171.Malabi with Orange Blossom and Candied Orange Peel:

Prep Time: 10 mins

Cook Time: 10 mins

Total Time: 2 hrs 20 mins (includes chilling time)

Servings: 4

Ingredients:

- 2 cups of whole milk
- 1/4 cup of cornstarch
- 1/4 cup of granulated sugar
- 1 tsp orange blossom water
- 1/4 cup of candied orange peel, chop-up
- 1/4 cup of pistachios, chop-up

Instructions:

1. Whisk together the whole milk, cornstarch, and granulated sugar in a saucepan up to well blended.
2. Cook, stirring constantly, over medium heat up to the Mixture thickens and reveryes a custard-like consistency.
3. Take the malabi Mixture off the stove and add the orange blossom water.
4. Divide the malabi among the cups of or bowls.
5. Refrigerate the malabi for at least 2 hrs, or up to completely cooled and set.
6. Garnish the malabi with candied orange peel and pistachios before serving.

Nutrition (per serving):

Cals: 230 kcal, Fat: 8g, Carbs: 33g, Fiber: 1g, Protein: 6g

172.Rugelach with Nutella and Pecans:

Prep Time: 20 mins

Cook Time: 20 mins

Total Time: 40 mins

Servings: 24

Ingredients:

- 2 cups of all-purpose flour
- 1 cup of unsalted butter, melted
- 1 cup of cream cheese, melted
- 1/4 cup of granulated sugar
- 1 tsp vanilla extract
- 1/2 cup of Nutella
- 1/2 cup of chop-up pecans
- 1/4 cup of powdered sugar (for dusting)

Instructions:

1. In a Big combining bowl, combine the melted butter, cream cheese, granulated sugar, and vanilla extract up to smooth.
2. Add the all-purpose flour gradually to the creamed Mixture and combine up to a soft dough forms.
3. Divide the dough into two equal parts and form every into a disc.
4. Wrap the dough discs in plastic wrap and place them in the refrigerator for at least 1 hr to firm up.

5. Preheat the oven to 180 Ds Celsius (350 Ds Fahrenheit) and line a baking sheet with parchment paper.
6. Roll out one cold dough disc into a circle approximately 1/8-inch thick on a floured surface.
7. Cover the rolled-out dough with Nutella, leaving a tiny border around the edges.
8. Over the Nutella layer, scatter chop-up pecans.
9. Slice the dough circle into 12 equal triangles with a knife or pizza sliceter.
10. Roll up every triangle to form rugelach, beginning with the wider end, and set them on the prepared baking sheet.
11. Steps 6–10 are repeated with the second cold dough disc.
12. Rugelach Must be baked in a preheated oven for 18-20 mins, or up to lightly golden.
13. Let the rugelach to cool on a wire rack before dusting with powdered sugar and serving.

Nutrition (per serving - 1 rugelach):
Cals: 160 kcal, Fat: 10g, Carbs: 15g, Fiber: 1g, Protein: 2g

173.Tahini Overnight Oats with Chia Seeds and Maple Syrup:

Prep Time: 5 mins
Total Time: 5 mins (+ overnight chilling time)
Servings: 2

Ingredients:
- 1 cup of rolled oats
- 2 tbsp chia seeds
- 2 tbsp tahini
- 2 tbsp maple syrup
- 1 cup of almond milk (or any milk of your choice)
- 1/4 tsp vanilla extract
- Pinch of salt
- Split bananas and crushed pistachios for topping

Instructions:
1. In a medium-sized combining dish, combine the rolled oats and chia seeds.
2. Whisk together the tahini, maple syrup, almond milk, vanilla essence, and a pinch of salt in a separate mini bowl.
3. Stir the tahini Mixture into the oats and chia seeds up to fully incorporated.
4. Refrigerate the bowl, covered with plastic wrap or a lid, overnight (or at least 4-6 hrs) to let the oats and chia seeds to soak and soften.
5. Stir the tahini overnight oats and divide them into serving bowls before serving.

6. Before serving, top the oats with split bananas and crushed pistachios.

Nutrition (per serving - half of the recipe):
Cals: 350 kcal, Fat: 18g, Carbs: 38g, Fiber: 10g, Protein: 9g

174.Israeli Spinach and Cheese Stuffed Mushrooms:

Prep Time: 15 mins
Cook Time: 20 mins
Total Time: 35 mins
Servings: 4

Ingredients:
- 16 Big button mushrooms
- 1 tbsp olive oil
- 1 mini onion, lightly chop-up
- 2 cloves garlic, chop-up
- 2 cups of fresh spinach, chop-up
- 1/2 cup of cut up feta cheese
- 1/4 cup of finely finely grated Parmesan cheese
- 1/4 cup of breadcrumbs
- Salt and pepper as needed
- Fresh parsley for garnish

Instructions:
1. Preheat the oven to 200 Ds Celsius (400 Ds Fahrenheit) and line a baking sheet with parchment paper.
2. Take out the stems from the mushrooms and set aside the caps.
3. Chop the mushroom stems lightly.
4. Warm the olive oil in a pan over medium heat.
5. Sauté the lightly chop-up onion up to it gets translucent.
6. Sauté for another min after adding the chop-up garlic.
7. Cook the mushroom stems in the skillet up to they release their liquid.
8. Cook the chop-up fresh spinach in the skillet up to it wilts.
9. Stir in the cut up feta cheese, finely finely grated Parmesan cheese, and breadcrumbs after the skillet has been take outd from the heat.
10. Season the spinach and cheese combination as needed with salt and pepper.
11. Stuff a tbsp of the spinach and cheese Mixture into every mushroom cap.
12. Place the stuffed mushrooms on the baking sheet that has been prepared.
13. Bake the stuffed mushrooms for 15-20 mins in a preheated oven, or up to the mushrooms are soft and the filling is brown.

14. Before serving, sprinkle the stuffed mushrooms with fresh parsley.

175.Falafel Sliders with Pickles and Tahini Mayo:

Prep Time: 20 mins

Cook Time: 15 mins

Total Time: 35 mins

Servings: 4 (makes 8 sliders)

Ingredients:

- 16 mini falafel patties (store-bought or homemade)
- 8 slider buns
- 1/2 cup of tahini sauce (store-bought or homemade)
- 1 cup of dill pickles, split
- Lettuce leaves
- Split tomatoes
- Split red onion

Instructions:

1. If using store-bought falafel, fry the falafel patties according to box/pkg directions up to heated through and crispy.
2. If you're making your own falafel, follow the directions on the box/pkg.
3. If desired, slice the slider buns in half and lightly toast them.
4. Spread tahini sauce generously on the bottom half of every slider bread.
5. On every bun, place two falafel patties.
6. Serve with split dill pickles, lettuce leaves, split tomatoes, and split red onion on top of the falafel.
7. Cover the sliders with the bun top halves.
8. Serve the falafel sliders immediately with pickles and tahini mayo.

176.Shakshuka with Kale and Chickpeas:

Prep Time: 10 mins

Cook Time: 25 mins

Total Time: 35 mins

Servings: 4

Ingredients:

- 2 tbsp olive oil
- 1 Big onion, lightly chop-up
- 2 cloves garlic, chop-up
- 1 red bell pepper, diced
- 1 yellow bell pepper, diced
- 2 cups of chop-up kale leaves
- 1 can (14 oz) diced tomatoes
- 1 can (14 oz) chickpeas, drained and rinsed
- 1 tsp ground cumin
- 1 tsp ground paprika
- 1/4 tsp cayenne pepper (non-compulsory, for heat)
- Salt and pepper as needed
- 4-6 Big eggs
- Fresh cilantro or parsley for garnish

Instructions:

1. Heat the olive oil in a big skillet or frying pan over medium heat.
2. Sauté the lightly chop-up onion up to it gets translucent.
3. Sauté for another min after adding the chop-up garlic.
4. Cook up to the diced red and yellow bell peppers begin to soften in the skillet.
5. Cook up to the kale leaves wilt, stirring frequently.
6. Add the diced tomatoes with their juices.
7. Add the chickpeas, cumin, paprika, cayenne pepper (if using), salt, and pepper as needed.
8. Let the shakshuka Mixture to boil for 10 mins.
9. Make mini wells in the shakshuka and crack the eggs into them.
10. Cook the eggs in a covered skillet over low heat up to they are done to your liking.
11. Before serving, garnish the shakshuka with fresh cilantro or parsley.

177.Malabi with Passionfruit and Coconut Flakes:

Prep Time: 10 mins

Cook Time: 10 mins

Total Time: 2 hrs 20 mins (includes chilling time)

Servings: 4

Ingredients:

- 2 cups of coconut milk
- 2 tbsp cornstarch
- 1/4 cup of granulated sugar
- 1 tsp vanilla extract

- 1/4 cup of passionfruit pulp (from about 4 passionfruits)
- 1/4 cup of coconut flakes

Instructions:
1. In a mini saucepan, combine the coconut milk, cornstarch, granulated sugar, and vanilla essence.
2. Cook, stirring constantly, over medium heat up to the Mixture thickens and revereyes a custard-like consistency.
3. Stir in the passionfruit pulp after removing the malabi Mixture from the heat.
4. Divide the malabi among the cups of or bowls.
5. Refrigerate the malabi for at least 2 hrs, or up to completely cooled and set.
6. Garnish the malabi with coconut flakes before serving.

Nutrition (per serving):
Cals: 220 kcal, Fat: 15g, Carbs: 20g, Fiber: 3g, Protein: 2g

178.Rugelach with Blueberry and Lemon Zest Filling:

Prep Time: 20 mins

Cook Time: 20 mins

Total Time: 40 mins

Servings: 24

Ingredients:
- 2 cups of all-purpose flour
- 1 cup of unsalted butter, melted
- 1 cup of cream cheese, melted
- 1/4 cup of granulated sugar
- 1 tsp vanilla extract
- 1/2 cup of blueberry preserves or jam
- Zest of 1 lemon
- 1/4 cup of powdered sugar (for dusting)

Instructions:
1. In a Big combining bowl, combine the melted butter, cream cheese, granulated sugar, and vanilla extract up to smooth.
2. Add the all-purpose flour gradually to the creamed Mixture and combine up to a soft dough forms.
3. Divide the dough into two equal parts and form every into a disc.
4. Wrap the dough discs in plastic wrap and place them in the refrigerator for at least 1 hr to firm up.
5. Preheat the oven to 180 Ds Celsius (350 Ds Fahrenheit) and line a baking sheet with parchment paper.

6. Roll out one cold dough disc into a circle approximately 1/8-inch thick on a floured surface.
7. Blueberry preserves or jam Must be spread over the rolled-out dough, leaving a tiny border around the edges.
8. Sprinkle the blueberry layer with lemon zest.
9. Slice the dough circle into 12 equal triangles with a knife or pizza sliceter.
10. Roll up every triangle to form rugelach, beginning with the wider end, and set them on the prepared baking sheet.
11. Steps 6–10 are repeated with the second cold dough disc.
12. Rugelach Must be baked in a preheated oven for 18-20 mins, or up to lightly golden.
13. Let the rugelach to cool on a wire rack before dusting with powdered sugar and serving.

Nutrition (per serving - 1 rugelach):
Cals: 160 kcal, Fat: 10g, Carbs: 15g, Fiber: 1g, Protein: 2g

179.Tahini Date Smoothie with Almond Milk:

Prep Time: 5 mins

Total Time: 5 mins

Servings: 2

Ingredients:
- 2 ripe bananas
- 6 Big dates, pitted
- 2 tbsp tahini
- 2 cups of unsweetened almond milk (or any milk of your choice)
- 1/2 tsp ground cinnamon
- 1/4 tsp vanilla extract
- Ice cubes (non-compulsory)

Instructions:
1. Blend together the ripe bananas, pitted dates, tahini, unsweetened almond milk, ground cinnamon, and vanilla essence in a blender.
2. Blend the ingredients up to the smoothie is smooth and creamy.
3. Add a few ice cubes to the blender and process up to the smoothie is cold, if desired.
4. Pour the tahini date smoothie into serving cups of and serve right away.

Nutrition (per serving - half of the recipe):
Cals: 300 kcal, Fat: 11g, Carbs: 50g, Fiber: 8g, Protein: 5g

180.Israeli Stuffed Tomatoes with Rice and Herbs:

Prep Time: 20 mins

Cook Time: 40 mins

Total Time: 1 hr

Servings: 4

Ingredients:

- 4 Big tomatoes
- 1 cup of cooked rice (white or brown)
- 1/4 cup of chop-up fresh parsley
- 1/4 cup of chop-up fresh mint
- 1/4 cup of chop-up fresh dill
- 1/4 cup of chop-up red onion
- 2 tbsp olive oil
- 2 tbsp lemon juice
- Salt and pepper as needed

Instructions:

1. Preheat the oven to 180°C (350°F) and butter a baking dish lightly.
2. Take out the tops of the tomatoes and use a spoon to carefully scoop out the pulp and seeds, forming hollow tomato shells.
3. Combine the cooked rice, chop-up fresh parsley, chop-up fresh mint, chop-up fresh dill, chop-up red onion, olive oil, lemon juice, salt, and pepper in a combining dish.
4. Combine the ingredients up to the rice filling is evenly coated with the herbs and seasonings.
5. Fill every tomato hollow with the rice and herb filling.
6. Place the stuffed tomatoes in a baking dish that has been buttered.
7. Bake the stuffed tomatoes for 30-40 mins in a preheated oven, or up to the tomatoes are soft.
8. As a delightful side dish or light supper, serve the Israeli stuffed tomatoes with rice and spices.

Nutrition (per serving - 1 stuffed tomato):

Cals: 180 kcal, Fat: 7g, Carbs: 27g, Fiber: 4g, Protein: 3g

181. Bourekas with Potato and Caramelized Onions:

Prep Time: 25 mins

Cook Time: 30 mins

Total Time: 55 mins

Servings: 12

Ingredients:

- 2 sheets puff pastry, thawed (10x10 inches every)
- 2 medium potatoes, boiled and mashed
- 2 Big onions, thinly split
- 2 tbsp olive oil
- 1 tsp ground cumin
- Salt and pepper as needed
- 1/4 cup of chop-up fresh parsley
- 1 egg, beaten (for egg wash)
- Sesame seeds for sprinkling

Instructions:

1. Preheat the oven to 200 Ds Celsius (400 Ds Fahrenheit) and line a baking sheet with parchment paper.
2. Warm the olive oil in a pan over medium heat.
3. Cook the thinly split onions in the skillet, turning regularly, up to they caramelize and turn golden brown.
4. Combine the mashed potatoes, caramelized onions, ground cumin, salt, pepper, and fresh parsley in a combining bowl. To make the filling, thoroughly combine all of the ingredients.
5. On a floured surface, place one sheet of puff pastry.
6. Make 6 equal squares out of the pastry sheet.
7. Fill every square with a tbsp of the potato and onion filling.
8. To seal the bourekas, fold one corner of every square over the filling to form a triangle and press the sides together.
9. Steps 5–8 Must be repeated with the second sheet of puff pastry.
10. Place the bourekas on the baking sheet that has been prepared.
11. For a golden finish, brush the tops of the bourekas with beaten egg and sprinkle with sesame seeds.
12. Bake the bourekas in a preheated oven for 20-25 mins, or up to puffy and golden brown.
13. Warm bourekas with potato and caramelized onions filling make an excellent appetizer or snack.

Nutrition (per serving - 1 boureka):

Cals: 190 kcal, Fat: 11g, Carbs: 18g, Fiber: 1g, Protein: 4g

182. Falafel Pita Bowl with Hummus and Tabouli:

Prep Time: 20 mins

Cook Time: 20 mins

Total Time: 40 mins

Servings: 4

Ingredients:

- 16 falafel balls (store-bought or homemade)
- 4 whole wheat pita bread
- 1 cup of hummus
- 2 cups of tabouli salad (a Mixture of bulgur, parsley, tomatoes, cucumber, lemon juice, olive oil, and spices)

- Combined salad greens
- Split cucumbers
- Split tomatoes
- Split red onion
- Tahini sauce for drizzling

Instructions:

1. If using store-bought falafel, fry the falafel balls according to box/pkg directions up to heated through and crispy.
2. If you're making your own falafel, follow the directions on the box/pkg.
3. Warm the pita bread in the oven or toaster.
4. To make pockets, slice the pita bread in half.
5. Fill every pita pocket with two falafel balls.
6. Insert a healthy amount of hummus into every pita pocket.
7. Place tabouli salad and combined salad leaves in pita pockets.
8. Salad Must be topped with split cucumbers, tomatoes, and red onion.
9. Before serving, drizzle the tahini sauce over the falafel pita bowls.

Nutrition (per serving - 1 falafel pita bowl):
Cals: 450 kcal, Fat: 15g, Carbs: 60g, Fiber: 12g, Protein: 15g

183.Shakshuka with Spinach and Feta:

Prep Time: 10 mins

Cook Time: 20 mins

Total Time: 30 mins

Servings: 4

Ingredients:

- 2 tbsp olive oil
- 1 Big onion, lightly chop-up
- 2 cloves garlic, chop-up
- 1 red bell pepper, diced
- 1 yellow bell pepper, diced
- 2 cups of chop-up fresh spinach
- 1 can (14 oz) diced tomatoes
- 1 tsp ground cumin
- 1 tsp ground paprika
- 1/4 tsp cayenne pepper (non-compulsory, for heat)
- Salt and pepper as needed
- 1/2 cup of cut up feta cheese
- Fresh parsley for garnish

Instructions:

1. Heat the olive oil in a big skillet or frying pan over medium heat.
2. Sauté the lightly chop-up onion up to it gets translucent.

3. Sauté for another min after adding the chop-up garlic.
4. Cook up to the diced red and yellow bell peppers begin to soften in the skillet.
5. Cook up to the fresh spinach wilts, stirring frequently.
6. Add the diced tomatoes with their juices.
7. Add the cumin, paprika, cayenne pepper (if using), salt, and pepper as needed.
8. Let the shakshuka Mixture to boil for 10 mins.
9. Make mini wells in the shakshuka and crack the eggs into them.
10. Cook the eggs in a covered skillet over low heat up to they are done to your liking.
11. Before serving, top the shakshuka with cut up feta cheese and sprinkle with fresh parsley.

Nutrition (per serving):
Cals: 250 kcal, Fat: 15g, Carbs: 20g, Fiber: 5g, Protein: 11g

184.Malabi with Pistachio and Rosewater Syrup:

Prep Time: 5 mins

Cook Time: 10 mins

Total Time: 2 hrs 15 mins (includes chilling time)

Servings: 4

Ingredients:

- 2 cups of whole milk
- 1/4 cup of cornstarch
- 1/4 cup of granulated sugar
- 1 tsp rosewater
- Crushed pistachios for garnish

Instructions:

1. Whisk together the whole milk, cornstarch, and granulated sugar in a saucepan up to well blended.
2. Cook, stirring constantly, over medium heat up to the Mixture thickens and reveryes a custard-like consistency.
3. Stir in the rosewater after removing the malabi Mixture from the heat.
4. Divide the malabi among the cups of or bowls.
5. Refrigerate the malabi for at least 2 hrs, or up to completely cooled and set.
6. Garnish the malabi with crushed pistachios before serving.

Nutrition (per serving):
Cals: 180 kcal, Fat: 7g, Carbs: 25g, Fiber: 1g, Protein: 4g

185. Rugelach with Raspberry and Almond Filling:

Prep Time: 30 mins

Cook Time: 20 mins

Total Time: 50 mins

Servings: 24

Ingredients:

- 2 cups of all-purpose flour
- 1 cup of unsalted butter, melted
- 1 cup of cream cheese, melted
- 1/4 cup of granulated sugar
- 1 tsp vanilla extract
- 1/2 cup of raspberry preserves or jam
- 1/2 cup of lightly chop-up almonds
- 1/4 cup of powdered sugar (for dusting)

Instructions:

1. In a Big combining bowl, combine the melted butter, cream cheese, granulated sugar, and vanilla extract up to smooth.
2. Add the all-purpose flour gradually to the creamed Mixture and combine up to a soft dough forms.
3. Divide the dough into two equal parts and form every into a disc.
4. Wrap the dough discs in plastic wrap and place them in the refrigerator for at least 1 hr to firm up.
5. Preheat the oven to 180 Ds Celsius (350 Ds Fahrenheit) and line a baking sheet with parchment paper.
6. Roll out one cold dough disc into a circle approximately 1/8-inch thick on a floured surface.
7. Cover the rolled-out dough with raspberry preserves or jam, leaving a tiny border around the borders.
8. Over the raspberry layer, scatter lightly chop-up almonds.
9. Slice the dough circle into 12 equal triangles with a knife or pizza sliceter.
10. Roll up every triangle to form rugelach, beginning with the wider end, and set them on the prepared baking sheet.
11. Steps 6–10 are repeated with the second cold dough disc.
12. Rugelach Must be baked in a preheated oven for 18-20 mins, or up to lightly golden.
13. Let the rugelach to cool on a wire rack before dusting with powdered sugar and serving.

Nutrition (per serving - 1 rugelach):
Cals: 150 kcal, Fat: 9g, Carbs: 14g, Fiber: 1g, Protein: 2g

186. Tahini Chia Seed Pudding with Berries:

Prep Time: 10 mins

Total Time: 2 hrs 10 mins (includes chilling time)

Servings: 4

Ingredients:

- 1/2 cup of chia seeds
- 2 cups of unsweetened almond milk (or any milk of your choice)
- 3 tbsp tahini
- 2 tbsp honey or maple syrup
- 1 tsp vanilla extract
- Fresh berries for topping (such as strawberries, blueberries, or raspberries)

Instructions:

1. In a combining bowl, combine the chia seeds, unsweetened almond milk, tahini, honey or maple syrup, and vanilla extract.
2. Refrigerate the chia seed pudding Mixture, covered, for at least 2 hrs or overnight to thicken.
3. Before serving, give the chia seed pudding a good stir to ensure that it has thickened evenly.
4. Serve the tahini chia seed pudding in glasses or bowls.
5. Before serving, top the pudding with fresh berries.

Nutrition (per serving):
Cals: 250 kcal, Fat: 14g, Carbs: 22g, Fiber: 10g, Protein: 8g

187. Israeli Stuffed Artichokes with Lemon and Olive Oil:

Prep Time: 20 mins

Cook Time: 45 mins

Total Time: 1 hr 5 mins

Servings: 4

Ingredients:

- 4 Big artichokes
- 1 cup of breadcrumbs
- 1/2 cup of finely finely grated Parmesan cheese
- 1/4 cup of chop-up fresh parsley
- 2 cloves garlic, chop-up
- Zest of 1 lemon
- 1/4 cup of olive oil
- 1 cup of vegetable or chicken broth
- Salt and pepper as needed

Instructions:

1. Preheat the oven to 180 Ds Celsius (350 Ds Fahrenheit).
2. Trim every artichoke's stem and take out any tough outer leaves.
3. Snip the spiky tips of the artichoke leaves using kitchen scissors.
4. Spread the artichoke leaves open gently to make room for the contents.
5. To make the filling, combine the breadcrumbs, finely finely grated Parmesan cheese, chop-up fresh parsley, chop-up garlic, lemon zest, olive oil, salt, and pepper in a combining bowl.
6. Fill the artichoke leaves with the filling Mixture, pushing firmly to keep it in place.
7. Pour the vegetable or chicken broth over the stuffed artichokes in a baking dish.
8. Cover the baking dish with aluminum foil and bake the artichokes for about 30 mins in a preheated oven.
9. Take out the foil and bake for another 15 mins, or up to the artichokes are soft and the filling is golden brown.
10. As an appetizer or side dish, serve the Israeli stuffed artichokes with lemon and olive oil.

Nutrition (per serving - 1 artichoke):
Cals: 300 kcal, Fat: 16g, Carbs: 30g, Fiber: 8g, Protein: 10g

188.Bourekas with Cheese and Dill Filling:

Prep Time: 20 mins

Cook Time: 25 mins

Total Time: 45 mins

Servings: 12

Ingredients:

- 2 sheets puff pastry, thawed (10x10 inches every)
- 1 cup of cut up feta cheese
- 1 cup of shredded mozzarella cheese
- 1/4 cup of chop-up fresh dill
- 1 egg, beaten (for egg wash)
- Sesame seeds for sprinkling

Instructions:

1. Preheat the oven to 200 Ds Celsius (400 Ds Fahrenheit) and line a baking sheet with parchment paper.
2. To make the filling, combine the cut up feta cheese, shredded mozzarella cheese, and chop-up fresh dill in a combining dish.
3. On a floured surface, place one sheet of puff pastry.
4. Make 6 equal squares out of the pastry sheet.
5. Fill every square with a tbsp of the cheese and dill filling.
6. To seal the bourekas, fold one corner of every square over the filling to form a triangle and press the sides together.
7. Steps 3–6 Must be repeated with the second sheet of puff pastry.
8. Place the bourekas on the baking sheet that has been prepared.
9. For a golden finish, brush the tops of the bourekas with beaten egg and sprinkle with sesame seeds.
10. Bake the bourekas in a preheated oven for 20-25 mins, or up to puffy and golden brown.
11. Warm bourekas with cheese and dill filling make an excellent appetizer or snack.

Nutrition (per serving - 1 boureka):
Cals: 180 kcal, Fat: 10g, Carbs: 15g, Fiber: 1g, Protein: 7g

189.Falafel Salad with Tahini Dressing:

Prep Time: 15 mins

Cook Time: 10 mins

Total Time: 25 mins

Servings: 4

Ingredients:

- 16 falafel balls (store-bought or homemade)
- 4 cups of combined salad greens
- 1 cup of cherry tomatoes, halved
- 1 cucumber, split
- 1/2 red onion, thinly split
- 1/4 cup of chop-up fresh parsley
- 1/4 cup of chop-up fresh mint
- 1/4 cup of tahini
- 2 tbsp lemon juice
- 2 tbsp water
- 1 clove garlic, chop-up
- Salt and pepper as needed

Instructions:

1. If using store-bought falafel, fry the falafel balls according to box/pkg directions up to heated through and crispy.
2. If you're making your own falafel, follow the directions on the box/pkg.
3. To make the salad, combine the combined salad greens, halved cherry tomatoes, split cucumber, thinly split red onion, chop-up fresh parsley, and chop-up fresh mint in a Big combining dish.
4. Place the falafel balls on top of the salad and serve.
5. To make the tahini dressing, combine together

the tahini, lemon juice, water, chop-up garlic, salt, and pepper in a separate bowl.
6. Before serving, drizzle the tahini dressing over the falafel salad.

Nutrition (per serving - 1 falafel salad):
Cals: 350 kcal, Fat: 20g, Carbs: 30g, Fiber: 8g, Protein: 12g

190. Shakshuka with Roasted Eggplant and Za'atar:

Prep Time: 15 mins

Cook Time: 30 mins

Total Time: 45 mins

Servings: 4

Ingredients:
- 2 medium eggplants, diced
- 4 tbsp olive oil, slice up
- 1 Big onion, lightly chop-up
- 2 cloves garlic, chop-up
- 1 red bell pepper, diced
- 1 yellow bell pepper, diced
- 1 can (14 oz) diced tomatoes
- 2 tbsp tomato paste
- 1 tsp ground cumin
- 1 tsp ground paprika
- 1/4 tsp cayenne pepper (non-compulsory, for heat)
- Salt and pepper as needed
- 4-6 Big eggs
- Za'atar seasoning for sprinkling
- Fresh parsley for garnish

Instructions:
1. Preheat the oven to 200 Ds Celsius (400 Ds Fahrenheit).
2. Spread the chop-up eggplant on a baking sheet and drizzle with 2 tbsp olive oil. Toss the eggplant in the oil to coat evenly.
3. Roast the eggplant for 20 mins in a preheated oven, or up to golden and soft.
4. Heat the remaining 2 tbsp olive oil in a Big skillet or frying pan over medium heat.
5. Sauté the lightly chop-up onion up to it gets translucent.
6. Sauté for another min after adding the chop-up garlic.
7. Cook up to the diced red and yellow bell peppers begin to soften in the skillet.
8. Pour in the chop-up tomatoes and liquids, then add the tomato paste, cumin, paprika, cayenne pepper (if using), salt, and pepper.
9. Let the shakshuka Mixture to boil for 10 mins.
10. Stir the roasted eggplant into the shakshuka Mixture to incorporate.
11. Make mini wells in the shakshuka and crack the eggs into them.
12. Cook the eggs in a covered skillet over low heat up to they are done to your liking.
13. Before serving, sprinkle the shakshuka with za'atar seasoning and top with fresh parsley.

Nutrition (per serving):
Cals: 300 kcal, Fat: 18g, Carbs: 25g, Fiber: 8g, Protein: 11g

191. Malabi with Rosewater and Pomegranate Seeds:

Prep Time: 10 mins

Cook Time: 10 mins

Total Time: 2 hrs 20 mins (includes chilling time)

Servings: 4

Ingredients:
- 2 cups of whole milk
- 1/4 cup of cornstarch
- 1/4 cup of granulated sugar
- 1 tsp rosewater
- Pomegranate seeds for garnish

Instructions:
1. Whisk together the whole milk, cornstarch, and granulated sugar in a saucepan up to well blended.
2. Cook, stirring constantly, over medium heat up to the Mixture thickens and reveryes a custard-like consistency.
3. Stir in the rosewater after removing the malabi Mixture from the heat.
4. Divide the malabi among the cups of or bowls.
5. Refrigerate the malabi for at least 2 hrs, or up to completely cooled and set.
6. Garnish the malabi with pomegranate seeds before serving.

Nutrition (per serving):
Cals: 180 kcal, Fat: 7g, Carbs: 25g, Fiber: 1g, Protein: 4g

192. Rugelach with Cinnamon Sugar Filling:

Prep Time: 30 mins

Cook Time: 20 mins

Total Time: 50 mins

Servings: 24

Ingredients:
- 2 cups of all-purpose flour
- 1 cup of unsalted butter, melted

- 1 box/pkg (8 oz) cream cheese, melted
- 1/4 cup of granulated sugar
- 1 tsp vanilla extract
- 1/2 cup of cinnamon sugar (1/2 cup of granulated sugar combined with 1 tbsp ground cinnamon)
- 1/2 cup of lightly chop-up nuts (such as walnuts or pecans)

Instructions:

1. In a Big combining bowl, combine the melted butter, cream cheese, granulated sugar, and vanilla extract up to smooth.
2. Add the all-purpose flour gradually to the creamed Mixture and combine up to a soft dough forms.
3. Divide the dough into two equal parts and form every into a disc.
4. Wrap the dough discs in plastic wrap and place them in the refrigerator for at least 1 hr to firm up.
5. Preheat the oven to 180 Ds Celsius (350 Ds Fahrenheit) and line a baking sheet with parchment paper.
6. Roll out one cold dough disc into a circle approximately 1/8-inch thick on a floured surface.
7. Sprinkle half of the cinnamon sugar and chop-up nuts over the rolled-out dough, pressing softly into the dough.
8. Slice the dough circle into 12 equal triangles with a knife or pizza sliceter.
9. Roll up every triangle to form rugelach, beginning with the wider end, and set them on the prepared baking sheet.
10. Steps 6–9 are repeated with the second cold dough disc.
11. Rugelach Must be baked in a preheated oven for 18-20 mins, or up to lightly golden.
12. Before serving, chill the rugelach on a wire rack.

Nutrition (per serving - 1 rugelach):
Cals: 150 kcal, Fat: 10g, Carbs: 14g, Fiber: 1g, Protein: 2g

193.Tahini Chocolate Chip Blondies:

Prep Time: 15 mins

Cook Time: 25 mins

Total Time: 40 mins

Servings: 16

Ingredients:

- 1/2 cup of unsalted butter, dilute
- 1 cup of light brown sugar, packed
- 1/4 cup of tahini
- 1 Big egg

- 1 tsp vanilla extract
- 1 cup of all-purpose flour
- 1/2 tsp baking powder
- 1/4 tsp salt
- 1 cup of semi-sweet chocolate chips

Instructions:

1. Preheat the oven to 180°C (350°F) and grease an 8x8-inch baking tray with cooking spray.
2. Whisk together the dilute butter and brown sugar in a Big combining basin up to well combined.
3. Blend in the tahini, egg, and vanilla extract up to smooth.
4. Whisk together the all-purpose flour, baking powder, and salt in a separate bowl.
5. Add the dry ingredients to the liquid components gradually, stirring up to just blended.
6. Incorporate the semi-sweet chocolate chips.
7. Spread the blondie batter into the prepared baking pan evenly.
8. Bake the blondies for 20-25 mins, or up to a toothpick inserted into the center comes out with wet crumbs.
9. Let the blondies to completely cool in the pan before Cuttinginto squares.

Nutrition (per serving - 1 blondie):
Cals: 200 kcal, Fat: 10g, Carbs: 25g, Fiber: 1g, Protein: 2g

194.Israeli Spinach and Cheese Filo Pie:

Prep Time: 20 mins

Cook Time: 40 mins

Total Time: 1 hr

Servings: 8

Ingredients:

- 10 sheets filo pastry
- 1/4 cup of unsalted butter, dilute
- 1 Big onion, lightly chop-up
- 2 cloves garlic, chop-up
- 10 oz fresh spinach, chop-up
- 1 cup of feta cheese, cut up
- 1/2 cup of ricotta cheese
- 1/4 cup of finely finely grated Parmesan cheese
- 2 Big eggs, lightly beaten
- 1/4 tsp ground nutmeg
- Salt and pepper as needed

Instructions:

1. Preheat the oven to 180°C (350°F) and oil a 9-inch pie plate with cooking spray.
2. Sauté the lightly chop-up onion and chop-up garlic in a little olive oil in a Big skillet up to the onion becomes transparent.

3. Cook the chop-up fresh spinach in the skillet up to it wilts.
4. Combine the sautéed spinach, cut up feta cheese, ricotta cheese, finely finely grated Parmesan cheese, beaten eggs, ground nutmeg, salt, and pepper in a combining bowl.
5. Brush every sheet of filo pastry with dilute butter before adding the next one to the prepared pie dish.
6. Half of the spinach and cheese Mixture Must be spread over the filo pastry.
7. Layer the remaining 5 filo pastry sheets on top, coating every with dilute butter.
8. Cover the second layer of filo pastry with the remaining spinach and cheese Mixture.
9. To achieve a rustic look, fold any overhanging filo pastry over the top of the pie.
10. Bake the filo pie for 30-35 mins, or up to the filo is golden brown and the filling is set, in a preheated oven.
11. Let the pie to cool for a few mins before slicing and serving.

Nutrition (per serving - 1 slice):
Cals: 300 kcal, Fat: 18g, Carbs: 22g, Fiber: 2g, Protein: 12g

195.Falafel Tostadas with Avocado-Tahini Sauce:

Prep Time: 30 mins

Cook Time: 20 mins

Total Time: 50 mins

Servings: 4

Ingredients:
- 1 cup of dried chickpeas, soaked overnight and drained (or 1 can of cooked chickpeas, drained)
- 1 mini onion, chop-up
- 4 cloves garlic, chop-up
- 1 cup of fresh parsley leaves
- 1 cup of fresh cilantro leaves
- 1 tsp ground cumin
- 1 tsp ground coriander
- 1/2 tsp baking soda
- Salt and pepper as needed
- Vegetable oil for frying
- 4 tostada shells
- 1 cup of shredded lettuce
- 1 cup of diced tomatoes
- 1/2 cup of diced cucumber
- 1/4 cup of diced red onion
- Avocado-Tahini Sauce:
- 1 ripe avocado
- 1/4 cup of tahini
- 2 tbsp lemon juice
- 1/4 cup of water
- Salt and pepper as needed

Instructions:
1. Combine the soaked and drained chickpeas, chop-up onion, chop-up garlic, fresh parsley leaves, fresh cilantro leaves, ground cumin, ground coriander, baking soda, salt, and pepper in a mixer.
2. The Mixture Must be processed up to it forms a coarse paste. If the Mixture is too dry, a little water can be added to help it come together.
3. Make tiny patties or balls out of the falafel Mixture.
4. Heat the vegetable oil in a Big skillet over medium-high heat.
5. Fry the falafel patties or balls in batches up to the outsides are golden brown and crispy.
6. To take out excess oil, drain the fried falafel on paper towels.
7. To make the Avocado-Tahini Sauce, in a blender or mixer, combine the ripe avocado, tahini, lemon juice, water, salt, and pepper up to smooth and creamy.
8. Place a tostada shell on a platter and top with shredded lettuce, split tomatoes, diced cucumber, and diced red onion to make the falafel tostadas.
9. Top the vegetables with the fried falafel.
10. Over the falafel tostadas, drizzle with the Avocado-Tahini Sauce.
11. Serve the falafel tostadas right away.

Nutrition (per serving - 1 tostada):
Cals: 450 kcal, Fat: 24g, Carbs: 40g, Fiber: 9g, Protein: 15g

196.Shakshuka with Swiss Chard and Goat Cheese:

Prep Time: 10 mins

Cook Time: 25 mins

Total Time: 35 mins

Servings: 4

Ingredients:
- 2 tbsp olive oil
- 1 Big onion, thinly split
- 1 red bell pepper, thinly split
- 1 yellow bell pepper, thinly split
- 2 cups of Swiss chard leaves, chop-up
- 4 cloves garlic, chop-up
- 1 can (14 oz) diced tomatoes
- 1 tbsp tomato paste
- 1 tsp ground cumin

- 1 tsp ground paprika
- 1/4 tsp cayenne pepper (non-compulsory, for heat)
- Salt and pepper as needed
- 4 to 6 Big eggs
- 1/2 cup of cut up goat cheese
- Fresh parsley for garnish

Instructions:

1. Heat the olive oil in a big skillet or frying pan over medium heat.
2. Sauté the thinly split onion up to it turns translucent.
3. Cook up to the thinly split red and yellow bell peppers soften, about 5 mins.
4. Cook up to the chop-up Swiss chard leaves wilt in the skillet.
5. Sauté for another min after adding the chop-up garlic.
6. Pour in the chop-up tomatoes and liquids, then add the tomato paste, cumin, paprika, cayenne pepper (if using), salt, and pepper.
7. Let the shakshuka Mixture to boil for 10 mins.
8. Make mini wells in the shakshuka and crack the eggs into them.
9. Cook the eggs in a covered skillet over low heat up to they are done to your liking.
10. Before serving, top the shakshuka with cut up goat cheese and sprinkle with fresh parsley.

Nutrition (per serving):
Cals: 250 kcal, Fat: 16g, Carbs: 15g, Fiber: 4g, Protein: 12g

197.Malabi with Raspberry and Mint:

Prep Time: 10 mins

Cook Time: 10 mins

Total Time: 2 hrs 20 mins (includes chilling time)

Servings: 4

Ingredients:

- 2 cups of whole milk
- 1/4 cup of cornstarch
- 1/4 cup of granulated sugar
- 1 tsp rosewater (or substitute with vanilla extract)
- Fresh raspberries and mint leaves for garnish

Instructions:

1. Whisk together the whole milk, cornstarch, and granulated sugar in a saucepan up to well blended.
2. Cook, stirring constantly, over medium heat up to the Mixture thickens and reveryes a custard-like consistency.

3. Stir in the rosewater (or vanilla essence) after removing the malabi Mixture from the heat.
4. Divide the malabi among the cups of or bowls.
5. Refrigerate the malabi for at least 2 hrs, or up to completely cooled and set.
6. Garnish the malabi with fresh raspberries and mint leaves before serving.

Nutrition (per serving):
Cals: 150 kcal, Fat: 5g, Carbs: 23g, Fiber: 1g, Protein: 5g

198.Rugelach with Apricot and Almond Filling:

Prep Time: 30 mins

Cook Time: 20 mins

Total Time: 50 mins

Servings: 24

Ingredients:

- 2 cups of all-purpose flour
- 1 cup of unsalted butter, melted
- 1 box/pkg (8 oz) cream cheese, melted
- 1/4 cup of granulated sugar
- 1 tsp vanilla extract
- 1/2 cup of apricot preserves
- 1/2 cup of lightly chop-up almonds

Instructions:

1. In a Big combining bowl, combine the melted butter, cream cheese, granulated sugar, and vanilla extract up to smooth.
2. Add the all-purpose flour gradually to the creamed Mixture and combine up to a soft dough forms.
3. Divide the dough into two equal parts and form every into a disc.
4. Wrap the dough discs in plastic wrap and place them in the refrigerator for at least 1 hr to firm up.
5. Preheat the oven to 180 Ds Celsius (350 Ds Fahrenheit) and line a baking sheet with parchment paper.
6. Roll out one cold dough disc into a circle approximately 1/8-inch thick on a floured surface.
7. Half of the apricot preserves Must be spread over the rolled-out dough, leaving a tiny border around the borders.
8. Half of the coarsely chop-up almonds Must be sprinkled over the apricot preserves.
9. Slice the dough circle into 12 equal triangles with a knife or pizza sliceter.
10. Roll up every triangle to form rugelach, beginning

with the wider end, and set them on the prepared baking sheet.

11. Steps 6–10 are repeated with the second cold dough disc.
12. Rugelach Must be baked in a preheated oven for 18-20 mins, or up to lightly golden.
13. Before serving, chill the rugelach on a wire rack.

Nutrition (per serving - 1 rugelach):
Cals: 160 kcal, Fat: 10g, Carbs: 15g, Fiber: 1g, Protein: 2g

199.Tahini Banana Bread with Walnuts:

Prep Time: 15 mins

Cook Time: 1 hr

Total Time: 1 hr 15 mins

Servings: 10

Ingredients:

- 1 3/4 cups of all-purpose flour
- 1 tsp baking soda
- 1/2 tsp salt
- 1/2 cup of unsalted butter, melted
- 1/2 cup of granulated sugar
- 1/2 cup of packed light brown sugar
- 2 Big eggs
- 1 tsp vanilla extract
- 1/4 cup of tahini
- 3 ripe bananas, mashed
- 1/2 cup of chop-up walnuts

Instructions:

1. Preheat the oven to 180°C (350°F) and grease a 9x5-inch loaf pan with cooking spray.
2. In a medium combining bowl, combine the all-purpose flour, baking soda, and salt.
3. Cream together the melted butter, granulated sugar, and light brown sugar in a separate Big combining basin up to light and fluffy.
4. One at a time, beat in the eggs, followed by the vanilla essence and tahini.
5. Add the dry ingredients to the liquid components gradually, combining up to just combined.
6. Combine in the mashed bananas and walnuts.
7. Smooth the top of the banana bread batter into the prepared loaf pan.
8. Bake the banana bread for approximately an hr, or up to a toothpick inserted into the center comes out clean.
9. Let the banana bread to cool for 10 mins in the pan before moving it to a wire rack to cool entirely.

Nutrition (per serving - 1 slice):
Cals: 300 kcal, Fat: 15g, Carbs: 39g, Fiber: 2g, Protein: 4g

200.Israeli Stuffed Mushrooms with Herbed Breadcrumbs:

Prep Time: 20 mins

Cook Time: 25 mins

Total Time: 45 mins

Servings: 4

Ingredients:

- 16 Big white mushrooms, stems take outd and reserved
- 1 tbsp olive oil
- 1 mini onion, lightly chop-up
- 2 cloves garlic, chop-up
- 1/2 cup of breadcrumbs
- 1/4 cup of finely finely grated Parmesan cheese
- 1 tbsp chop-up fresh parsley
- 1 tbsp chop-up fresh thyme
- 1 tbsp chop-up fresh rosemary
- Salt and pepper as needed
- Olive oil for drizzling

Instructions:

1. Preheat the oven to 180 Ds Celsius (350 Ds Fahrenheit) and line a baking sheet with parchment paper.
2. Set aside the mushroom stems, which have been lightly chop-up.
3. Warm the olive oil in a Big skillet over medium heat.
4. Sauté the lightly chop-up onion up to it gets translucent.
5. Sauté for another 2-3 mins after adding the chop-up garlic and chop-up mushroom stems.
6. To the skillet, add the breadcrumbs, finely finely grated Parmesan cheese, chop-up fresh parsley, chop-up fresh thyme, chop-up fresh rosemary, salt, and pepper.
7. Cook for a few mins more, or up to the breadcrumbs are gently browned and everything is well combined.
8. Take out the skillet from the heat and set aside to cool.
9. Place every mushroom cap on the prepared baking sheet and stuff with the breadcrumb Mixture.
10. Drizzle a little olive oil over the stuffed mushrooms.
11. Bake the stuffed mushrooms for 20-25 mins, or up to the mushrooms are soft and the tops are golden brown.

12. As an appetizer or side dish, serve the Israeli Stuffed Mushrooms with Herbed Breadcrumbs.

Nutrition (per serving - 4 stuffed mushrooms):
Cals: 180 kcal, Fat: 8g, Carbs: 21g, Fiber: 2g, Protein: 8g

201.Bourekas with Potato and Onion Filling:

Prep Time: 30 mins

Cook Time: 25 mins

Total Time: 55 mins

Servings: 12

Ingredients:
- 1 box/pkg (17.3 oz) puff pastry sheets, thawed according to box/pkg instructions
- 2 Big potatoes, peel off and diced
- 1 Big onion, lightly chop-up
- 2 tbsp olive oil
- 1 tsp ground cumin
- 1/2 tsp paprika
- Salt and pepper as needed
- 1 egg, lightly beaten (for egg wash)

Instructions:
1. Preheat the oven to 200 Ds Celsius (400 Ds Fahrenheit) and line a baking sheet with parchment paper.
2. Warm the olive oil in a Big skillet over medium heat.
3. Sauté the lightly chop-up onion in the skillet up to it turns translucent.
4. Cook up to the potatoes are soft, stirring in the diced potatoes, ground cumin, paprika, salt, and pepper.
5. Take out the skillet from the heat and set aside to cool slightly.
6. On a floured board, roll out the thawed puff pastry sheets and slice them into squares.
7. Fill every puff pastry square with a tbsp of the potato filling.
8. Fold the puff pastry over the filling and press the sides together to seal.
9. Crimp the edges with a fork for a decorative touch.
10. Place the filled bourekas on the baking sheet that has been prepared.
11. For a golden finish, brush the tops of the bourekas with the beaten egg.
12. Bake the bourekas for 20-25 mins, or up to puffy and golden brown in a preheated oven.
13. As a savory snack or appetizer, serve the Bourekas with Potato and Onion Filling.

Nutrition (per serving - 1 boureka):
Cals: 200 kcal, Fat: 12g, Carbs: 18g, Fiber: 1g, Protein: 3g

202.Falafel Tabbouleh Salad with Lemon-Tahini Dressing:

- Prep Time: 20 mins
- Cook Time: 10 mins
- Total Time: 30 mins
- Servings: 4

Ingredients:
- 1 cup of falafel, cooked and cut up
- 1 cup of cooked quinoa
- 1 cup of cherry tomatoes, halved
- 1 cucumber, diced
- 1/2 cup of fresh parsley, chop-up
- 1/4 cup of fresh mint leaves, chop-up
- 1/4 cup of red onion, lightly chop-up
- 1/4 cup of lemon juice
- 3 tbsp tahini
- 2 tbsp olive oil
- 2 cloves garlic, chop-up
- Salt and pepper as needed

Instructions:
1. Combine the cut up falafel, cooked quinoa, cherry tomatoes, split cucumber, chop-up parsley, chop-up mint leaves, and lightly chop-up red onion in a Big combining dish.
2. To make the lemon-tahini dressing, combine together the lemon juice, tahini, olive oil, chop-up garlic, salt, and pepper in a separate mini bowl.
3. Toss the salad with the lemon-tahini dressing up to everything is well incorporated.
4. Enjoy the Falafel Tabbouleh Salad with Lemon-Tahini Dressing!

Nutrition (per serving):
Cals: 350 kcal, Fat: 18g, Carbs: 35g, Fiber: 7g, Protein: 12g

203.Shakshuka with Spinach and Feta:

Prep Time: 10 mins

Cook Time: 20 mins

Total Time: 30 mins

Servings: 4

Ingredients:
- 2 tbsp olive oil
- 1 Big onion, thinly split
- 1 red bell pepper, thinly split
- 2 cups of baby spinach leaves

- 4 cloves garlic, chop-up
- 1 can (14 oz) diced tomatoes
- 1 tbsp tomato paste
- 1 tsp ground cumin
- 1/2 tsp smoked paprika
- Salt and pepper as needed
- 4 to 6 Big eggs
- 1/2 cup of cut up feta cheese
- Fresh parsley for garnish

Instructions:

1. Heat the olive oil in a big skillet or frying pan over medium heat.
2. Sauté the thinly split onion up to it turns translucent.
3. Cook up to the thinly split red bell pepper softens, about 5 mins.
4. Cook up to the young spinach leaves wilt in the skillet.
5. Sauté for another min after adding the chop-up garlic.
6. Pour in the chop-up tomatoes and liquids, then add the tomato paste, ground cumin, smoked paprika, salt, and pepper as needed.
7. Let the shakshuka Mixture to boil for 10 mins.
8. Make mini wells in the shakshuka and crack the eggs into them.
9. Cook the eggs in a covered skillet over low heat up to they are done to your liking.
10. Before serving, top the shakshuka with cut up feta cheese and sprinkle with fresh parsley.

Nutrition (per serving):

Cals: 250 kcal, Fat: 15g, Carbs: 15g, Fiber: 4g, Protein: 12g

204.Malabi with Coconut Milk and Mango Sauce:

Prep Time: 5 mins

Cook Time: 10 mins

Chill Time: 2 hrs

Total Time: 2 hrs 15 mins

Servings: 4

Ingredients:

- 2 cups of coconut milk
- 1/4 cup of cornstarch
- 1/4 cup of granulated sugar
- 1 tsp rosewater (non-compulsory)
- Mango Sauce:
- 1 ripe mango, peel off and diced
- 1 tbsp honey or maple syrup
- 1 tbsp lemon juice
- 1/4 tsp ground cardamom

- Fresh mint leaves for garnish

Instructions:

1. Whisk together the coconut milk, cornstarch, and granulated sugar in a saucepan up to well blended.
2. Cook, stirring constantly, over medium heat up to the Mixture thickens and reveryes a custard-like consistency.
3. Take out the malabi Mixture from the heat and, if using, whisk in the rosewater.
4. Divide the malabi among the cups of or bowls.
5. Refrigerate the malabi for at least 2 hrs, or up to completely cooled and set.
6. To make the mango sauce, in a blender, combine the diced mango, honey or maple syrup, lemon juice, and ground cardamom up to smooth.
7. Spoon the mango sauce over the cold malabi and sprinkle with fresh mint leaves before serving.

Nutrition (per serving):

Cals: 300 kcal, Fat: 20g, Carbs: 30g, Fiber: 2g, Protein: 3g

205.Rugelach with Chocolate and Raspberry Filling:

Prep Time: 30 mins

Chill Time: 1 hr

Cook Time: 20 mins

Total Time: 1 hr 50 mins

Servings: 24

Ingredients:

- 2 cups of all-purpose flour
- 1/2 cup of granulated sugar
- 1 cup of unsalted butter, melted
- 1 tsp vanilla extract
- 1/2 cup of raspberry preserves
- 1/2 cup of mini chocolate chips
- 1/2 cup of chop-up toasted almonds
- 1 egg, lightly beaten (for egg wash)
- Powdered sugar for dusting (non-compulsory)

Instructions:

1. Cream together the melted butter, granulated sugar, and vanilla extract in a Big combining bowl up to light and fluffy.
2. Add the all-purpose flour gradually to the creamed Mixture and combine up to a soft dough forms.
3. Divide the dough into two equal parts and form every into a disc.
4. Wrap the dough discs in plastic wrap and place them in the refrigerator for at least 1 hr to firm up.

5. Preheat the oven to 180 Ds Celsius (350 Ds Fahrenheit) and line a baking sheet with parchment paper.
6. Roll out one cold dough disc into a circle approximately 1/8-inch thick on a floured surface.
7. Half of the raspberry preserves Must be spread over the rolled-out dough, leaving a little border around the borders.
8. Over the raspberry preserves, scatter half of the mini chocolate chips and chop-up toasted almonds.
9. Slice the dough circle into 12 equal triangles with a knife or pizza sliceter.
10. Roll up every triangle to form rugelach, beginning with the wider end, and set them on the prepared baking sheet.
11. Steps 6–10 are repeated with the second cold dough disc.
12. For a lustrous finish, brush the rugelach with beaten egg.
13. Rugelach Must be baked in a preheated oven for 18-20 mins, or up to lightly golden.
14. Let the rugelach to cool completely on a wire rack before dusting with powdered sugar, if desired.

Nutrition (per serving - 1 rugelach):
Cals: 150 kcal, Fat: 9g, Carbs: 16g, Fiber: 1g, Protein: 2g

206.Tahini Date Energy Balls with Coconut:

Prep Time: 15 mins

Chill Time: 30 mins

Total Time: 45 mins

Servings: 12

Ingredients:

- 1 cup of pitted dates
- 1/2 cup of almond meal
- 1/4 cup of tahini
- 1/4 cup of shredded coconut, + extra for rolling
- 1/2 tsp vanilla extract
- Pinch of salt

Instructions:

1. Blend the pitted dates, almond meal, tahini, shredded coconut, vanilla essence, and a pinch of salt in a mixer up to the Mixture becomes a sticky dough.
2. Scoop out tbsp of the Mixture and roll it into balls with your palms.
3. Roll the energy balls in additional crushed coconut to coat.
4. Place the energy balls on a parchment-lined plate or baking sheet.

5. Refrigerate the energy balls for around 30 mins before serving to firm up.

Nutrition (per serving - 1 energy ball):
Cals: 100 kcal, Fat: 6g, Carbs: 11g, Fiber: 2g, Protein: 2g

207.Israeli Stuffed Bell Peppers with Quinoa and Chickpeas:

Prep Time: 20 mins

Cook Time: 30 mins

Total Time: 50 mins

Servings: 4

Ingredients:

- 4 Big bell peppers, any color
- 1 cup of cooked quinoa
- 1 can (14 oz) chickpeas, drained and rinsed
- 1/2 cup of cherry tomatoes, halved
- 1/4 cup of chop-up fresh parsley
- 2 tbsp lemon juice
- 2 tbsp olive oil
- 2 cloves garlic, chop-up
- 1 tsp ground cumin
- 1/2 tsp paprika
- Salt and pepper as needed

Instructions:

1. Preheat the oven to 200°C (400°F) and lightly grease a baking dish.
2. Take out the tops of the bell peppers and scoop out the seeds and membranes.
3. Combine cooked quinoa, chickpeas, halved cherry tomatoes, chop-up fresh parsley, lemon juice, olive oil, chop-up garlic, ground cumin, paprika, salt, and pepper in a combining bowl.
4. Stuff the quinoa and chickpea Mixture into every bell pepper.
5. Place the stuffed bell peppers in the baking dish that has been prepared.
6. Cover the baking dish with foil and bake the stuffed bell peppers for about 25-30 mins, or up to the peppers are soft.
7. Take out the cover and continue baking for 5 mins more to lightly brown the tops of the stuffed peppers.
8. As a filling and nutritious supper, serve the Israeli Stuffed Bell Peppers with Quinoa and Chickpeas.

Nutrition (per serving):
Cals: 300 kcal, Fat: 10g, Carbs: 45g, Fiber: 9g, Protein: 10g

208.Bourekas with Cheese and Spinach Filling:

Prep Time: 30 mins

Cook Time: 25 mins

Total Time: 55 mins

Servings: 12

Ingredients:

- 1 box/pkg (17.3 oz) puff pastry sheets, thawed according to box/pkg instructions
- 1 cup of refrigerate chop-up spinach, thawed and drained
- 1 cup of cut up feta cheese
- 1/2 cup of shredded mozzarella cheese
- 1/4 cup of chop-up fresh parsley
- 1/4 tsp ground nutmeg
- Salt and pepper as needed
- 1 egg, lightly beaten (for egg wash)

Instructions:

1. Preheat the oven to 200 Ds Celsius (400 Ds Fahrenheit) and line a baking sheet with parchment paper.
2. To make the cheese and spinach filling, combine the refrigerate and drained chop-up spinach, cut up feta cheese, shredded mozzarella cheese, chop-up fresh parsley, ground nutmeg, salt, and pepper in a combining dish.
3. On a floured board, roll out the thawed puff pastry sheets and slice them into squares.
4. Fill every puff pastry square with a tbsp of the cheese and spinach filling.
5. Fold the puff pastry over the filling and press the sides together to seal.
6. Crimp the edges with a fork for a decorative touch.
7. Place the filled bourekas on the baking sheet that has been prepared.
8. For a golden finish, brush the tops of the bourekas with the beaten egg.
9. Bake the bourekas for 20-25 mins, or up to puffy and golden brown in a preheated oven.
10. As an appetizer or snack, serve the Bourekas with Cheese and Spinach Filling.

Nutrition (per serving - 1 boureka):

Cals: 200 kcal, Fat: 14g, Carbs: 14g, Fiber: 1g, Protein: 6g

209.Falafel Sliders with Pickles and Spicy Tahini Mayo:

Prep Time: 20 mins

Cook Time: 10 mins

Total Time: 30 mins

Servings: 4

Ingredients:

- 8 mini falafel patties
- 4 mini slider buns, halved
- 4 tbsp spicy tahini mayo (store-bought or homemade)
- 4 slices of pickles
- Lettuce leaves

Instructions:

1. Cook the tiny falafel patties according to the box/pkg or recipe directions.
2. Spread a spoonful of spicy tahini mayo on the bottom half of every slider bread before assembling.
3. On top of the mayo, place a cooked falafel patty.
4. On top of the falafel, place a piece of pickle and lettuce leaves.
5. The top half of the buns Must be used to cover the sliders.
6. As a fun and savory supper, serve the Falafel Sliders with Pickles & Spicy Tahini Mayo.

Nutrition (per serving - 1 slider):

Cals: 200 kcal, Fat: 8g, Carbs: 25g, Fiber: 3g, Protein: 8g

210.Shakshuka with Roasted Red Peppers and Feta:

Prep Time: 15 mins

Cook Time: 25 mins

Total Time: 40 mins

Servings: 4

Ingredients:

- 2 tbsp olive oil
- 1 Big onion, thinly split
- 2 roasted red bell peppers, split
- 4 cloves garlic, chop-up
- 1 can (14 oz) diced tomatoes
- 1 tbsp tomato paste
- 1 tsp ground cumin
- 1/2 tsp smoked paprika
- Salt and pepper as needed
- 4 to 6 Big eggs
- 1/2 cup of cut up feta cheese
- Fresh parsley for garnish

Instructions:

1. Heat the olive oil in a big skillet or frying pan over medium heat.
2. Sauté the thinly split onion up to it turns translucent.
3. Cook up to the roasted red bell pepper slices are cooked through, about 5 mins.

4. Cook for another min after adding the chop-up garlic.
5. Pour in the chop-up tomatoes and liquids, then add the tomato paste, ground cumin, smoked paprika, salt, and pepper as needed.
6. Let the shakshuka Mixture to boil for 10 mins.
7. Make mini wells in the shakshuka and crack the eggs into them.
8. Cook the eggs in a covered skillet over low heat up to they are done to your liking.
9. Before serving, top the shakshuka with cut up feta cheese and sprinkle with fresh parsley.

Nutrition (per serving):
Cals: 250 kcal, Fat: 15g, Carbs: 18g, Fiber: 4g, Protein: 12g

211.Malabi with Orange Blossom and Citrus Salad:

Prep Time: 10 mins

Cook Time: 10 mins

Chill Time: 2 hrs

Total Time: 2 hrs 20 mins

Servings: 4

Ingredients:
- 2 cups of whole milk
- 1/4 cup of cornstarch
- 1/4 cup of granulated sugar
- 1 tsp orange blossom water
- Citrus Salad:
- 1 orange, peel off and segmented
- 1 grapefruit, peel off and segmented
- 1 tbsp honey or maple syrup
- 1 tbsp lemon juice
- Fresh mint leaves for garnish

Instructions:
1. Whisk together the whole milk, cornstarch, and granulated sugar in a saucepan up to well blended.
2. Cook, stirring constantly, over medium heat up to the Mixture thickens and reverdes a custard-like consistency.
3. Take the malabi Mixture off the stove and add the orange blossom water.
4. Divide the malabi among the cups of or bowls.
5. Refrigerate the malabi for at least 2 hrs, or up to completely cooled and set.
6. To make the citrus salad, combine the orange and grapefruit segments in a bowl.
7. Drizzle the citrus salad with honey or maple syrup and lemon juice, tossing lightly to incorporate.
8. Spoon the citrus salad over the cold malabi and sprinkle with fresh mint leaves before serving.

Nutrition (per serving):
Cals: 180 kcal, Fat: 5g, Carbs: 30g, Fiber: 4g, Protein: 5g

212.Rugelach with Chocolate and Pecan Filling:

Prep Time: 20 mins

Cook Time: 25 mins

Total Time: 45 mins

Servings: 12

Ingredients:
- 1 box/pkg (17.3 oz) puff pastry sheets, thawed according to box/pkg instructions
- 1/2 cup of chocolate chips
- 1/2 cup of chop-up pecans
- 1/4 cup of granulated sugar
- 1 tsp ground cinnamon
- 1 egg, lightly beaten (for egg wash)

Instructions:
1. Preheat the oven to 200 Ds Celsius (400 Ds Fahrenheit) and line a baking sheet with parchment paper.
2. To create the filling, combine the chop-up pecans, granulated sugar, and ground cinnamon in a mini bowl.
3. On a floured board, roll out the thawed puff pastry sheets and slice them into circles or triangles.
4. Spread the chocolate chips and pecan filling evenly over the pastry dough.
5. Roll up every circle or triangle to form rugelach, starting from the widest end, and lay them on the prepared baking sheet.
6. For a lustrous finish, brush the rugelach with beaten egg.
7. Rugelach Must be baked in a preheated oven for 20-25 mins, or up to golden brown and flaky.
8. Before serving, chill the rugelach on a wire rack.

Nutrition (per serving - 1 rugelach):
Cals: 180 kcal, Fat: 12g, Carbs: 15g, Fiber: 1g, Protein: 3g

213.Tahini Oat Cookies with Raisins:

Prep Time: 15 mins

Cook Time: 12 mins

Total Time: 27 mins

Servings: 18 cookies

Ingredients:
- 1/2 cup of tahini
- 1/2 cup of brown sugar

- 1/4 cup of unsalted butter, melted
- 1 Big egg
- 1 tsp vanilla extract
- 1 cup of rolled oats
- 1/2 cup of all-purpose flour
- 1/2 tsp baking soda
- 1/4 tsp salt
- 1/2 cup of raisins

Instructions:

1. Preheat the oven to 180 Ds Celsius (350 Ds Fahrenheit) and line a baking sheet with parchment paper.
2. Cream together the tahini, brown sugar, and melted butter in a combining bowl up to completely combined.
3. Combine in the egg and vanilla extract up to well combined.
4. Whisk together the rolled oats, all-purpose flour, baking soda, and salt in a separate dish.
5. Combine the dry ingredients into the wet components up to a dough forms.
6. Incorporate the raisins into the dough up to they are uniformly distributed.
7. Scoop out tbsp of cookie dough and roll them into balls with your palms.
8. Place the cookie dough balls on the baking sheet that has been prepared, leaving some space between every cookie.
9. With the back of a fork, slightly flatten the cookie dough balls.
10. Bake the cookies for 10-12 mins, or up to gently golden, in a preheated oven.
11. Let the cookies to cool on a wire rack before serving.

Nutrition (per serving - 1 cookie):
Cals: 140 kcal, Fat: 8g, Carbs: 16g, Fiber: 1g, Protein: 2g

214.Israeli Stuffed Zucchini with Lamb and Rice:

Prep Time: 30 mins

Cook Time: 1 hr

Total Time: 1 hr 30 mins

Servings: 4

Ingredients:

- 2 Big zucchinis
- 250g ground lamb
- 1/2 cup of long-grain rice
- 1 onion, lightly chop-up
- 2 cloves garlic, chop-up
- 1 tomato, diced
- 1/4 cup of chop-up fresh parsley

- 1/4 cup of chop-up fresh mint
- 1/4 tsp ground cinnamon
- 1/4 tsp ground cumin
- Salt and pepper as needed
- 2 cups of chicken or vegetable broth
- 1 tbsp olive oil

Instructions:

1. Preheat the oven to 180 Ds Celsius (350 Ds Fahrenheit).
2. To make boats, slice the zucchinis in half lengthwise and scoop out the centers. Set the zucchini flesh aside for later use.
3. Warm the olive oil in a pan over medium heat. Sauté the chop-up onion and chop-up garlic up to melted.
4. Cook up to the ground lamb is browned and cooked through, breaking it up into mini pieces.
5. Combine the chop-up tomato, zucchini flesh, long-grain rice, chop-up fresh parsley, chop-up fresh mint, ground cinnamon, ground cumin, salt, and pepper in a combining bowl. Cook for a few mins, stirring frequently, up to the flavors are fully blended.
6. Fill the zucchini halves that have been hollowed out with the meat and rice Mixture.
7. Place the packed zucchinis in a baking dish and cover with the chicken or vegetable stock.
8. Cover the baking dish with foil and bake for 45 mins to 1 hr, or up to the zucchinis are soft and the rice is done.
9. As a robust and fulfilling main course, serve the Israeli Stuffed Zucchini with Lamb and Rice.

Nutrition (per serving):
Cals: 350 kcal, Fat: 18g, Carbs: 22g, Fiber: 3g, Protein: 25g

215.Falafel Buddha Bowl with Hummus and Avocado:

Prep Time: 20 mins

Cook Time: 15 mins

Total Time: 35 mins

Servings: 2

Ingredients:

- 8 falafel patties (store-bought or homemade)
- 2 cups of cooked quinoa or rice
- 1 cup of combined salad greens
- 1 cucumber, split
- 1 Big tomato, diced
- 1/2 avocado, split
- 1/4 cup of hummus
- 2 tbsp tahini sauce
- Lemon wedges for garnish

- Fresh parsley for garnish

Instructions:
1. Prepare the falafel patties as directed on the box/pkg or in the recipe.
2. Arrange the cooked quinoa or rice, combined salad greens, split cucumber, diced tomato, and split avocado in two serving bowls.
3. Fill the bowls with the cooked falafel patties.
4. Drizzle the falafel and vegetables with the hummus and tahini sauce.
5. Serve the Falafel Buddha Bowls garnished with lemon wedges and fresh parsley.
6. As a healthful and filling supper, serve the Buddha bowls.

Nutrition (per serving):
Cals: 550 kcal, Fat: 25g, Carbs: 60g, Fiber: 12g, Protein: 20g

216.Shakshuka with Swiss Chard and Za'atar:

Prep Time: 10 mins

Cook Time: 25 mins

Total Time: 35 mins

Servings: 4

Ingredients:
- 2 tbsp olive oil
- 1 onion, thinly split
- 2 cloves garlic, chop-up
- 1 bunch Swiss chard, leaves chop-up and stems discarded
- 1 can (14 oz) diced tomatoes
- 1 tbsp tomato paste
- 1 tsp ground cumin
- 1 tsp za'atar spice blend
- Salt and pepper as needed
- 4 to 6 Big eggs
- Fresh parsley for garnish

Instructions:
1. Heat the olive oil in a big skillet or frying pan over medium heat.
2. Sauté the thinly split onion up to it turns translucent.
3. Sauté for another min after adding the chop-up garlic.
4. Cook up to the chop-up Swiss chard leaves wilt in the skillet.
5. Pour in the chop-up tomatoes and liquids, then add the tomato paste, ground cumin, za'atar spice blend, salt, and pepper as needed.
6. Let the shakshuka Mixture to boil for 10 mins.

7. Make mini wells in the shakshuka and crack the eggs into them.
8. Cook the eggs in a covered skillet over low heat up to they are done to your liking.
9. Before serving, garnish the Shakshuka with Swiss chard and Za'atar with fresh parsley.

Nutrition (per serving):
Cals: 180 kcal, Fat: 10g, Carbs: 14g, Fiber: 4g, Protein: 9g

217.Malabi with Raspberry Coulis and Pistachios:

Prep Time: 5 mins

Cook Time: 10 mins

Chill Time: 2 hrs

Total Time: 2 hrs 15 mins

Servings: 4

Ingredients:
- 2 cups of coconut milk
- 3 tbsp cornstarch
- 1/4 cup of granulated sugar
- 1 tsp rose water
- 1/4 cup of raspberry coulis (store-bought or homemade)
- 2 tbsp chop-up pistachios
- Fresh raspberries for garnish

Instructions:
1. Whisk together the coconut milk, cornstarch, and granulated sugar in a saucepan up to well blended.
2. Cook, stirring constantly, over medium heat up to the Mixture thickens and reveryes a custard-like consistency.
3. Take the malabi Mixture off the stove and add the rose water.
4. Divide the malabi among the cups of or bowls.
5. Refrigerate the malabi for at least 2 hrs, or up to completely cooled and set.
6. Drizzle raspberry coulis over cold malabi and top with chop-up pistachios before serving.
7. Garnish the Malabi with Raspberry Coulis and fresh raspberries on the pistachios.

Nutrition (per serving):
Cals: 230 kcal, Fat: 15g, Carbs: 21g, Fiber: 2g, Protein: 2g

218.Rugelach with Fig and Walnut Filling:

Prep Time: 25 mins

Cook Time: 25 mins

Total Time: 50 mins

Servings: 12

Ingredients:

- 1 box/pkg (17.3 oz) puff pastry sheets, thawed according to box/pkg instructions
- 1/2 cup of fig preserves or jam
- 1/2 cup of chop-up walnuts
- 1/4 cup of granulated sugar
- 1 tsp ground cinnamon
- 1 egg, lightly beaten (for egg wash)

Instructions:

1. Preheat the oven to 200 Ds Celsius (400 Ds Fahrenheit) and line a baking sheet with parchment paper.
2. To create the filling, combine the chop-up walnuts, granulated sugar, and ground cinnamon in a mini bowl.
3. On a floured board, roll out the thawed puff pastry sheets and slice them into circles or triangles.
4. Over the pastry dough, spread a thin layer of fig preserves or jam.
5. Evenly distribute the walnut filling over the fig preserves.
6. Roll up every circle or triangle to form rugelach, starting from the widest end, and lay them on the prepared baking sheet.
7. For a lustrous finish, brush the rugelach with beaten egg.
8. Rugelach Must be baked in a preheated oven for 20-25 mins, or up to golden brown and flaky.
9. Before serving, chill the rugelach on a wire rack.

Nutrition (per serving - 1 rugelach):
Cals: 200 kcal, Fat: 12g, Carbs: 20g, Fiber: 1g, Protein: 3g

219.Tahini Chocolate Banana Smoothie:

Prep Time: 5 mins

Total Time: 5 mins

Servings: 2

Ingredients:

- 2 ripe bananas
- 2 tbsp tahini
- 2 tbsp cocoa powder
- 1 cup of milk (dairy or plant-based)
- 1 tbsp honey or maple syrup
- 1/2 tsp vanilla extract
- Ice cubes (non-compulsory)

Instructions:

1. Ripe bananas Must be peel off and split.

2. Blend the split bananas, tahini, chocolate powder, milk, honey or maple syrup, and vanilla extract in a blender.
3. Blend the ingredients up to the smoothie is smooth and creamy.
4. To make a cooled smoothie, add ice cubes to the blender and process again.
5. Serve the Tahini Chocolate Banana Smoothie immediately in glasses.

Nutrition (per serving):
Cals: 250 kcal, Fat: 10g, Carbs: 35g, Fiber: 4g,Protein: 6g

220.Israeli Stuffed Artichokes with Lemon and Olive Oil:

Prep Time: 20 mins

Cook Time: 1 hr

Total Time: 1 hr 20 mins

Servings: 4

Ingredients:

- 4 Big artichokes
- 1 cup of breadcrumbs
- 1/2 cup of finely finely grated Parmesan cheese
- 2 cloves garlic, chop-up
- 1/4 cup of chop-up fresh parsley
- 1/4 cup of chop-up fresh mint
- 1/4 cup of chop-up fresh dill
- Zest of 1 lemon
- Juice of 1 lemon
- 1/4 cup of olive oil
- Salt and pepper as needed

Instructions:

1. Trim the stems and take out any tough outer leaves from the artichokes.
2. Take out the top 1 inch of every artichoke and scrape out the interior choke with a spoon.
3. To make the stuffing, combine the breadcrumbs, finely finely grated Parmesan cheese, chop-up garlic, fresh parsley, fresh mint, fresh dill, lemon zest, lemon juice, olive oil, salt, and pepper in a combining bowl.
4. Fill the center of every artichoke and between the leaves with the Mixture.
5. Place the stuffed artichokes in a big pot and cover with water halfway.
6. Cook the artichokes for about 1 hr, or up to soft and readily punctured with a fork, in a covered pot over low heat.
7. As a savory and distinctive side dish, serve the Israeli Stuffed Artichokes with Lemon and Olive Oil.

Nutrition (per serving):
Cals: 280 kcal, Fat: 15g, Carbs: 28g, Fiber: 10g, Protein: 10g

221.Bourekas with Potato and Mushroom Filling:

Prep Time: 30 mins

Cook Time: 25 mins

Total Time: 55 mins

Servings: 12

Ingredients:

- 1 box/pkg (17.3 oz) puff pastry sheets, thawed according to box/pkg instructions
- 2 Big potatoes, boiled and mashed
- 1 cup of mushrooms, lightly chop-up
- 1 onion, lightly chop-up
- 2 cloves garlic, chop-up
- 1 tbsp olive oil
- Salt and pepper as needed
- 1/4 cup of chop-up fresh parsley
- 1/4 cup of cut up feta cheese (non-compulsory)
- 1 egg, lightly beaten (for egg wash)

Instructions:

1. Preheat the oven to 200 Ds Celsius (400 Ds Fahrenheit) and line a baking sheet with parchment paper.
2. Warm the olive oil in a pan over medium heat. Sauté the lightly chop-up onion and chop-up garlic up to melted.
3. Cook up to the mushrooms release their moisture and become soft in the skillet with the lightly chop-up mushrooms.
4. Combine the boiling and mashed potatoes, sautéed mushrooms, chop-up fresh parsley, cut up feta cheese (if using), salt, and pepper in a combining bowl. To create the filling, thoroughly combine all of the ingredients.
5. On a floured board, roll out the thawed puff pastry sheets and slice them into squares or rectangles.
6. Fill every piece of pastry dough with a spoonful of the potato and mushroom filling.
7. Fold the pastry over the filling to form triangles or rectangles and seal the bourekas with a fork.
8. For a lustrous finish, brush the bourekas with the beaten egg.
9. Bake the bourekas for 20-25 mins, or up to golden brown and flaky, in a preheated oven.
10. Before serving, chill the bourekas on a wire rack.

Nutrition (per serving - 1 boureka):
Cals: 190 kcal, Fat: 10g, Carbs: 20g, Fiber: 2g, Protein: 4g

222.Falafel Tacos with Avocado-Lime Sauce

Prep Time: 20 mins

Cook Time: 20 mins

Total Time: 40 mins

Servings: 4

Ingredients:

- 1 cup of cooked chickpeas
- 1 mini onion, chop-up
- 3 cloves garlic
- 1/4 cup of fresh parsley, chop-up
- 1/4 cup of fresh cilantro, chop-up
- 1 tsp ground cumin
- 1/2 tsp ground coriander
- 1/4 tsp baking soda
- Salt and pepper as needed
- 1 tbsp all-purpose flour
- 2 tbsp olive oil
- 8 mini taco shells or tortillas
- 1 cup of shredded lettuce
- 1 cup of diced tomatoes
- 1/2 cup of diced cucumber
- Avocado-Lime Sauce:
- 1 ripe avocado, peel off and pitted
- 1/4 cup of plain Greek yogurt
- 2 tbsp lime juice
- 1 tbsp fresh cilantro, chop-up
- Salt and pepper as needed

Instructions:

1. Combine the chickpeas, onion, garlic, parsley, cilantro, cumin, coriander, baking soda, salt, and pepper in a mixer. Pulse up to everything is well blended but not pureed.
2. Pour the Mixture into a combining basin and toss in the all-purpose flour. Make tiny patties out of the Mixture.
3. In a skillet over medium heat, heat the olive oil. Cook for 2-3 mins per side, or up to golden brown and crispy.
4. To make the avocado-lime sauce, combine the avocado, Greek yogurt, lime juice, cilantro, salt, and pepper in a mixer and puree up to smooth.
5. Warm the taco shells or tortillas and put a few falafel patties in every shell to make the falafel tacos. Serve with shredded lettuce, split tomatoes, diced cucumber, and an avocado-lime sauce drizzle.

NUTRITION INFO (per serving):
Cals: 380 kcal, Carbs: 45g, Protein: 12g, Fat: 18g, Saturated Fat: 3g, Fiber: 10g, Sugar: 4g, Sodium: 360mg

223.Shakshuka with Roasted Eggplant and Labneh

Prep Time: 15 mins

Cook Time: 35 mins

Total Time: 50 mins

Servings: 4

Ingredients:

- 2 Big eggplants, diced
- 4 tbsp olive oil
- 1 Big onion, lightly chop-up
- 3 cloves garlic, chop-up
- 1 red bell pepper, diced
- 1 yellow bell pepper, diced
- 1 tsp ground cumin
- 1 tsp ground paprika
- 1 tsp ground coriander
- 1/2 tsp ground cayenne pepper (non-compulsory, adjust as needed)
- 1 can (400g) crushed tomatoes
- 4-6 Big eggs
- 1/2 cup of labneh (strained yogurt)
- Fresh parsley, chop-up (for garnish)
- Salt and pepper as needed

Instructions:

1. Preheat the oven to 400 Ds Fahrenheit (200 Ds Celsius). Spread the diced eggplant on a baking sheet and toss it with 2 tbsp olive oil. Roast for 20-25 mins, or up to tender and gently browned.
2. Heat the remaining 2 tbsp olive oil in a Big skillet over medium heat. Sauté the chop-up onion up to transparent.
3. In the skillet, combine the chop-up garlic, diced red bell pepper, and yellow bell pepper. Cook for a few mins, or up to the peppers begin to soften.
4. Add the cumin, paprika, coriander, cayenne pepper (if using), salt, and pepper as needed. Cook for another min, or up to the Mixture is aromatic.
5. Pour in the crushed tomatoes and cook for about 10 mins, or up to the liquid thickens slightly.
6. Make mini wells in the tomato Mixture and place the eggs inside. Cook, covered, for 5-7 mins, or up to the egg whites are set but the yolks are still runny.
7. Take out from the fire and top with the roasted eggplant. Sprinkle with chop-up fresh parsley and dollops of labneh.

NUTRITION INFO (per serving):

Cals: 310 kcal, Carbs: 22g, Protein: 12g, Fat: 20g, Saturated Fat: 5g, Fiber: 8g, Sugar: 12g, Sodium: 310mg

224.Malabi with Rosewater and Raspberry Sauce

Prep Time: 5 mins

Cook Time: 10 mins

Total Time: 15 mins

Servings: 4

Ingredients:

- 1/2 cup of cornstarch
- 4 cups of milk (or plant-based milk for a vegan version)
- 1/2 cup of sugar
- 2 tbsp rosewater
- Fresh raspberries (for garnish)
- Crushed pistachios (for garnish)
- Raspberry Sauce:
- 1 cup of fresh or refrigerate raspberries
- 2 tbsp sugar
- 1 tbsp water

Instructions:

1. In a mini dish, combine the cornstarch with 1/2 cup of milk to make a smooth slurry.
2. Heat the remaining 3 1/2 cups of milk in a saucepan over medium heat. Stir in the sugar up to it is completely dissolved.
3. Pour in the cornstarch slurry slowly while constantly swirling to avoid lumps. Cook and stir up to the Mixture thickens and begins to boil.
4. Cook for another min after adding the rosewater.
5. Take out the malabi from the heat and divide it among individual serving dishes or a Big serving bowl. Let it cool to room temperature before refrigerating for at least 2 hrs, or up to set.
6. In a mini saucepan, combine the raspberries, sugar, and water to make the raspberry sauce. Mash the berries with a spoon over medium heat up to they break down and the sauce thickens slightly.
7. Drizzle the raspberry sauce over the top of the malabi and decorate with fresh raspberries and cut up pistachios.

NUTRITION INFO (per serving):

Cals: 280 kcal, Carbs: 53g, Protein: 6g, Fat: 5g, Saturated Fat: 2g, Fiber: 4g, Sugar: 34g, Sodium: 90mg

225.Rugelach with Apricot and Coconut Filling

Prep Time: 30 mins

Cook Time: 20 mins

Total Time: 50 mins

Servings: 24 cookies

Ingredients:

- 2 cups of all-purpose flour
- 1/4 tsp salt
- 1 cup of unsalted butter, melted
- 8 ozs cream cheese, melted
- 1/2 cup of granulated sugar
- 1 tsp vanilla extract
- 1 cup of apricot jam
- 1 cup of sweetened shredded coconut
- 1/2 cup of chop-up walnuts
- 1 egg, beaten (for egg wash)
- Powdered sugar (for dusting)

Instructions:

1. Whisk together the flour and salt in a Big combining dish. Place aside.
2. In a separate combining dish, combine the melted butter and cream cheese up to smooth and creamy.
3. To the butter Mixture, add the granulated sugar and vanilla essence and stir well.
4. Add the flour Mixture to the wet ingredients gradually, combining up to a soft dough forms.
5. Divide the dough into four equal pieces, shape into disks, and cover every in plastic wrap. Chill the dough for at least 30 mins in the refrigerator.
6. Preheat the oven to 350 Ds Fahrenheit (175 Ds Celsius) and line baking sheets with parchment paper.
7. Roll out one cold dough disk into a circle approximately 1/8 inch thick on a floured surface.
8. Cover the rolled-out dough with about 1/4 cup of apricot jam, leaving a tiny border around the borders.
9. Sprinkle the jam with 1/4 cup of sweetened shredded coconut and 2 tbsp chop-up walnuts.
10. Slice the dough into 6 to 8 triangular wedges with a pizza sliceter or a sharp knife.
11. Roll every wedge carefully from the wide end to the pointed end to produce a rugelach crescent. Repeat with the rest of the dough and filling.
12. Place the rugelach on the baking sheets that have been prepared. Brush the beaten egg wash over every cookie.
13. Bake for 18 to 20 mins, or up to the rugelach turns golden brown, in a preheated oven.
14. Place the cookies on a wire rack to cool. When completely cool, dust with powdered sugar before serving.

NUTRITION INFO (per cookie):

Cals: 180 kcal, Carbs: 17g, Protein: 2g, Fat: 12g, Saturated Fat: 7g, Fiber: 1g, Sugar: 8g, Sodium: 60mg

226. Tahini Swirl Brownies with Sea Salt

Prep Time: 15 mins

Cook Time: 25 mins

Total Time: 40 mins

Servings: 16 brownies

Ingredients:

- 1/2 cup of unsalted butter, dilute
- 1 cup of granulated sugar
- 2 Big eggs
- 1 tsp vanilla extract
- 1/2 cup of all-purpose flour
- 1/3 cup of cocoa powder
- 1/4 tsp baking powder
- 1/4 tsp salt
- 1/4 cup of tahini
- Sea salt flakes (for topping)

Instructions:

1. Preheat the oven to 350 Ds Fahrenheit (175 Ds Celsius). Line an 8x8-inch baking dish with parchment paper, providing an overhang on all sides for easy removal.
2. Whisk together the dilute butter and granulated sugar in a Big combining basin up to completely combined.
3. Whisk in the eggs one at a time, one at a time. Incorporate the vanilla extract.
4. Whisk together the flour, cocoa powder, baking powder, and salt in a separate basin.
5. Add the dry ingredients to the liquid components gradually, stirring up to just blended.
6. Spread the brownie batter evenly in the prepared baking dish.
7. Add tahini spoonfuls to the brownie batter. Swirl the tahini into the batter with a knife or toothpick to create a marbled look.
8. Sprinkle the top of the brownie batter with sea salt flakes.
9. Bake for approximately 25 mins, or up to a toothpick inserted into the center comes out with a few wet crumbs.
10. Let the brownies to cool completely before Cuttinginto squares and serving.

NUTRITION INFO (per brownie):

Cals: 180 kcal, Carbs: 22g, Protein: 3g, Fat: 10g, Saturated Fat: 5g, Fiber: 1g, Sugar: 15g, Sodium: 80mg

227. Israeli Stuffed Cabbage Rolls with Rice and Lentils

Prep Time: 30 mins

Cook Time: 1 hr 15 mins

Total Time: 1 hr 45 mins

Servings: 6

Ingredients:

- 12 Big cabbage leaves
- 1 cup of cooked brown rice
- 1 cup of cooked lentils
- 1 mini onion, lightly chop-up
- 2 cloves garlic, chop-up
- 1 tbsp olive oil
- 1 can (400g) crushed tomatoes
- 1 tbsp tomato paste
- 1 tsp ground cumin
- 1 tsp ground coriander
- 1/2 tsp ground cinnamon
- Salt and pepper as needed
- 2 cups of vegetable broth or water

Instructions:

1. A big saucepan of salted water Must be brought to a boil. Blanch the cabbage leaves for about 3 mins in boiling water, or up to they become flexible. Set aside after draining.
2. Warm the olive oil in a pan over medium heat. Sauté the chop-up onion up to transparent.
3. Cook for another min after adding the chop-up garlic to the skillet.
4. Cooked brown rice, cooked lentils, ground cumin, ground coriander, ground cinnamon, salt, and pepper are all good additions. Cook for a few mins to enable the flavors to blend.
5. Fill every cabbage leaf with roughly 2 tbsp of the rice and lentil filling. Fold the leaf's sides over the filling and roll it up like a burrito.
6. Combine the crushed tomatoes, tomato paste, and vegetable broth or water in a separate saucepan. Season as needed with salt and pepper.
7. Combine the stuffed cabbage rolls with the tomato sauce in a saucepan. Cook for about 1 hr, or up to the cabbage rolls are soft and the flavors have permeated.
8. If preferred, serve the Israeli stuffed cabbage rolls with more tomato sauce.

NUTRITION INFO (per serving, 2 cabbage rolls):

Cals: 280 kcal, Carbs: 45g, Protein: 12g, Fat: 5g, Saturated Fat: 1g, Fiber: 10g, Sugar: 8g, Sodium: 590mg

228.Falafel Salad Bowl with Tahini Dressing

Prep Time: 20 mins

Cook Time: 15 mins

Total Time: 35 mins

Servings: 4

Ingredients:

- 1 cup of dry chickpeas (or 1 can of cooked chickpeas, drained)
- 1 mini onion, chop-up
- 3 cloves garlic
- 1/4 cup of fresh parsley, chop-up
- 1/4 cup of fresh cilantro, chop-up
- 1 tsp ground cumin
- 1/2 tsp ground coriander
- 1/4 tsp baking soda
- Salt and pepper as needed
- 2 tbsp all-purpose flour
- 2 tbsp olive oil
- 4 cups of combined salad greens
- 1 cucumber, split
- 1 cup of cherry tomatoes, halved
- 1/4 cup of split red onion
- 1/4 cup of cut up feta cheese (non-compulsory)
- Tahini Dressing:
- 1/4 cup of tahini
- 2 tbsp lemon juice
- 2 tbsp water
- 1 clove garlic, chop-up
- Salt and pepper as needed

Instructions:

1. Soak dry chickpeas overnight if using. Before usage, drain and rinse the soaked chickpeas.
2. Combine the chickpeas, onion, garlic, parsley, cilantro, cumin, coriander, baking soda, salt, and pepper in a mixer. Pulse up to everything is well blended but not pureed.
3. Pour the Mixture into a combining basin and toss in the all-purpose flour. Make mini falafel patties out of the ingredients.
4. In a skillet over medium heat, heat the olive oil. Cook for 2-3 mins per side, or up to golden brown and crispy.
5. To create the tahini dressing, combine together the tahini, lemon juice, water, chop-up garlic, salt, and pepper in a mini bowl.
6. In serving bowls, arrange the combined salad greens, split cucumber, halved cherry tomatoes, and split red onion.
7. Drizzle the tahini dressing over the salad and top with the falafel patties.
8. Before serving, top with cut up feta cheese if preferred.

NUTRITION INFO (per serving):

Cals: 350 kcal, Carbs: 30g, Protein: 12g, Fat: 22g, Saturated Fat: 3g, Fiber: 9g, Sugar: 7g, Sodium: 420mg

229.Shakshuka with Swiss Chard and Labneh

Prep Time: 15 mins

Cook Time: 30 mins

Total Time: 45 mins

Servings: 4

Ingredients:

- 1 tbsp olive oil
- 1 Big onion, lightly chop-up
- 2 cloves garlic, chop-up
- 1 red bell pepper, diced
- 1 yellow bell pepper, diced
- 1 tsp ground cumin
- 1 tsp ground paprika
- 1/2 tsp ground cayenne pepper (non-compulsory, adjust as needed)
- 1 can (400g) crushed tomatoes
- 4-6 Big eggs
- 1 bunch Swiss chard, stems take outd and leaves chop-up
- 1/2 cup of labneh (strained yogurt)
- Fresh parsley, chop-up (for garnish)
- Salt and pepper as needed

Instructions:

1. Warm the olive oil in a Big skillet over medium heat. Sauté the chop-up onion up to transparent.
2. In the skillet, combine the chop-up garlic, diced red bell pepper, and yellow bell pepper. Cook for a few mins, or up to the peppers begin to soften.
3. Add the cumin, paprika, cayenne pepper (if using), salt, and pepper as needed. Cook for another min, or up to the Mixture is aromatic.
4. Pour in the crushed tomatoes and cook for about 10 mins, or up to the liquid thickens slightly.
5. Stir in the chop-up Swiss chard to the tomato sauce in the skillet. Cook for a few mins, or up to the chard begins to wilt.
6. Make mini wells in the tomato-chard Mixture and place the eggs inside. Cook, covered, for 5-7 mins, or up to the egg whites are set but the yolks are still runny.
7. Take out from the heat and serve with labneh. Garnish with fresh parsley, if desired.

NUTRITION INFO (per serving):

Cals: 250 kcal, Carbs: 16g, Protein: 10g, Fat: 17g, Saturated Fat: 6g, Fiber: 4g, Sugar: 9g, Sodium: 340mg

230.Malabi with Passionfruit and Coconut

Prep Time: 5 mins

Cook Time: 10 mins

Total Time: 15 mins

Servings: 4

Ingredients:

- 1/2 cup of cornstarch
- 4 cups of coconut milk (or regular milk for a non-coconut version)
- 1/4 cup of sugar
- 2 tbsp rosewater
- Fresh passionfruit pulp (seeds and juice)
- Shredded coconut (for garnish)

Instructions:

1. In a mini dish, combine the cornstarch and 1/2 cup of coconut milk to make a smooth slurry.
2. Heat the remaining 3 1/2 cups of coconut milk in a saucepan over medium heat. Stir in the sugar up to it is completely dissolved.
3. Pour in the cornstarch slurry slowly while constantly swirling to avoid lumps. Cook and stir up to the Mixture thickens and begins to boil.
4. Cook for another min after adding the rosewater.
5. Take out the malabi from the heat and divide it among individual serving dishes or a Big serving bowl. Let it cool to room temperature before refrigerating for at least 2 hrs, or up to set.
6. To serve, garnish the malabi with fresh passionfruit pulp and shredded coconut.

NUTRITION INFO (per serving):

Cals: 280 kcal, Carbs: 23g, Protein: 2g, Fat: 20g, Saturated Fat: 18g, Fiber: 1g, Sugar: 15g, Sodium: 30mg

231.Rugelach with Cherry and Almond Filling

Prep Time: 30 mins

Cook Time: 20 mins

Total Time: 50 mins

Servings: 24 cookies

Ingredients:

- 2 cups of all-purpose flour
- 1/4 tsp salt
- 1 cup of unsalted butter, melted
- 8 ozs cream cheese, melted
- 1/2 cup of granulated sugar
- 1 tsp vanilla extract
- 1 cup of cherry jam or preserves
- 1/2 cup of chop-up almonds
- 1 egg, beaten (for egg wash)
- Powdered sugar (for dusting)

Instructions:

1. Whisk together the flour and salt in a Big combining dish. Place aside.

2. In a separate combining dish, combine the melted butter and cream cheese up to smooth and creamy.
3. To the butter Mixture, add the granulated sugar and vanilla essence and stir well.
4. Add the flour Mixture to the wet ingredients gradually, combining up to a soft dough forms.
5. Divide the dough into four equal pieces, shape into disks, and cover every in plastic wrap. Chill the dough for at least 30 mins in the refrigerator.
6. Preheat the oven to 350 Ds Fahrenheit (175 Ds Celsius) and line baking sheets with parchment paper.
7. Roll out one cold dough disk into a circle approximately 1/8 inch thick on a floured surface.
8. Cover the rolled-out dough with about 1/4 cup of cherry jam, leaving a tiny border around the borders.
9. Sprinkle 2 tbsp of chop-up almonds over the jam.
10. Slice the dough into 6 to 8 triangular wedges with a pizza sliceter or a sharp knife.
11. Roll every wedge carefully from the wide end to the pointed end to produce a rugelach crescent. Repeat with the rest of the dough and filling.
12. Place the rugelach on the baking sheets that have been prepared. Brush the beaten egg wash over every cookie.
13. Bake for 18 to 20 mins, or up to the rugelach turns golden brown, in a preheated oven.
14. Place the cookies on a wire rack to cool. When completely cool, dust with powdered sugar before serving.

NUTRITION INFO (per cookie):
Cals: 190 kcal, Carbs: 17g, Protein: 2g, Fat: 13g, Saturated Fat: 7g, Fiber: 1g, Sugar: 8g, Sodium: 45mg

232.Tahini Maple Granola Bars with Sunflower Seeds

Prep Time: 15 mins

Cook Time: 25 mins

Total Time: 40 mins

Servings: 12 bars

Ingredients:
- 2 cups of rolled oats
- 1/2 cup of sunflower seeds
- 1/2 cup of almond butter
- 1/3 cup of pure maple syrup
- 1/4 cup of tahini
- 1 tsp vanilla extract
- Pinch of salt

Instructions:
1. Preheat the oven to 350 Ds Fahrenheit (175 Ds Celsius). Line an 8x8-inch baking dish with parchment paper, providing an overhang on all sides to facilitate removal.
2. Combine the rolled oats and sunflower seeds in a Big combining basin.
3. Heat the almond butter, maple syrup, tahini, vanilla extract, and a bit of salt in a separate microwave-safe bowl up to smooth and well blended.
4. Pour the wet Mixture over the dry ingredients and stir to coat everything evenly.
5. Using the back of a spoon or your hands, press the Mixture firmly into the prepared baking dish.
6. Bake for 20-25 mins, or up to the edges are golden brown, in a preheated oven.
7. Let the granola bars to cool completely before Cuttinginto 12 bars.
8. Keep the bars at room temperature in an airtight container for up to a week.

NUTRITION INFO (per bar):
Cals: 200 kcal, Carbs: 17g, Protein: 5g, Fat: 14g, Saturated Fat: 2g, Fiber: 3g, Sugar: 6g, Sodium: 10mg

233.Israeli Stuffed Artichokes with Quinoa and Herbs

Prep Time: 20 mins

Cook Time: 1 hr 15 mins

Total Time: 1 hr 35 mins

Servings: 4

Ingredients:
- 4 Big artichokes
- 1 cup of cooked quinoa
- 1/2 cup of chop-up fresh parsley
- 1/4 cup of chop-up fresh mint
- 1/4 cup of chop-up fresh dill
- 1/4 cup of chop-up green onions
- 2 cloves garlic, chop-up
- 1/4 cup of lemon juice
- 1/4 cup of olive oil
- Salt and pepper as needed
- Lemon wedges (for serving)

Instructions:
1. Take out the stems and about 1 inch of the top of the artichokes. Take out any stiff outer leaves and use scissors to trim the tips of the remaining leaves.
2. Bring water to a boil in a big pot and add a squeeze of lemon juice. Cook for 30-40 mins, or

up to the artichokes' leaves are soft. Set aside after draining.

3. Combine the cooked quinoa, chop-up parsley, mint, dill, green onions, chop-up garlic, lemon juice, olive oil, salt, and pepper in a combining bowl. Combine thoroughly.
4. Gently separate the artichoke leaves and insert the quinoa-herb Mixture into the centers and between the leaves of every artichoke.
5. Serve the Israeli stuffed artichokes alongside lemon wedges.

NUTRITION INFO (per serving, 1 artichoke):
Cals: 230 kcal, Carbs: 27g, Protein: 5g, Fat: 13g, Saturated Fat: 2g, Fiber: 10g, Sugar: 2g, Sodium: 210mg

234. Falafel Sliders with Pickles and Garlic Sauce

Prep Time: 20 mins

Cook Time: 20 mins

Total Time: 40 mins

Servings: 4 (4 sliders every)

Ingredients:
- 16 mini falafel patties
- 8 slider buns or mini pitas, split
- 1 cup of split pickles
- 1 cup of shredded lettuce
- 1 cup of split tomatoes
- 1/2 cup of chop-up red onions
- 1/2 cup of garlic sauce (store-bought or homemade)

Instructions:
1. Preheat the oven to 375°F (190°C) or cook the falafel patties according to the box/pkg directions.
2. Cook the refrigerate falafel patties according to the box/pkg directions.
3. Placing a falafel patty on the bottom half of every sandwich or pita makes the sliders.
4. Add split cucumbers, shredded lettuce, split tomatoes, and chop-up red onions to the falafel.
5. Drizzle the garlic sauce over the salad ingredients.
6. To finish the sliders, place the top half of the buns or pitas over the fillings.
7. Serve the falafel sliders alongside extra pickles, lettuce, and garlic sauce.

NUTRITION INFO (per serving, 4 sliders):
Cals: 430 kcal, Carbs: 65g, Protein: 16g, Fat: 11g, Saturated Fat: 2g, Fiber: 10g, Sugar: 7g, Sodium: 740mg

235. Shakshuka with Roasted Red Peppers and Spinach

Prep Time: 15 mins

Cook Time: 30 mins

Total Time: 45 mins

Servings: 4

Ingredients:
- 2 tbsp olive oil
- 1 Big onion, lightly chop-up
- 2 cloves garlic, chop-up
- 2 roasted red peppers, split
- 1 tsp ground cumin
- 1 tsp ground paprika
- 1/2 tsp ground cayenne pepper (non-compulsory, adjust as needed)
- 1 can (400g) crushed tomatoes
- 4-6 Big eggs
- 2 cups of baby spinach
- Salt and pepper as needed
- Fresh parsley, chop-up (for garnish)

Instructions:
1. Warm the olive oil in a Big skillet over medium heat. Sauté the chop-up onion up to transparent.
2. Cook for another min after adding the chop-up garlic to the skillet.
3. Add the split roasted red peppers, cumin, paprika, cayenne pepper (if using), salt, and pepper as needed. Cook for another min, or up to the Mixture is aromatic.
4. Pour in the crushed tomatoes and cook for about 10 mins, or up to the liquid thickens slightly.
5. Let the young spinach to wilt in the tomato Mixture.
6. Make mini wells in the tomato-spinach Mixture and place the eggs inside. Cook, covered, for 5-7 mins, or up to the egg whites are set but the yolks are still runny.
7. Take out from the heat and garnish with fresh parsley.

NUTRITION INFO (per serving):
Cals: 240 kcal, Carbs: 17g, Protein: 10g, Fat: 14g, Saturated Fat: 3g, Fiber: 5g, Sugar: 8g
Sodium: 430mg

236. Malabi with Orange Blossom and Pistachio

Prep Time: 5 mins

Cook Time: 10 mins

Total Time: 15 mins

Servings: 4

Ingredients:

- 1/2 cup of cornstarch
- 4 cups of milk (or plant-based milk for a vegan version)
- 1/4 cup of sugar
- 1 tbsp orange blossom water
- Crushed pistachios (for garnish)

Instructions:

1. In a mini dish, combine the cornstarch with 1/2 cup of milk to make a smooth slurry.
2. Heat the remaining 3 1/2 cups of milk in a saucepan over medium heat. Stir in the sugar up to it is completely dissolved.
3. Pour in the cornstarch slurry slowly while constantly swirling to avoid lumps. Cook and stir up to the Mixture thickens and begins to boil.
4. Cook for another min after adding the orange blossom water.
5. Take out the malabi from the heat and divide it among individual serving dishes or a Big serving bowl.
6. Let it cool to room temperature before refrigerating for at least 2 hrs, or up to set.
7. Before serving, sprinkle with cut up pistachios.

NUTRITION INFO (per serving):
Cals: 250 kcal, Carbs: 40g, Protein: 8g, Fat: 8g, Saturated Fat: 5g, Fiber: 0g, Sugar: 28g, Sodium: 120mg

237. Rugelach with Raspberry and Pecan Filling

Prep Time: 30 mins

Cook Time: 20 mins

Total Time: 50 mins

Servings: 24 cookies

Ingredients:

- 2 cups of all-purpose flour
- 1/4 tsp salt
- 1 cup of unsalted butter, melted
- 8 ozs cream cheese, melted
- 1/2 cup of granulated sugar
- 1 tsp vanilla extract
- 1 cup of raspberry preserves
- 1/2 cup of chop-up pecans
- 1 egg, beaten (for egg wash)
- Powdered sugar (for dusting)

Instructions:

1. Whisk together the flour and salt in a Big combining dish. Place aside.
2. In a separate combining dish, combine the melted butter and cream cheese up to smooth and creamy.
3. To the butter Mixture, add the granulated sugar and vanilla essence and stir well.
4. Add the flour Mixture to the wet ingredients gradually, combining up to a soft dough forms.
5. Divide the dough into four equal pieces, shape into disks, and cover every in plastic wrap. Chill the dough for at least 30 mins in the refrigerator.
6. Preheat the oven to 350 Ds Fahrenheit (175 Ds Celsius) and line baking sheets with parchment paper.
7. Roll out one cold dough disk into a circle approximately 1/8 inch thick on a floured surface.
8. Cover the rolled-out dough with about 1/4 cup of raspberry preserves, leaving a tiny border around the borders.
9. Sprinkle 2 tbsp chop-up pecans over the preserves.
10. Slice the dough into 6 to 8 triangular wedges with a pizza sliceter or a sharp knife.
11. Roll every wedge carefully from the wide end to the pointed end to produce a rugelach crescent. Repeat with the rest of the dough and filling.
12. Place the rugelach on the baking sheets that have been prepared. Brush the beaten egg wash over every cookie.
13. Bake for 18 to 20 mins, or up to the rugelach turns golden brown, in a preheated oven.
14. Place the cookies on a wire rack to cool. When completely cool, dust with powdered sugar before serving.

NUTRITION INFO (per cookie):
Cals: 220 kcal, Carbs: 18g, Protein: 3g, Fat: 15g, Saturated Fat: 7g, Fiber: 1g, Sugar: 8g, Sodium: 45mg

238. Tahini Banana Muffins with Chocolate Chips

Prep Time: 15 mins

Cook Time: 20 mins

Total Time: 35 mins

Servings: 12 muffins

Ingredients:

- 1 1/2 cups of all-purpose flour
- 1 tsp baking powder
- 1/2 tsp baking soda
- Pinch of salt
- 3 ripe bananas, mashed
- 1/2 cup of tahini
- 1/2 cup of brown sugar

- 1 Big egg
- 1 tsp vanilla extract
- 1/2 cup of milk (or plant-based milk)
- 1/2 cup of chocolate chips

Instructions:

1. Preheat the oven to 375 Ds Fahrenheit (190 Ds Celsius). Line the muffin cups of with paper liners or oil them.
2. Whisk together the flour, baking powder, baking soda, and a pinch of salt in a Big combining basin.
3. In a separate bowl, add the mashed bananas, tahini, brown sugar, egg, and vanilla essence.
4. Gradually combine the wet and dry ingredients, alternating with the milk. Combine up to everything is just blended.
5. Add the chocolate chips and combine well.
6. Fill every muffin cup of about two-thirds of the way full with batter.
7. Bake for 18-20 mins, or up to a toothpick inserted in the center of a muffin comes out clean.
8. Let the muffins to cool for a few mins in the pan before transferring to a wire rack to cool completely.

NUTRITION INFO (per muffin):
Cals: 260 kcal, Carbs: 33g, Protein: 4g, Fat: 12g, Saturated Fat: 3g, Fiber: 2g, Sugar: 16g, Sodium: 120mg

239. Israeli Stuffed Tomatoes with Couscous and Mint

Prep Time: 30 mins

Cook Time: 25 mins

Total Time: 55 mins

Servings: 4

Ingredients:

- 4 Big tomatoes
- 1 cup of couscous
- 1 1/4 cups of vegetable broth or water
- 1/4 cup of chop-up fresh mint
- 1/4 cup of chop-up fresh parsley
- 1/4 cup of chop-up fresh dill
- 1/4 cup of chop-up green onions
- 1/4 cup of lemon juice
- 2 tbsp olive oil
- Salt and pepper as needed

Instructions:

1. Using a spoon, carefully scrape off the seeds and pulp from every tomato. Set aside the hollowed tomatoes.
2. Bring the vegetable broth or water to a boil in a saucepan. Cover and take out from heat after

stirring in the couscous. Let for 5 mins, or up to the couscous absorbs the liquid.
3. Let the couscous to cool slightly before fluffing with a fork.
4. Combine the cooked couscous, chop-up mint, parsley, dill, green onions, lemon juice, olive oil, salt, and pepper in a combining bowl. Combine thoroughly.
5. Fill every tomato hollow with the couscous-herb Mixture, carefully pressing it down.
6. The Israeli stuffed tomatoes can be served at room temperature or chilled.

NUTRITION INFO (per serving, 1 stuffed tomato):
Cals: 290 kcal, Carbs: 49g, Protein: 8g, Fat: 8g, Saturated Fat: 1g, Fiber: 6g, Sugar: 6g, Sodium: 240mg

240. Falafel Tabbouleh Bowl with Lemon-Tahini Dressing

Prep Time: 25 mins

Cook Time: 20 mins

Total Time: 45 mins

Servings: 4

Ingredients:

- 16 mini falafel patties
- 2 cups of cooked quinoa
- 1 cucumber, diced
- 1 cup of cherry tomatoes, halved
- 1 cup of chop-up fresh parsley
- 1/2 cup of chop-up fresh mint
- 1/4 cup of chop-up fresh dill
- 1/4 cup of chop-up green onions
- 1/4 cup of lemon juice
- 1/4 cup of tahini
- 2 cloves garlic, chop-up
- Salt and pepper as needed
- Lemon wedges (for serving)

Instructions:

1. Preheat the oven to 375°F (190°C) or cook the falafel patties according to the box/pkg directions.
2. Cook the refrigerate falafel patties according to the box/pkg directions.
3. Combine the cooked quinoa, diced cucumber, halved cherry tomatoes, chop-up parsley, mint, dill, and green onions in a Big combining dish.
4. To make the lemon-tahini dressing, combine together the lemon juice, tahini, chop-up garlic, salt, and pepper in a separate bowl.
5. Toss the quinoa tabbouleh with the lemon-tahini dressing to coat evenly.

6. Place 4 falafel patties on top of every quinoa tabbouleh portion to make the falafel tabbouleh bowls.

7. Serve the falafel tabbouleh bowls alongside lemon wedges.

NUTRITION INFO (per serving, 1 bowl):
Cals: 460 kcal, Carbs: 48g, Protein: 15g, Fat: 24g, Saturated Fat: 3g, Fiber: 10g, Sugar: 6g, Sodium: 570mg

241.Shakshuka with Swiss Chard and Harissa

Prep Time: 15 mins

Cook Time: 30 mins

Total Time: 45 mins

Servings: 4

Ingredients:

- 2 tbsp olive oil
- 1 Big onion, lightly chop-up
- 2 cloves garlic, chop-up
- 1 bunch Swiss chard, stems take outd and leaves chop-up
- 1 tsp ground cumin
- 1 tsp ground paprika
- 1/2 tsp ground cayenne pepper (non-compulsory, adjust as needed)
- 1 can (400g) crushed tomatoes
- 4-6 Big eggs
- 2 tbsp harissa paste (adjust as needed)
- Salt and pepper as needed
- Fresh cilantro, chop-up (for garnish)

Instructions:

1. Warm the olive oil in a Big skillet over medium heat. Sauté the chop-up onion up to transparent.

2. Cook for another min after adding the chop-up garlic to the skillet.

3. Cook up to the Swiss chard is wilted, about 5 mins.

4. To the skillet, add the cumin, paprika, cayenne pepper (if using), salt, and pepper. Cook for another min, or up to the Mixture is aromatic.

5. Combine the crushed tomatoes and harissa paste in a combining bowl. Let the Mixture to simmer for 10 mins, or up to it thickens slightly.

6. Make mini wells in the tomato-chard Mixture and place the eggs inside. Cook, covered, for 5-7 mins, or up to the egg whites are set but the yolks are still runny.

7. Take out from the heat and garnish with fresh cilantro.

NUTRITION INFO (per serving):
Cals: 240 kcal, Carbs: 15g, Protein: 10g, Fat: 16g, Saturated Fat: 3g, Fiber: 4g, Sugar: 6g, Sodium: 480mg

242.Malabi with Rosewater and Strawberry Sauce

Prep Time: 5 mins

Cook Time: 10 mins

Total Time: 15 mins

Servings: 4

Ingredients:

- 1/2 cup of cornstarch
- 4 cups of milk (or plant-based milk for a vegan version)
- 1/4 cup of sugar
- 1 tsp rosewater
- Fresh strawberries, split (for sauce and garnish)
- Crushed pistachios (for garnish)

Instructions:

1. In a mini dish, combine the cornstarch with 1/2 cup of milk to make a smooth slurry.

2. Heat the remaining 3 1/2 cups of milk in a saucepan over medium heat. Stir in the sugar up to it is completely dissolved.

3. Pour in the cornstarch slurry slowly while constantly swirling to avoid lumps. Cook and stir up to the Mixture thickens and begins to boil.

4. Cook for another min after adding the rosewater.

5. Take out the malabi from the heat and divide it among individual serving dishes or a Big serving bowl.

6. Let it cool to room temperature before refrigerating for at least 2 hrs, or up to set.

7. Serve the malabi topped with split strawberries and crushed pistachios.

NUTRITION INFO (per serving):
Cals: 250 kcal, Carbs: 40g, Protein: 8g, Fat: 8g, Saturated Fat: 5g, Fiber: 1g, Sugar: 28g, Sodium: 120mg

243.Rugelach with Blueberry and Almond Filling

Prep Time: 30 mins

Cook Time: 20 mins

Total Time: 50 mins

Servings: 24 cookies

Ingredients:

- 2 cups of all-purpose flour
- 1/4 tsp salt
- 1 cup of unsalted butter, melted

- 8 ozs cream cheese, melted
- 1/2 cup of granulated sugar
- 1 tsp vanilla extract
- 1/2 cup of blueberry preserves
- 1/2 cup of chop-up almonds
- 1 egg, beaten (for egg wash)
- Powdered sugar (for dusting)

Instructions:

1. Whisk together the flour and salt in a Big combining dish. Place aside.
2. In a separate combining dish, combine the melted butter and cream cheese up to smooth and creamy.
3. To the butter Mixture, add the granulated sugar and vanilla essence and stir well.
4. Add the flour Mixture to the wet ingredients gradually, combining up to a soft dough forms.
5. Divide the dough into four equal pieces, shape into disks, and cover every in plastic wrap. Chill the dough for at least 30 mins in the refrigerator.
6. Preheat the oven to 350 Ds Fahrenheit (175 Ds Celsius) and line baking sheets with parchment paper.
7. Roll out one cold dough disk into a circle approximately 1/8 inch thick on a floured surface.
8. Cover the rolled-out dough with about 1/4 cup of blueberry preserves, leaving a tiny border around the borders.
9. Sprinkle 2 tbsp chop-up almonds over the preserves.
10. Slice the dough into 6 to 8 triangular wedges with a pizza sliceter or a sharp knife.
11. Roll every wedge carefully from the wide end to the pointed end to produce a rugelach crescent. Repeat with the rest of the dough and filling.
12. Place the rugelach on the baking sheets that have been prepared. Brush the beaten egg wash over every cookie.
13. Bake for 18 to 20 mins, or up to the rugelach turns golden brown, in a preheated oven.
14. Place the cookies on a wire rack to cool. When completely cool, dust with powdered sugar before serving.

NUTRITION INFO (per cookie):
Cals: 220 kcal, Carbs: 18g, Protein: 3g, Fat: 15g, Saturated Fat: 7g, Fiber: 1g, Sugar: 8g, Sodium: 45mg

244. Tahini Coconut Energy Bites

Prep Time: 15 mins

Total Time: 15 mins

Servings: 12 energy bites

Ingredients:

- 1 cup of old-fashioned rolled oats
- 1/2 cup of shredded coconut
- 1/2 cup of almond butter
- 1/4 cup of honey (or maple syrup for a vegan version)
- 1/4 cup of tahini
- 1 tsp vanilla extract
- Pinch of salt
- 1/4 cup of mini chocolate chips (non-compulsory)

Instructions:

1. Combine the rolled oats and shredded coconut in a Big combining basin.
2. Heat the almond butter, honey (or maple syrup), tahini, vanilla essence, and a bit of salt in a separate microwave-safe bowl up to smooth and well blended.
3. Pour the wet Mixture over the dry ingredients and stir to coat everything evenly.
4. Stir micro chocolate chips into the Mixture if using.
5. Using your hands, form the Mixture into mini energy bites by pressing it firmly.
6. Place the energy bits on a tray or plate lined with parchment paper.
7. Refrigerate the energy bites for at least 30 mins before serving to firm up.
8. Refrigerate the energy bites in an airtight jar for up to two weeks.

NUTRITION INFO (per energy bite):
Cals: 170 kcal, Carbs: 15g, Protein: 4g, Fat: 11g, Saturated Fat: 3g, Fiber: 2g, Sugar: 6g, Sodium: 40mg

245. Israeli Stuffed Mushrooms with Quinoa and Pesto

Prep Time: 20 mins

Cook Time: 25 mins

Total Time: 45 mins

Servings: 4

Ingredients:

- 16 Big button mushrooms
- 1 cup of cooked quinoa
- 1/4 cup of pesto sauce
- 1/4 cup of finely finely grated Parmesan cheese (non-compulsory, omit for a vegan version)
- Salt and pepper as needed
- Fresh basil leaves (for garnish)

Instructions:

1. Preheat the oven to 375 Ds Fahrenheit (190 Ds Celsius).

2. Take out the stems and clean the mushrooms. Set aside the mushroom caps.
3. Combine the cooked quinoa, pesto sauce, and finely finely grated Parmesan cheese (if using) in a combining bowl. Combine thoroughly.
4. Season the quinoa Mixture as needed with salt and pepper.
5. Fill every mushroom cap with the quinoa Mixture, carefully pressing it down.
6. Place the stuffed mushrooms on a parchment-lined baking sheet.
7. Bake for 20-25 mins, or up to the mushrooms are soft and the filling is slightly browned, in a preheated oven.
8. Before serving, garnish with fresh basil leaves.

NUTRITION INFO (per serving, 4 stuffed mushrooms):
Cals: 150 kcal, Carbs: 12g, Protein: 6g, Fat: 8g, Saturated Fat: 2g, Fiber: 2g, Sugar: 1g, Sodium: 260mg

246.Falafel Wrap with Hummus and Cucumber Salad

Prep Time: 20 mins

Cook Time: 10 mins

Total Time: 30 mins

Servings: 4 wraps

Ingredients:
- 16 mini falafel patties
- 4 Big whole wheat or spinach wraps
- 1 cup of hummus
- 1 cucumber, split
- 1 cup of cherry tomatoes, halved
- 1/2 cup of chop-up red onions
- Fresh parsley, chop-up (for garnish)

Instructions:
1. Preheat the oven to 375°F (190°C) or cook the falafel patties according to the box/pkg directions.
2. Cook the refrigerate falafel patties according to the box/pkg directions.
3. To make the whole wheat or spinach wraps more malleable for wrapping, warm them in the microwave or on the stovetop.
4. Cover every wrap with about 1/4 cup of hummus, leaving a tiny border around the borders.
5. Place four falafel patties on every roll, equally spaced.
6. Add split cucumbers, split cherry tomatoes, and chop-up red onions to the falafel.
7. Sprinkle the contents with fresh parsley.

8. To make the falafel wrap, fold the sides of the wrap toward the center and roll it up securely.
9. If necessary, secure the wrap with a toothpick.
10. Serve immediately or wrap the falafel wraps in parchment paper or foil for a portable lunch.

NUTRITION INFO (per wrap):
Cals: 480 kcal, Carbs: 60g, Protein: 15g, Fat: 20g, Saturated Fat: 3g, Fiber: 12g, Sugar: 7g, Sodium: 840mg

247.Shakshuka with Roasted Eggplant and Herbs

Prep Time: 15 mins

Cook Time: 35 mins

Total Time: 50 mins

Servings: 4

Ingredients:
- 2 tbsp olive oil
- 1 Big onion, lightly chop-up
- 2 cloves garlic, chop-up
- 1 Big eggplant, diced
- 1 tsp ground cumin
- 1 tsp ground paprika
- 1/2 tsp ground cayenne pepper (non-compulsory, adjust as needed)
- 1 can (400g) crushed tomatoes
- 4-6 Big eggs
- 1/4 cup of chop-up fresh parsley
- 1/4 cup of chop-up fresh cilantro
- Salt and pepper as needed

Instructions:
1. Preheat the oven to 400 Ds Fahrenheit (200 Ds Celsius).
2. 1 tbsp olive oil, heated in a Big skillet over medium heat. Sauté the chop-up onion up to transparent.
3. Cook for another min after adding the chop-up garlic to the skillet.
4. Cook the diced eggplant in the skillet up to it is soft and slightly browned.
5. Add the cumin, paprika, cayenne pepper (if using), salt, and pepper as needed. Cook for another min, or up to the Mixture is aromatic.
6. Pour in the crushed tomatoes and cook for about 10 mins, or up to the liquid thickens slightly.
7. Place the eggplant-tomato Mixture in a baking dish that is oven-safe.
8. Make mini wells in the Mixture, then crack the eggs into them.
9. Bake for 10-15 mins, or up to the egg whites are set but the yolks are still runny, in a preheated oven.

10. Before serving, take out the shakshuka from the oven and top with chop-up fresh parsley and cilantro.

NUTRITION INFO (per serving):
Cals: 230 kcal, Carbs: 18g, Protein: 10g, Fat: 14g, Saturated Fat: 2g, Fiber: 6g, Sugar: 9g, Sodium: 350mg

248.Malabi with Passionfruit and Mango

Prep Time: 5 mins

Cook Time: 10 mins

Total Time: 15 mins

Servings: 4

Ingredients:
- 1/2 cup of cornstarch
- 4 cups of coconut milk (or regular milk for a non-coconut version)
- 1/4 cup of sugar
- 1 tsp vanilla extract
- Pulp of 2 ripe passionfruits (for sauce and garnish)
- 1 ripe mango, diced (for sauce and garnish)

Instructions:
1. In a mini dish, combine the cornstarch and 1/2 cup of coconut milk to make a smooth slurry.
2. Heat the remaining 3 1/2 cups of coconut milk in a saucepan over medium heat. Stir in the sugar up to it is completely dissolved.
3. Pour in the cornstarch slurry slowly while constantly swirling to avoid lumps. Cook and stir up to the Mixture thickens and begins to boil.
4. Cook for another min after adding the vanilla essence.
5. Take out the malabi from the heat and divide it among individual serving dishes or a Big serving bowl.
6. Let it cool to room temperature before refrigerating for at least 2 hrs, or up to set.
7. To serve, top the malabi with ripe passionfruit pulp and chop-up mango.

NUTRITION INFO (per serving):
Cals: 250 kcal, Carbs: 40g, Protein: 4g, Fat: 10g, Saturated Fat: 8g, Fiber: 3g, Sugar: 26g, Sodium: 25mg

249.Rugelach with Apricot and Walnut Filling

Prep Time: 30 mins

Cook Time: 20 mins

Total Time: 50 mins

Servings: 24 cookies

Ingredients:
- 2 cups of all-purpose flour
- 1/4 tsp salt
- 1 cup of unsalted butter, melted
- 8 ozs cream cheese, melted
- 1/2 cup of granulated sugar
- 1 tsp vanilla extract
- 1/2 cup of apricot preserves
- 1/2 cup of chop-up walnuts
- 1 egg, beaten (for egg wash)
- Powdered sugar (for dusting)

Instructions:
1. Whisk together the flour and salt in a Big combining dish. Place aside.
2. In a separate combining dish, combine the melted butter and cream cheese up to smooth and creamy.
3. To the butter Mixture, add the granulated sugar and vanilla essence and stir well.
4. Add the flour Mixture to the wet ingredients gradually, combining up to a soft dough forms.
5. Divide the dough into four equal pieces, shape into disks, and cover every in plastic wrap. Chill the dough for at least 30 mins in the refrigerator.
6. Preheat the oven to 350 Ds Fahrenheit (175 Ds Celsius) and line baking sheets with parchment paper.
7. Roll out one cold dough disk into a circle approximately 1/8 inch thick on a floured surface.
8. Cover the rolled-out dough with about 1/4 cup of apricot preserves, leaving a tiny border around the sides.
9. Sprinkle 2 tbsp of chop-up walnuts over the preserves.
10. Slice the dough into 6 to 8 triangular wedges with a pizza sliceter or a sharp knife.
11. Roll every wedge carefully from the wide end to the pointed end to produce a rugelach crescent. Repeat with the rest of the dough and filling.
12. Place the rugelach on the baking sheets that have been prepared. Brush the beaten egg wash over every cookie.
13. Bake for 18-20 mins, or up to the rugelach turns golden brown, in a preheated oven.
14. Place the cookies on a wire rack to cool. When completely cool, dust with powdered sugar before serving.

NUTRITION INFO (per cookie):
Cals: 200 kcal, Carbs: 16g, Protein: 3g, Fat: 13g, Saturated Fat: 7g, Fiber: 1g, Sugar: 7g, Sodium: 55mg

250. Tahini Rice Pudding with Cinnamon and Dates

Prep Time: 5 mins

Cook Time: 25 mins

Total Time: 30 mins

Servings: 4

Ingredients:

- 1 cup of white rice
- 2 cups of milk (or plant-based milk for a vegan version)
- 2 tbsp tahini
- 2 tbsp honey (or maple syrup for a vegan version)
- 1 tsp vanilla extract
- 1/2 tsp ground cinnamon
- 1/4 cup of chop-up dates
- Crushed pistachios (for garnish)

Instructions:

1. Cold water Must be used to rinse the white rice.
2. Bring the milk to a simmer in a saucepan over medium heat. Reduce the heat to low and add the washed rice.
3. Cook the rice in milk, stirring periodically, for about 20 mins, or up to soft and most of the milk has been absorbed.
4. Combine the tahini, honey (or maple syrup), vanilla essence, ground cinnamon, and chop-up dates in a combining bowl. Combine thoroughly.
5. Cook for 5 mins more to enable the flavors to mingle.
6. Take out the tahini rice pudding from the heat and divide it into individual serving bowls.
7. Before serving, top every bowl with cut up pistachios.

NUTRITION INFO (per serving):

Cals: 310 kcal, Carbs: 57g, Protein: 7g, Fat: 7g, Saturated Fat: 2g, Fiber: 2g, Sugar: 20g, Sodium: 85mg

251. Israeli Stuffed Bell Peppers with Quinoa and Chickpeas

Prep Time: 30 mins

Cook Time: 35 mins

Total Time: 1 hr 5 mins

Servings: 4

Ingredients:

- 4 Big bell peppers (any color)
- 1 cup of cooked quinoa
- 1 can (15 oz) chickpeas, drained and rinsed
- 1/2 cup of diced tomatoes (canned or fresh)
- 1/4 cup of chop-up fresh parsley
- 1/4 cup of chop-up fresh mint
- 1/4 cup of chop-up fresh dill
- 1/4 cup of chop-up green onions
- 2 tbsp lemon juice
- 2 tbsp olive oil
- Salt and pepper as needed

Instructions:

1. Preheat the oven to 375 Ds Fahrenheit (190 Ds Celsius).
2. Take out the tops of the bell peppers and scoop out the seeds and membranes.
3. Combine the cooked quinoa, chickpeas, diced tomatoes, chop-up parsley, mint, dill, green onions, lemon juice, olive oil, salt, and pepper in a combining dish. Combine thoroughly.
4. Fill every bell pepper with the quinoa-chickpea Mixture, gently pushing it down.
5. In a baking dish, place the filled bell peppers.
6. Cover the baking dish with aluminum foil and bake for 25 mins in a preheated oven.
7. Take out the foil and bake for 10 mins more, or up to the bell peppers are soft and slightly browned.
8. Serve the filled Israeli bell peppers hot.

NUTRITION INFO (per serving, 1 stuffed bell pepper):

Cals: 370 kcal, Carbs: 56g, Protein: 13g, Fat: 11g, Saturated Fat: 1g, Fiber: 15g, Sugar: 10g, Sodium: 90mg

252. Falafel Tacos with Cilantro-Lime Sauce

Prep Time: 20 mins

Cook Time: 20 mins

Total Time: 40 mins

Servings: 4

Ingredients: Falafel:

- 16 mini falafel patties (store-bought or homemade)
- 4 soft taco-sized flour tortillas or pita bread
- Cilantro-Lime Sauce:
- 1 cup of Greek yogurt (or vegan yogurt for a dairy-free version)
- 1/4 cup of chop-up fresh cilantro
- 2 tbsp lime juice
- 1 clove garlic, chop-up
- Salt and pepper as needed
- Taco Toppings:
- Shredded lettuce
- Diced tomatoes
- Split cucumbers
- Split red onions

- Pickled turnips or pickles (non-compulsory)

Instructions:

1. Cook the falafel patties according to the box/pkg directions if using store-bought falafel patties. Cook homemade falafel till golden brown and crispy on the exterior.
2. Microwave or heat the flour tortillas or pita bread on the stovetop.
3. To make the cilantro-lime sauce, combine the Greek yogurt, chop-up cilantro, lime juice, chop-up garlic, salt, and pepper in a mini bowl.
4. Place 4 falafel patties in the center of every warm tortilla or pita bread to make the falafel tacos.
5. Shredded lettuce, chop-up tomatoes, split cucumbers, and split red onions go on top of the falafel.
6. Drizzle the cilantro-lime sauce over the salad ingredients.
7. Add pickled turnips or pickles for added flavor if desired.
8. To make the falafel taco, fold the sides of the tortilla or pita bread over the filling and roll it up securely.
9. Serve the falafel tacos right away.

NUTRITION INFO (per serving, 1 taco):
Cals: 420 kcal, Carbs: 56g, Protein: 18g, Fat: 13g, Saturated Fat: 4g, Fiber: 7g, Sugar: 5g, Sodium: 720mg

253. Shakshuka with Swiss Chard and Chickpeas

Prep Time: 15 mins

Cook Time: 25 mins

Total Time: 40 mins

Servings: 4

Ingredients:

- 2 tbsp olive oil
- 1 Big onion, lightly chop-up
- 2 cloves garlic, chop-up
- 1 bunch Swiss chard, stems take outd and leaves chop-up
- 1 tsp ground cumin
- 1 tsp ground paprika
- 1/2 tsp ground cayenne pepper (non-compulsory, adjust as needed)
- 1 can (400g) crushed tomatoes
- 1 can (400g) cooked chickpeas, drained and rinsed
- 4-6 Big eggs
- Salt and pepper as needed
- Fresh parsley, chop-up (for garnish)

Instructions:

1. Warm the olive oil in a Big skillet over medium heat. Sauté the chop-up onion up to transparent.
2. Cook for another min after adding the chop-up garlic to the skillet.
3. Cook up to the Swiss chard is wilted, about 5 mins.
4. To the skillet, add the cumin, paprika, cayenne pepper (if using), salt, and pepper. Cook for another min, or up to the Mixture is aromatic.
5. Add the cooked chickpeas and the smashed tomatoes. Let the Mixture to simmer for 10 mins, or up to it thickens slightly.
6. Make mini wells in the tomato-chard Mixture and place the eggs inside.
7. Cook, covered, for 5-7 mins, or up to the egg whites are set but the yolks are still runny.
8. Take out from the heat and garnish with fresh parsley.

NUTRITION INFO (per serving):
Cals: 320 kcal, Carbs: 33g, Protein: 14g, Fat: 15g, Saturated Fat: 3g, Fiber: 9g, Sugar: 9g, Sodium: 410mg

254. Malabi with Rosewater and Pevery Sauce

Prep Time: 5 mins

Cook Time: 10 mins

Total Time: 15 mins

Servings: 4

Ingredients:

- 1/2 cup of cornstarch
- 4 cups of milk (or plant-based milk for a vegan version)
- 1/4 cup of sugar
- 1 tsp rosewater
- Fresh peveryes, split (for sauce and garnish)
- Crushed pistachios (for garnish)

Instructions:

1. In a mini dish, combine the cornstarch with 1/2 cup of milk to make a smooth slurry.
2. Heat the remaining 3 1/2 cups of milk in a saucepan over medium heat. Stir in the sugar up to it is completely dissolved.
3. Pour in the cornstarch slurry slowly while constantly swirling to avoid lumps. Cook and stir up to the Mixture thickens and begins to boil.
4. Cook for another min after adding the rosewater.
5. Take out the malabi from the heat and divide it among individual serving dishes or a Big serving bowl.

6. Let it cool to room temperature before refrigerating for at least 2 hrs, or up to set.
7. Serve the malabi topped with split peveryes and cut up pistachios.

NUTRITION INFO (per serving):
Cals: 240 kcal, Carbs: 42g, Protein: 8g, Fat: 5g, Saturated Fat: 3g, Fiber: 1g, Sugar: 28g, Sodium: 120mg

255.Rugelach with Chocolate and Coconut Filling

Prep Time: 30 mins

Cook Time: 20 mins

Total Time: 50 mins

Servings: 24 cookies

Ingredients:
- 2 cups of all-purpose flour
- 1/4 tsp salt
- 1 cup of unsalted butter, melted
- 8 ozs cream cheese, melted
- 1/2 cup of granulated sugar
- 1 tsp vanilla extract
- 1/2 cup of chocolate chips
- 1/2 cup of shredded coconut
- 1 egg, beaten (for egg wash)
- Powdered sugar (for dusting)

Instructions:
1. Whisk together the flour and salt in a Big combining dish. Place aside.
2. In a separate combining dish, combine the melted butter and cream cheese up to smooth and creamy.
3. To the butter Mixture, add the granulated sugar and vanilla essence and stir well.
4. Add the flour Mixture to the wet ingredients gradually, combining up to a soft dough forms.
5. Divide the dough into four equal pieces, shape into disks, and cover every in plastic wrap. Chill the dough for at least 30 mins in the refrigerator.
6. Preheat the oven to 350 Ds Fahrenheit (175 Ds Celsius) and line baking sheets with parchment paper.
7. Roll out one cold dough disk into a circle approximately 1/8 inch thick on a floured surface.
8. Sprinkle chocolate chips and shredded coconut over the rolled-out dough, gently pushing them in.
9. Slice the dough into 6 to 8 triangular wedges with a pizza sliceter or a sharp knife.
10. Roll every wedge carefully from the wide end to the pointed end to produce a rugelach crescent. Repeat with the rest of the dough and filling.

11. Place the rugelach on the baking sheets that have been prepared. Brush the beaten egg wash over every cookie.
12. Bake for 18-20 mins, or up to the rugelach turns golden brown, in a preheated oven.
13. Place the cookies on a wire rack to cool. When completely cool, dust with powdered sugar before serving.

NUTRITION INFO (per cookie):
Cals: 210 kcal, Carbs: 16g, Protein: 3g, Fat: 15g, Saturated Fat: 9g, Fiber: 1g, Sugar: 7g, Sodium: 70mg

256.Tahini Fig Bars with Oat Crust

Prep Time: 20 mins

Cook Time: 25 mins

Total Time: 45 mins

Servings: 12 bars

Ingredients: Oat Crust:
- 1 cup of rolled oats
- 1 cup of all-purpose flour
- 1/2 cup of brown sugar
- 1/4 tsp baking soda
- 1/4 tsp salt
- 1/2 cup of unsalted butter, dilute (or coconut oil for a dairy-free version)
- 1 tsp vanilla extract
- Fig Filling:
- 1 cup of dried figs, stems take outd and chop-up
- 1/2 cup of water
- 1/4 cup of tahini
- 1 tbsp honey (or maple syrup for a vegan version)
- 1/2 tsp ground cinnamon
- Pinch of salt

Instructions:
1. Preheat the oven to 350°F (175°C) and grease or line a 9x9-inch baking sheet with parchment paper.
2. To prepare the oat crust, combine the rolled oats, all-purpose flour, brown sugar, baking soda, and salt in a combining bowl.
3. Combine the dilute butter and vanilla essence in a combining bowl. Combine up to the ingredients are well incorporated and the Mixture is crumbly.
4. To make a uniform layer, press two-thirds of the oat crust Mixture into the bottom of the prepared baking pan.
5. Combine the chop-up dried figs and water in a saucepan. Cook, stirring occasionally, up to the figs soften and absorb most of the water.
6. In a blender or mixer, combine the melted figs. Combine the tahini, honey (or maple syrup),

ground cinnamon, and a pinch of salt in a combining bowl. Blend up to the filling is smooth.

7. In the baking pan, spread the fig filling over the oat crust.
8. Sprinkle the remaining oat crust Mixture over the fig filling.
9. Bake for 20-25 mins, or up to the oat crust is golden brown, in a preheated oven.
10. Let the fig bars to cool completely in the pan before Cuttinginto bars.

NUTRITION INFO (per bar, 1/12 of the pan):
Cals: 240 kcal, Carbs: 31g, Protein: 3g, Fat: 12g, Saturated Fat: 6g, Fiber: 2g, Sugar: 16g, Sodium: 100mg

257. Israeli Stuffed Zucchini with Quinoa and Feta

Prep Time: 30 mins

Cook Time: 35 mins

Total Time: 1 hr 5 mins

Servings: 4

Ingredients:

- 4 Big zucchini
- 1 cup of cooked quinoa
- 1/2 cup of cut up feta cheese
- 1/4 cup of chop-up fresh parsley
- 1/4 cup of chop-up fresh mint
- 1/4 cup of chop-up fresh dill
- 1/4 cup of chop-up green onions
- 2 tbsp lemon juice
- 2 tbsp olive oil
- Salt and pepper as needed

Instructions:

1. Preheat the oven to 375 Ds Fahrenheit (190 Ds Celsius).
2. Take out the zucchini tops and scoop out the seeds to make a hollow area for stuffing.
3. Combine the cooked quinoa, cut up feta cheese, chop-up parsley, mint, dill, green onions, lemon juice, olive oil, salt, and pepper in a combining bowl. Combine thoroughly.
4. Fill every hollowed-out zucchini with the quinoa-feta Mixture, carefully pressing it down.
5. In a baking dish, place the stuffed zucchini.
6. Cover the baking dish with aluminum foil and bake for 25 mins in a preheated oven.
7. Take out the cover and continue baking for another 10 mins, or up to the zucchini is soft and slightly browned.
8. Serve the Israeli stuffed zucchini immediately.

NUTRITION INFO (per serving):
Cals: 280 kcal, Carbs: 25g, Protein: 9g, Fat: 16g, Saturated Fat: 5g, Fiber: 5g, Sugar: 7g, Sodium: 330mg

258. Falafel Salad with Lemon-Tahini Dressing

Prep Time: 20 mins

Cook Time: 10 mins

Total Time: 30 mins

Servings: 4

Ingredients: Falafel:

- 16 mini falafel patties (store-bought or homemade)
- Salad:
- 4 cups of combined salad greens (lettuce, spinach, arugula, etc.)
- 1 cup of cherry tomatoes, halved
- 1 cucumber, split
- 1/2 red onion, thinly split
- 1/4 cup of chop-up fresh parsley
- 1/4 cup of chop-up fresh mint
- 1/4 cup of chop-up fresh dill
- Lemon-Tahini Dressing:
- 1/4 cup of tahini
- 1/4 cup of water
- 2 tbsp lemon juice
- 1 clove garlic, chop-up
- Salt and pepper as needed

Instructions:

1. Cook the falafel patties according to the box/pkg directions if using store-bought falafel patties. Cook homemade falafel till golden brown and crispy on the exterior.
2. To make the salad, put the combined salad greens, cherry tomatoes, cucumber, thinly split red onion, chop-up parsley, mint, and dill in a Big salad bowl.
3. To make the lemon-tahini dressing, combine together the tahini, water, lemon juice, chop-up garlic, salt, and pepper in a separate mini bowl. If necessary, add more water to get the required consistency.
4. Cooked falafel patties can be combined into the salad or served separately.
5. Drizzle the salad and falafel with the lemon-tahini dressing.
6. Gently toss the salad with the dressing to coat the contents.
7. Serve the falafel salad right away.

Cals: 320 kcal, Carbs: 31g, Protein: 12g, Fat: 18g, Saturated Fat: 3g, Fiber: 9g, Sugar: 8g, Sodium: 480mg

259.Shakshuka with Roasted Red Peppers and Olives

Prep Time: 15 mins

Cook Time: 25 mins

Total Time: 40 mins

Servings: 4

Ingredients:

- 2 tbsp olive oil
- 1 Big onion, lightly chop-up
- 2 cloves garlic, chop-up
- 2 roasted red peppers, chop-up (from a jar or freshly roasted)
- 1 tsp ground cumin
- 1 tsp ground paprika
- 1/2 tsp ground cayenne pepper (non-compulsory, adjust as needed)
- 1 can (400g) crushed tomatoes
- 1/4 cup of split black olives
- 4-6 Big eggs
- Salt and pepper as needed
- Fresh parsley, chop-up (for garnish)

Instructions:

1. Warm the olive oil in a Big skillet over medium heat. Sauté the chop-up onion up to transparent.
2. Cook for another min after adding the chop-up garlic to the skillet.
3. Cook for a few mins after adding the chop-up roasted red peppers.
4. To the skillet, add the cumin, paprika, cayenne pepper (if using), salt, and pepper. Cook for another min, or up to the Mixture is aromatic.
5. Add the smashed tomatoes and split black olives. Let the Mixture to simmer for 10 mins, or up to it thickens slightly.
6. Make mini wells in the tomato-pepper Mixture and place the eggs inside.
7. Cook, covered, for 5-7 mins, or up to the egg whites are set but the yolks are still runny.
8. Take out from the heat and garnish with fresh parsley.

NUTRITION INFO (per serving):

Cals: 250 kcal, Carbs: 15g, Protein: 10g, Fat: 16g, Saturated Fat: 3g, Fiber: 4g, Sugar: 8g, Sodium: 380mg

260.Malabi with Orange Blossom and Kiwi

Prep Time: 5 mins

Cook Time: 10 mins

Total Time: 15 mins

Servings: 4

Ingredients:

- 1/2 cup of cornstarch
- 4 cups of coconut milk (or regular milk for a non-coconut version)
- 1/4 cup of sugar
- 1 tsp orange blossom water
- 2 kiwis, peel off and split (for sauce and garnish)
- Toasted coconut flakes (for garnish)

Instructions:

1. In a mini dish, combine the cornstarch and 1/2 cup of coconut milk to make a smooth slurry.
2. Heat the remaining 3 1/2 cups of coconut milk in a saucepan over medium heat. Stir in the sugar up to it is completely dissolved.
3. Pour in the cornstarch slurry slowly while constantly swirling to avoid lumps. Cook and stir up to the Mixture thickens and begins to boil.
4. Cook for another min after adding the orange blossom water.
5. Take out the malabi from the heat and divide it among individual serving dishes or a Big serving bowl.
6. Let it cool to room temperature before refrigerating for at least 2 hrs, or up to set.
7. Top the malabi with split kiwis and toasted coconut flakes to serve.

NUTRITION INFO (per serving):

Cals: 270 kcal, Carbs: 32g, Protein: 3g, Fat: 15g, Saturated Fat: 13g, Fiber: 2g, Sugar: 15g, Sodium: 20mg

261.Rugelach with Raspberry and Macadamia Nut Filling

Prep Time: 30 mins

Cook Time: 20 mins

Total Time: 50 mins

Servings: 24 cookies

Ingredients:

- 2 cups of all-purpose flour
- 1/4 tsp salt
- 1 cup of unsalted butter, melted
- 8 ozs cream cheese, melted
- 1/2 cup of granulated sugar
- 1 tsp vanilla extract
- 1/2 cup of raspberry preserves
- 1/2 cup of chop-up macadamia nuts
- 1 egg, beaten (for egg wash)
- Powdered sugar (for dusting)

1. Whisk together the flour and salt in a Big combining dish. Place aside.
2. In a separate combining dish, combine the melted butter and cream cheese up to smooth and creamy.
3. To the butter Mixture, add the granulated sugar and vanilla essence and stir well.
4. Add the flour Mixture to the wet ingredients gradually, combining up to a soft dough forms.
5. Divide the dough into four equal pieces, shape into disks, and cover every in plastic wrap. Chill the dough for at least 30 mins in the refrigerator.
6. Preheat the oven to 350 Ds Fahrenheit (175 Ds Celsius) and line baking sheets with parchment paper.
7. Roll out one cold dough disk into a circle approximately 1/8 inch thick on a floured surface.
8. Cover the rolled-out dough with roughly 2 tbsp raspberry preserves, leaving a tiny border around the borders.
9. Sprinkle 2 tbsp of chop-up macadamia nuts over the preserves.
10. Slice the dough into 6 to 8 triangular wedges with a pizza sliceter or a sharp knife.
11. Roll every wedge carefully from the wide end to the pointed end to produce a rugelach crescent. Repeat with the rest of the dough and filling.
12. Place the rugelach on the baking sheets that have been prepared. Brush the beaten egg wash over every cookie.
13. Bake for 18-20 mins, or up to the rugelach turns golden brown, in a preheated oven.
14. Place the cookies on a wire rack to cool. When completely cool, dust with powdered sugar before serving.

NUTRITION INFO (per cookie):
Cals: 190 kcal, Carbs: 16g, Protein: 3g, Fat: 12g, Saturated Fat: 6g, Fiber: 1g, Sugar: 6g, Sodium: 70mg

262.Tahini Chai Latte with Honey

Prep Time: 5 mins

Cook Time: 5 mins

Total Time: 10 mins

Servings: 2

Ingredients:

- 2 cups of milk (dairy or plant-based)
- 2 tbsp tahini
- 2 tbsp honey
- 2 chai tea bags
- Ground cinnamon (for garnish)

Instructions:

1. Heat the milk in a mini saucepan over medium heat up to it begins to steam.
2. Whisk in the tahini and honey up to they are completely combined with the milk.
3. Add the chai tea bags to the milk Mixture and steep for 3-5 mins, or as directed on the chai tea packaging.
4. Take out and discard the tea bags.
5. Pour the tahini chai latte into two mugs and decorate with ground cinnamon.
6. Serve the tahini chai latte immediately.

NUTRITION INFO (per serving):
Cals: 220 kcal, Carbs: 23g, Protein: 8g, Fat: 11g, Saturated Fat: 3g, Fiber: 1g, Sugar: 20g, Sodium: 100mg

263.Israeli Stuffed Portobello Mushrooms with Couscous and Herbs

Prep Time: 15 mins

Cook Time: 25 mins

Total Time: 40 mins

Servings: 4

Ingredients:

- 4 Big Portobello mushrooms, stems take outd
- 1 cup of cooked couscous
- 1/2 cup of chop-up cherry tomatoes
- 1/4 cup of chop-up fresh parsley
- 1/4 cup of chop-up fresh mint
- 1/4 cup of chop-up fresh dill
- 1/4 cup of chop-up green onions
- 2 tbsp lemon juice
- 2 tbsp olive oil
- Salt and pepper as needed

Instructions:

1. Preheat the oven to 375 Ds Fahrenheit (190 Ds Celsius).
2. Place the Portobello mushrooms, gill side up, on a baking sheet.
3. Combine the cooked couscous, chop-up cherry tomatoes, chop-up parsley, mint, dill, green onions, lemon juice, olive oil, salt, and pepper in a combining bowl. Combine thoroughly.
4. Fill every Portobello mushroom with the couscous-herb Mixture, carefully pushing it down.
5. Bake the stuffed Portobello mushrooms for 20-25 mins, or up to the mushrooms are soft.
6. Serve the filled Israeli Portobello mushrooms hot.

NUTRITION INFO (per serving):
Cals: 200 kcal, Carbs: 24g, Protein: 6g, Fat: 10g, Saturated Fat: 1g, Fiber: 4g, Sugar: 2g, Sodium: 15mg

264.Falafel Pita Bowl with Hummus and Tomato-Cucumber Salad

Prep Time: 20 mins

Cook Time: 15 mins

Total Time: 35 mins

Servings: 2

Ingredients: Falafel:

- 16 mini falafel patties (store-bought or homemade)
- Tomato-Cucumber Salad:
- 1 cup of cherry tomatoes, halved
- 1 cucumber, diced
- 1/4 cup of chop-up fresh parsley
- 1/4 cup of chop-up fresh mint
- 2 tbsp lemon juice
- 2 tbsp olive oil
- Salt and pepper as needed
- Pita Bowl:
- 2 whole wheat pita breads, slice in half to form pockets
- 1 cup of hummus
- Falafel patties
- Tomato-cucumber salad

Instructions:

1. Cook the falafel patties according to the box/pkg directions if using store-bought falafel patties. Cook homemade falafel till golden brown and crispy on the exterior.
2. To make the tomato-cucumber salad, add the split cherry tomatoes, diced cucumber, chop-up parsley, mint, lemon juice, olive oil, salt, and pepper in a combining bowl.
3. Open the pita bread pockets and generously spread hummus within every pocket.
4. Fill every pita pocket with falafel patties and the tomato-cucumber salad.
5. Serve the falafel pita bowl right away.

NUTRITION INFO (per serving, 1 pita bowl):
Cals: 480 kcal, Carbs: 47g, Protein: 16g, Fat: 28g, Saturated Fat: 4g, Fiber: 11g, Sugar: 6g, Sodium: 480mg

265.Shakshuka with Swiss Chard and Olives

Prep Time: 15 mins

Cook Time: 25 mins

Total Time: 40 mins

Servings: 4

Ingredients:

- 2 tbsp olive oil
- 1 Big onion, lightly chop-up
- 2 cloves garlic, chop-up
- 1 bunch Swiss chard, stems take outd and leaves chop-up
- 1 tsp ground cumin
- 1 tsp ground paprika
- 1/2 tsp ground cayenne pepper (non-compulsory, adjust as needed)
- 1 can (400g) crushed tomatoes
- 1/4 cup of split black olives
- 4-6 Big eggs
- Salt and pepper as needed
- Fresh parsley, chop-up (for garnish)

Instructions:

1. Warm the olive oil in a Big skillet over medium heat. Sauté the chop-up onion up to transparent.
2. Cook for another min after adding the chop-up garlic to the skillet.
3. Cook up to the Swiss chard is wilted, about 5 mins.
4. To the skillet, add the cumin, paprika, cayenne pepper (if using), salt, and pepper. Cook for another min, or up to the Mixture is aromatic.
5. Add the smashed tomatoes and split black olives. Let the Mixture to simmer for 10 mins, or up to it thickens slightly.
6. Make mini wells in the tomato-chard Mixture and place the eggs inside.
7. Cook, covered, for 5-7 mins, or up to the egg whites are set but the yolks are still runny.
8. Take out from the heat and garnish with fresh parsley.

NUTRITION INFO (per serving):
Cals: 240 kcal, Carbs: 15g, Protein: 10g, Fat: 16g, Saturated Fat: 3g, Fiber: 4g, Sugar: 8g, Sodium: 380mg

266.Malabi with Passionfruit and Coconut Milk

Prep Time: 5 mins

Cook Time: 10 mins

Total Time: 15 mins

Servings: 4

Ingredients:

- 1/2 cup of cornstarch
- 4 cups of coconut milk (or regular milk for a non-coconut version)
- 1/4 cup of sugar
- 1 tsp vanilla extract

- Pulp of 2 passionfruits
- Unsweetened shredded coconut (for garnish)

Instructions:

1. In a mini dish, combine the cornstarch and 1/2 cup of coconut milk to make a smooth slurry.
2. Heat the remaining 3 1/2 cups of coconut milk in a saucepan over medium heat. Stir in the sugar up to it is completely dissolved.
3. Pour in the cornstarch slurry slowly while constantly swirling to avoid lumps. Cook and stir up to the Mixture thickens and begins to boil.
4. Incorporate the vanilla extract and the pulp from two passionfruits. Cook for 1 min more.
5. Take out the malabi from the heat and divide it among individual serving dishes or a Big serving bowl.
6. Let it cool to room temperature before refrigerating for at least 2 hrs, or up to set.
7. To serve, sprinkle unsweetened shredded coconut on top of the malabi.

NUTRITION INFO (per serving):

Cals: 280 kcal, Carbs: 30g, Protein: 3g, Fat: 18g, Saturated Fat: 16g, Fiber: 1g, Sugar: 15g, Sodium: 20mg

267. Rugelach with Blueberry and Walnut Filling

Prep Time: 30 mins

Cook Time: 20 mins

Total Time: 50 mins

Servings: 24 cookies

Ingredients:

- 2 cups of all-purpose flour
- 1/4 tsp salt
- 1 cup of unsalted butter, melted
- 8 ozs cream cheese, melted
- 1/2 cup of granulated sugar
- 1 tsp vanilla extract
- 1/2 cup of blueberry preserves
- 1/2 cup of chop-up walnuts
- 1 egg, beaten (for egg wash)
- Powdered sugar (for dusting)

Instructions:

1. Whisk together the flour and salt in a Big combining dish. Place aside.
2. In a separate combining dish, combine the melted butter and cream cheese up to smooth and creamy.
3. To the butter Mixture, add the granulated sugar and vanilla essence and stir well.

4. Add the flour Mixture to the wet ingredients gradually, combining up to a soft dough forms.
5. Divide the dough into four equal pieces, shape into disks, and cover every in plastic wrap. Chill the dough for at least 30 mins in the refrigerator.
6. Preheat the oven to 350 Ds Fahrenheit (175 Ds Celsius) and line baking sheets with parchment paper.
7. Roll out one cold dough disk into a circle approximately 1/8 inch thick on a floured surface.
8. Cover the rolled-out dough with roughly 2 tbsp blueberry preserves, leaving a tiny border around the borders.
9. Sprinkle 2 tbsp of chop-up walnuts over the preserves.
10. Slice the dough into 6 to 8 triangular wedges with a pizza sliceter or a sharp knife.
11. Roll every wedge carefully from the wide end to the pointed end to produce a rugelach crescent. Repeat with the rest of the dough and filling.
12. Place the rugelach on the baking sheets that have been prepared. Brush the beaten egg wash over every cookie.
13. Bake for 18-20 mins, or up to the rugelach turns golden brown, in a preheated oven.
14. Place the cookies on a wire rack to cool. When completely cool, dust with powdered sugar before serving.

NUTRITION INFO (per cookie):

Cals: 190 kcal, Carbs: 16g, Protein: 3g, Fat: 12g, Saturated Fat: 6g, Fiber: 1g, Sugar: 6g, Sodium: 70mg

268. Tahini Date Bars with Almond Flour Crust

Prep Time: 20 mins

Cook Time: 25 mins

Total Time: 45 mins

Servings: 12 bars

Ingredients: Almond Flour Crust:

- 1 1/2 cups of almond flour
- 1/4 cup of coconut oil, dilute
- 2 tbsp honey (or maple syrup for a vegan version)
- 1 tsp vanilla extract
- Pinch of salt
- Tahini Date Filling:
- 1 cup of tahini
- 1 cup of pitted dates, soaked in hot water for 10 mins and drained
- 2 tbsp honey (or maple syrup for a vegan version)
- 1/2 cup of water
- 1 tsp vanilla extract

- Pinch of salt

Instructions:

1. Preheat the oven to 350°F (175°C) and grease or line a 9x9-inch baking sheet with parchment paper.
2. To prepare the almond flour crust, combine the almond flour, dilute coconut oil, honey, vanilla essence, and a bit of salt in a combining bowl.
3. To make an even layer, press the almond flour crust Mixture into the bottom of the prepared baking pan.
4. Bake the crust for 10 mins, or up to golden brown, in a preheated oven.
5. To create the tahini date filling, combine the tahini, soaked dates, honey, water, vanilla essence, and a bit of salt in a blender or mixer. Blend up to the filling is smooth.
6. Spread the baked almond flour crust with the tahini date filling.
7. Bake the date bars for another 15 mins in the preheated oven.
8. Let the date bars to cool before Cuttinginto bars.

NUTRITION INFO (per bar, 1/12 of the pan):
Cals: 300 kcal, Carbs: 23g, Protein: 7g, Fat: 22g, Saturated Fat: 5g, Fiber: 4g, Sugar: 15g, Sodium: 35mg

269. Israeli Stuffed Cabbage Rolls with Quinoa and Mushrooms

Prep Time: 30 mins

Cook Time: 50 mins

Total Time: 1 hr 20 mins

Servings: 4

Ingredients: Cabbage Rolls:

- 1 Big cabbage head
- 1 cup of cooked quinoa
- 1 cup of chop-up mushrooms
- 1/2 cup of chop-up onion
- 2 cloves garlic, chop-up
- 1 tbsp olive oil
- 1 tsp ground cumin
- 1 tsp ground paprika
- 1/2 tsp ground coriander
- Salt and pepper as needed
- 1 can (400g) crushed tomatoes
- 1 cup of vegetable broth
- Sauce:
- 1 cup of tomato passata or tomato sauce
- 1 tbsp maple syrup or honey
- 1 tsp apple cider vinegar
- Salt and pepper as needed

Instructions:

1. Preheat the oven to 375 Ds Fahrenheit (190 Ds Celsius).
2. A Big pot of water Must be brought to a boil. Blanch the entire cabbage head in boiling water for around 5 mins. Take out the cabbage from the water with care and set it aside to cool slightly. Peel off the individual leaves gently, taking care not to harm them. Set aside the leaves.
3. Warm the olive oil in a pan over medium heat. Cook up to the onion is transparent, about 5 mins.
4. To the skillet, add the chop-up garlic, chop-up mushrooms, ground cumin, ground paprika, ground coriander, salt, and pepper. Cook, stirring occasionally, up to the mushrooms are cooked and any excess moisture has gone.
5. Combine the cooked quinoa and mushroom Mixture in a Big combining basin.
6. Place a cabbage leaf on a flat surface and fill with a dollop of the quinoa-mushroom filling. Fold the leaf's sides over the filling and roll it up to form a cabbage roll. Repeat with the rest of the leaves and filling.
7. Spread a layer of smashed tomatoes in a baking dish. On top of the tomato layer, place the stuffed cabbage rolls.
8. To prepare the sauce, combine the tomato passata or tomato sauce, maple syrup or honey, apple cider vinegar, salt, and pepper in a separate bowl. Serve the sauce on top of the stuffed cabbage rolls.
9. In the baking dish, pour the vegetable stock around the cabbage rolls.
10. Cover the baking dish tightly with aluminum foil and bake for 30-35 mins, or up to the cabbage rolls are soft.
11. Serve the stuffed Israeli cabbage rolls hot.

NUTRITION INFO (per serving):
Cals: 340 kcal, Carbs: 55g, Protein: 11g, Fat: 10g, Saturated Fat: 1g, Fiber: 10g, Sugar: 19g, Sodium: 560mg

270. Falafel Sliders with Pickles and Cilantro-Tahini Sauce

Prep Time: 20 mins

Cook Time: 15 mins

Total Time: 35 mins

Servings: 4 (3 sliders per serving)

Ingredients: Falafel Patties:

- 12 mini falafel patties (store-bought or homemade)

- Slider buns or mini pita breads
- Cilantro-Tahini Sauce:
- 1/2 cup of tahini
- 1/4 cup of water
- 1/4 cup of chop-up fresh cilantro
- 2 tbsp lemon juice
- 1 clove garlic, chop-up
- Salt and pepper as needed
- Pickles and Toppings:
- Split pickles
- Split tomatoes
- Split red onions
- Lettuce leaves

Instructions:

1. Cook the falafel patties according to the box/pkg directions if using store-bought falafel patties. Cook homemade falafel till golden brown and crispy on the exterior.
2. To make the cilantro-tahini sauce, combine together the tahini, water, chop-up cilantro, lemon juice, chop-up garlic, salt, and pepper in a mini basin. If necessary, add more water to get the required consistency.
3. Spread a liberal quantity of cilantro-tahini sauce on the bottom half of every slider bun or tiny pita bread before assembling the sliders.
4. On every bread, place three falafel patties.
5. Add split pickles, tomatoes, red onions, and lettuce leaves to the falafel patties.
6. The top half of the buns Must be used to cover the sliders.
7. Serve with pickles and cilantro-tahini sauce on the side.

NUTRITION INFO (per serving, 3 sliders):
Cals: 580 kcal, Carbs: 58g, Protein: 20g, Fat: 32g, Saturated Fat: 5g, Fiber: 10g, Sugar: 8g, Sodium: 780mg

271. Shakshuka with Roasted Eggplant and Tahini

Prep Time: 15 mins

Cook Time: 40 mins

Total Time: 55 mins

Servings: 4

Ingredients:

- 2 Big eggplants, slice into cubes
- 3 tbsp olive oil
- 1 Big onion, lightly chop-up
- 2 cloves garlic, chop-up
- 1 red bell pepper, chop-up
- 1 yellow bell pepper, chop-up

- 1 tsp ground cumin
- 1 tsp ground paprika
- 1/2 tsp ground cayenne pepper (non-compulsory, adjust as needed)
- 1 can (400g) crushed tomatoes
- 1/4 cup of tahini
- 1/4 cup of water
- 4-6 Big eggs
- Salt and pepper as needed
- Fresh parsley, chop-up (for garnish)

Instructions:

1. Preheat the oven to 400 Ds Fahrenheit (200 Ds Celsius).
2. Toss the cubed eggplant with 2 tbsp of olive oil on a baking sheet. Roast the eggplant for 20-25 mins in a preheated oven, or up to soft and slightly browned.
3. Heat the remaining 1 tbsp olive oil in a Big skillet over medium heat. Sauté the chop-up onion up to transparent.
4. To the skillet, add the chop-up garlic, chop-up red bell pepper, and chop-up yellow bell pepper. Cook the peppers up to they are soft.
5. Add the cumin, paprika, cayenne pepper (if using), salt, and pepper as needed. Cook for another min, or up to the Mixture is aromatic.
6. Add the roasted eggplant and the smashed tomatoes. Let the Mixture to simmer for 10 mins.
7. In a mini combining bowl, combine the tahini and water to make a smooth tahini sauce.
8. Make mini wells in the tomato-eggplant Mixture and place the eggs inside.
9. Drizzle the tahini sauce over the shakshuka, being careful not to get any on the eggs.
10. Cook, covered, for 8-10 mins, or up to the egg whites are set but the yolks are still runny.
11. Take out from the heat and garnish with fresh parsley.

NUTRITION INFO (per serving):
Cals: 370 kcal, Carbs: 20g, Protein: 11g, Fat: 29g, Saturated Fat: 4g, Fiber: 7g, Sugar: 10g, Sodium: 330mg

272. Malabi with Rosewater and Raspberry Sauce

Prep Time: 10 mins

Cook Time: 10 mins

Total Time: 20 mins

Servings: 4

Ingredients:

- 1/4 cup of cornstarch
- 2 cups of whole milk

- 1/4 cup of sugar
- 1 tsp rosewater
- Fresh raspberries (for garnish)
- Crushed pistachios (for garnish)
- Raspberry Sauce:
- 1 cup of fresh raspberries
- 2 tbsp sugar
- 1 tbsp water

Instructions:

1. In a mini dish, combine the cornstarch with 1/4 cup of milk to make a smooth slurry.
2. Warm the remaining 1 3/4 cups of milk in a saucepan over medium heat. Stir in the sugar up to it is completely dissolved.
3. Pour in the cornstarch slurry slowly while constantly swirling to avoid lumps. Cook and stir up to the Mixture thickens and begins to boil.
4. Cook for another min after adding the rosewater.
5. Take out the malabi from the heat and divide it among individual serving dishes or a Big serving bowl.
6. Let it cool to room temperature before refrigerating for at least 2 hrs, or up to set.
7. In a mini saucepan, combine the fresh raspberries, sugar, and water to make the raspberry sauce. Cook up to the raspberries have broken down and the sauce has thickened slightly over medium heat.
8. Take out the raspberry sauce from the heat and set it aside to cool.
9. Drizzle the rosewater malabi with the raspberry sauce before serving, then decorate with fresh raspberries and cut up pistachios.

NUTRITION INFO (per serving):

Cals: 220 kcal, Carbs: 37g, Protein: 5g, Fat: 6g, Saturated Fat: 3g, Fiber: 4g, Sugar: 26g, Sodium: 60mg

273. Rugelach with Apricot and Hazelnut Filling

Prep Time: 30 mins

Cook Time: 20 mins

Total Time: 50 mins

Servings: 24 cookies

Ingredients:

- 2 cups of all-purpose flour
- 1/4 tsp salt
- 1 cup of unsalted butter, melted
- 8 ozs cream cheese, melted
- 1/2 cup of granulated sugar
- 1 tsp vanilla extract
- 1/2 cup of apricot preserves

- 1/2 cup of chop-up hazelnuts
- 1 egg, beaten (for egg wash)
- Powdered sugar (for dusting)

Instructions:

1. Whisk together the flour and salt in a Big combining dish. Place aside.
2. In a separate combining dish, combine the melted butter and cream cheese up to smooth and creamy.
3. To the butter Mixture, add the granulated sugar and vanilla essence and stir well.
4. Add the flour Mixture to the wet ingredients gradually, combining up to a soft dough forms.
5. Divide the dough into four equal pieces, shape into disks, and cover every in plastic wrap. Chill the dough for at least 30 mins in the refrigerator.
6. Preheat the oven to 350 Ds Fahrenheit (175 Ds Celsius) and line baking sheets with parchment paper.
7. Roll out one cold dough disk into a circle approximately 1/8 inch thick on a floured surface.
8. 2 tbsp apricot preserves, spread evenly over the rolled-out dough, leaving a tiny border around the borders.
9. Sprinkle 2 tbsp of chop-up hazelnuts over the preserves.
10. Slice the dough into 6 to 8 triangular wedges with a pizza sliceter or a sharp knife.
11. Roll every wedge carefully from the wide end to the pointed end to produce a rugelach crescent. Repeat with the rest of the dough and filling.
12. Place the rugelach on the baking sheets that have been prepared. Brush the beaten egg wash over every cookie.
13. Bake for 18-20 mins, or up to the rugelach turns golden brown, in a preheated oven.
14. Place the cookies on a wire rack to cool. When completely cool, dust with powdered sugar before serving.

NUTRITION INFO (per cookie):

Cals: 160 kcal, Carbs: 14g, Protein: 2g, Fat: 10g, Saturated Fat: 5g, Fiber: 1g, Sugar: 7g, Sodium: 55mg

274. Tahini Chocolate Protein Smoothie

Prep Time: 5 mins

Cook Time: 0 mins

Total Time: 5 mins

Servings: 2

Ingredients:

- 2 ripe bananas
- 2 tbsp tahini

- 2 tbsp unsweetened cocoa powder
- 1 tbsp honey or maple syrup
- 1 cup of milk (dairy or plant-based)
- 1/2 cup of plain Greek yogurt
- 1/2 tsp vanilla extract
- Ice cubes (non-compulsory)

Instructions:

1. Blend the ripe bananas, tahini, unsweetened cocoa powder, honey or maple syrup, milk, Greek yogurt, and vanilla extract in a blender.
2. Blend up to all of the ingredients are well incorporated and the smoothie is the consistency you want.
3. Add a couple ice cubes and blend again for a richer smoothie.
4. Serve the tahini chocolate protein smoothie immediately in glasses.

NUTRITION INFO (per serving):

Cals: 280 kcal, Carbs: 41g, Protein: 11g, Fat: 11g, Saturated Fat: 2g, Fiber: 6g, Sugar: 24g, Sodium: 80mg

275.Israeli Stuffed Artichokes with Quinoa and Lemon-Herb Dressing

Prep Time: 20 mins

Cook Time: 45 mins

Total Time: 1 hr 5 mins

Servings: 4

Ingredients: Stuffed Artichokes:

- 4 Big artichokes
- 1 cup of cooked quinoa
- 1/2 cup of chop-up cherry tomatoes
- 1/4 cup of chop-up fresh parsley
- 1/4 cup of chop-up fresh mint
- 1/4 cup of chop-up fresh dill
- 1/4 cup of chop-up green onions
- 2 tbsp lemon juice
- 2 tbsp olive oil
- Salt and pepper as needed
- Lemon-Herb Dressing:
- 1/4 cup of olive oil
- 2 tbsp lemon juice
- 1 tbsp Dijon mustard
- 1 clove garlic, chop-up
- 1 tsp honey or maple syrup
- Salt and pepper as needed

Instructions:

1. Trim the artichoke stems and take out any tough outer leaves. Every artichoke Must have about 1 inch of its top take outd. Trim the pointed points of the remaining leaves using kitchen scissors.

2. Cook the artichokes in a Big pot of boiling water for 20-25 mins, or up to the base of the artichokes is tender when pierced with a fork. Let the artichokes to cool after draining.
3. To prepare the stuffing, combine cooked quinoa, chop-up cherry tomatoes, chop-up parsley, mint, dill, green onions, lemon juice, olive oil, salt, and pepper in a combining bowl.
4. Open the leaves of every artichoke carefully to make room for the stuffing. If there is a fuzzy choke in the center, take out it.
5. Fill every artichoke with the quinoa-herb Mixture, carefully pressing it down.
6. To create the lemon-herb dressing, whisk together the olive oil, lemon juice, Dijon mustard, chop-up garlic, honey or maple syrup, salt, and pepper in a separate bowl.
7. Dress the stuffed artichokes with the dressing.
8. Steam the stuffed artichokes for around 20 mins in a steamer basket.
9. Warm Israeli stuffed artichokes Must be served.

NUTRITION INFO (per serving):

Cals: 320 kcal, Carbs: 28g, Protein: 7g, Fat: 22g, Saturated Fat: 3g, Fiber: 9g, Sugar: 5g, Sodium: 80mg

276.Falafel Tabbouleh Salad with Lemon-Tahini Dressing

Prep Time: 20 mins

Cook Time: 0 mins

Total Time: 20 mins

Servings: 4

Ingredients: Falafel:

- 16 mini falafel patties (store-bought or homemade)
- Tabbouleh Salad:
- 1 cup of bulgur wheat, cooked and cooled
- 1 cup of chop-up fresh parsley
- 1/2 cup of chop-up fresh mint
- 1 cup of chop-up cucumber
- 1 cup of chop-up tomatoes
- 1/2 cup of chop-up red onion
- Juice of 1 lemon
- 2 tbsp olive oil
- Salt and pepper as needed
- Lemon-Tahini Dressing:
- 1/4 cup of tahini
- Juice of 1 lemon
- 2 tbsp water
- 1 clove garlic, chop-up
- Salt and pepper as needed

1. Cook the falafel patties according to the box/pkg directions if using store-bought falafel patties. Cook homemade falafel till golden brown and crispy on the exterior.
2. To make the tabbouleh salad, combine the cooked bulgur wheat, chop-up parsley, mint, cucumber, tomatoes, red onion, lemon juice, olive oil, salt, and pepper in a Big combining dish.
3. To make the lemon-tahini dressing, combine together the tahini, lemon juice, water, chop-up garlic, salt, and pepper in a separate bowl.
4. Place the falafel on top of the tabbouleh salad and drizzle with the lemon-tahini dressing to serve.

NUTRITION INFO (per serving):
Cals: 400 kcal, Carbs: 49g, Protein: 11g, Fat: 20g, Saturated Fat: 3g, Fiber: 11g, Sugar: 4g, Sodium: 440mg

277.Shakshuka with Swiss Chard and Za'atar

Prep Time: 15 mins

Cook Time: 25 mins

Total Time: 40 mins

Servings: 4

Ingredients:

- 2 tbsp olive oil
- 1 Big onion, lightly chop-up
- 2 cloves garlic, chop-up
- 1 bunch Swiss chard, stems take outd and leaves chop-up
- 1 tsp za'atar spice blend
- 1 tsp ground cumin
- 1 tsp ground paprika
- 1/2 tsp ground cayenne pepper (non-compulsory, adjust as needed)
- 1 can (400g) crushed tomatoes
- 4-6 Big eggs
- Salt and pepper as needed
- Fresh parsley, chop-up (for garnish)

Instructions:

1. Warm the olive oil in a Big skillet over medium heat. Sauté the chop-up onion up to transparent.
2. Cook for another min after adding the chop-up garlic to the skillet.
3. Cook up to the Swiss chard is wilted, about 5 mins.
4. To the skillet, add the za'atar spice combination, ground cumin, ground paprika, cayenne pepper (if using), salt, and pepper. Cook for another min, or up to the Mixture is aromatic.

5. Pour in the crushed tomatoes and cook for about 10 mins, or up to the liquid thickens slightly.
6. Make mini wells in the tomato-chard Mixture and place the eggs inside.
7. Cook, covered, for 5-7 mins, or up to the egg whites are set but the yolks are still runny.
8. Take out from the heat and garnish with fresh parsley.

NUTRITION INFO (per serving):
Cals: 250 kcal, Carbs: 14g, Protein: 10g, Fat: 17g, Saturated Fat: 3g, Fiber: 4g, Sugar: 6g, Sodium: 340mg

278.Malabi with Passionfruit and Mango Sauce

Prep Time: 10 mins

Cook Time: 10 mins

Total Time: 20 mins

Servings: 4

Ingredients:

- 1/4 cup of cornstarch
- 2 cups of coconut milk (or regular milk for a non-coconut version)
- 1/4 cup of sugar
- Pulp of 2 passionfruits
- Pulp of 1 ripe mango
- Fresh passionfruit and mango pieces (for garnish)

Instructions:

1. In a mini dish, combine the cornstarch and 1/4 cup of coconut milk to make a smooth slurry.
2. Heat the remaining 1 3/4 cups of coconut milk in a saucepan over medium heat. Stir in the sugar up to it is completely dissolved.
3. Pour in the cornstarch slurry slowly while constantly swirling to avoid lumps. Cook and stir up to the Mixture thickens and begins to boil.
4. Stir in the pulp from 2 passionfruits and 1 ripe mango. Cook for 1 min more.
5. Take out the malabi from the heat and divide it among individual serving dishes or a Big serving bowl.
6. Let it cool to room temperature before refrigerating for at least 2 hrs, or up to set.
7. Serve the malabi topped with fresh passionfruit and mango slices.

NUTRITION INFO (per serving):
Cals: 280 kcal, Carbs: 35g, Protein: 3g, Fat: 16g, Saturated Fat: 14g, Fiber: 3g, Sugar: 23g, Sodium: 20mg

279. Rugelach with Chocolate and Almond Filling

Prep Time: 30 mins

Cook Time: 20 mins

Total Time: 50 mins

Servings: 24 cookies

Ingredients:

- 2 cups of all-purpose flour
- 1/4 tsp salt
- 1 cup of unsalted butter, melted
- 8 ozs cream cheese, melted
- 1/2 cup of granulated sugar
- 1 tsp vanilla extract
- 1/2 cup of chocolate spread (Nutella or any other chocolate spread)
- 1/2 cup of chop-up almonds
- 1 egg, beaten (for egg wash)
- Powdered sugar (for dusting)

Instructions:

1. Whisk together the flour and salt in a Big combining dish. Place aside.
2. In a separate combining dish, combine the melted butter and cream cheese up to smooth and creamy.
3. To the butter Mixture, add the granulated sugar and vanilla essence and stir well.
4. Add the flour Mixture to the wet ingredients gradually, combining up to a soft dough forms.
5. Divide the dough into four equal pieces, shape into disks, and cover every in plastic wrap. Chill the dough for at least 30 mins in the refrigerator.
6. Preheat the oven to 350 Ds Fahrenheit (175 Ds Celsius) and line baking sheets with parchment paper.
7. Roll out one cold dough disk into a circle approximately 1/8 inch thick on a floured surface.
8. Cover the rolled-out dough with about 2 tbsp chocolate spread, leaving a tiny border around the borders.
9. Sprinkle 2 tbsp chop-up almonds over the chocolate spread.
10. Slice the dough into 6 to 8 triangular wedges with a pizza sliceter or a sharp knife.
11. Roll every wedge carefully from the wide end to the pointed end to produce a rugelach crescent. Repeat with the rest of the dough and filling.
12. Place the rugelach on the baking sheets that have been prepared. Brush the beaten egg wash over every cookie.
13. Bake for 18-20 mins, or up to the rugelach turns golden brown, in a preheated oven.
14. Place the cookies on a wire rack to cool. When completely cool, dust with powdered sugar before serving.

NUTRITION INFO (per cookie):

Cals: 180 kcal, Carbs: 15g, Protein: 3g, Fat: 12g, Saturated Fat: 7g, Fiber: 1g, Sugar: 7g, Sodium: 60mg

280. Tahini Chia Pudding with Coconut and Maple Syrup

Prep Time: 5 mins

Cook Time: 0 mins

Total Time: 5 mins

Servings: 2

Ingredients:

- 1/4 cup of chia seeds
- 1 cup of coconut milk (or any other milk of your choice)
- 2 tbsp tahini
- 2 tbsp maple syrup
- 1/2 tsp vanilla extract
- Unsweetened shredded coconut (for topping)

Instructions:

1. Combine the chia seeds, coconut milk, tahini, maple syrup, and vanilla extract in a combining dish.
2. Stir the Mixture thoroughly to spread the chia seeds evenly.
3. Refrigerate the bowl for at least 2 hrs or overnight to let the chia seeds to absorb the liquid and produce a pudding-like consistency.
4. Stir the chia pudding well before serving to break up any clumps.
5. Divide the tahini chia pudding among serving bowls and garnish with unsweetened shredded coconut.

NUTRITION INFO (per serving):

Cals: 300 kcal, Carbs: 24g, Protein: 6g, Fat: 21g, Saturated Fat: 11g, Fiber: 10g, Sugar: 10g, Sodium: 20mg

281. Israeli Stuffed Tomatoes with Quinoa and Herbs

Prep Time: 30 mins

Cook Time: 35 mins

Total Time: 1 hr 5 mins

Servings: 4

Ingredients:

- 8 Big tomatoes
- 1 cup of cooked quinoa

- 1/2 cup of chop-up fresh parsley
- 1/4 cup of chop-up fresh mint
- 1/4 cup of chop-up fresh dill
- 1/4 cup of chop-up green onions
- 2 tbsp lemon juice
- 2 tbsp olive oil
- Salt and pepper as needed

Instructions:

1. Take out the tops of the tomatoes and carefully scoop out the pulp and seeds using a spoon. Save the pulp and seeds for another time.
2. To prepare the stuffing, combine the cooked quinoa, chop-up parsley, mint, dill, green onions, lemon juice, olive oil, salt, and pepper in a Big combining dish.
3. Add the reserved tomato pulp and seeds to the quinoa-herb combination. Combine thoroughly.
4. Fill every hollowed-out tomato with the quinoa-herb Mixture, gently pressing it down.
5. Cover the stuffed tomatoes in a baking dish with foil.
6. Preheat the oven to 350 Ds Fahrenheit (175 Ds Celsius).
7. Bake the stuffed tomatoes for 25-30 mins in a preheated oven, or up to the tomatoes are soft.
8. Warm Israeli stuffed tomatoes Must be served.

NUTRITION INFO (per serving):
Cals: 200 kcal, Carbs: 24g, Protein: 5g, Fat: 10g, Saturated Fat: 2g, Fiber: 6g, Sugar: 9g, Sodium: 15mg

282.Falafel Tacos with Avocado-Tahini Sauce

Prep Time: 20 mins Cook

Time: 20 mins Total

Time: 40 mins

Servings: 4

Ingredients:

- 1 cup of dried chickpeas, soaked overnight
- 1 mini onion, roughly chop-up
- 3 garlic cloves
- 1 cup of fresh parsley leaves
- 1 cup of fresh cilantro leaves
- 1 tsp ground cumin
- 1 tsp ground coriander
- 1/2 tsp baking soda
- Salt and pepper as needed
- 1/4 cup of all-purpose flour (or chickpea flour for gluten-free)
- Oil for frying

- 8 mini taco shells
- 1 avocado, split
- 1/4 cup of tahini sauce

Instructions:

1. Combine soaked chickpeas, onion, garlic, parsley, cilantro, cumin, coriander, baking soda, salt, and pepper in a mixer. Pulse the ingredients up to a coarse Mixture formed.
2. Transfer the Mixture to a combining basin and toss in the flour up to it comes together.
3. Form the ingredients into mini patties and cook them in high oil up to golden brown and crispy.
4. Fill every taco shell with falafel patties, avocado slices, and tahini sauce.
5. Enjoy the falafel tacos while they're still warm!

NUTRITION INFO (per serving):
Cals: 380 kcal, Carbs: 47g, Protein: 13g, Fat: 17g, Fiber: 10g

283.Shakshuka with Roasted Red Peppers and Labneh

Prep Time: 10 mins Cook

Time: 30 mins Total

Time: 40 mins

Servings: 4

Ingredients:

- 2 tbsp olive oil
- 1 onion, chop-up
- 1 red bell pepper, roasted and split
- 2 garlic cloves, chop-up
- 1 tsp ground cumin
- 1 tsp ground paprika
- 1/2 tsp ground cayenne pepper (non-compulsory, for heat)
- 1 can (14 ozs) crushed tomatoes
- Salt and pepper as needed
- 4-6 Big eggs
- 1/2 cup of labneh (strained yogurt)

Instructions:

1. Warm the olive oil in a Big skillet over medium heat. Sauté the chop-up onions and roasted red peppers up to the onions are transparent.
2. Incorporate the chop-up garlic, cumin, paprika, and cayenne pepper (if using). Cook for one more min.
3. Pour in the crushed tomatoes, season with salt and pepper, and simmer for about 15 mins, or up to the sauce thickens.
4. With a spoon, make mini wells in the sauce and carefully crack the eggs into the wells.

5. Cook the eggs, covered, for 5-7 mins, or up to the whites are set but the yolks are still runny.
6. Shakshuka Must be served hot with dollops of labneh on top.

NUTRITION INFO (per serving):
Cals: 240 kcal, Carbs: 16g, Protein: 11g, Fat:15g, Fiber: 3g

284.Malabi with Orange Blossom and Pevery Sauce

Prep Time: 5 mins Cook
Time: 10 mins Total
Time: 4 hrs 15 mins
Servings: 6

Ingredients:
- 1/2 cup of cornstarch
- 4 cups of whole milk
- 1/2 cup of sugar
- 1 tsp orange blossom water
- 1 cup of ripe peveryes, peel off and diced
- Crushed pistachios for garnish

Instructions:
1. Combine the cornstarch with 1/2 cup of milk in a mini bowl up to completely dissolved.
2. Heat the remaining milk and sugar in a saucepan over medium heat up to the sugar melts.
3. Pour in the cornstarch Mixture and continue to stir continually up to the liquid thickens.
4. Take out from the heat and add the orange blossom water.
5. Let the malabi to cool to room temperature in individual serving bowls or a big serving dish.
6. Refrigerate for at least 4 hrs, or up to firm.
7. To make a sauce, combine the diced peveryes and a tsp of sugar in a separate bowl.
8. Top the malabi with the pevery sauce and garnish with crushed pistachios before serving.

NUTRITION INFO (per serving):
Cals: 220 kcal, Carbs: 38g, Protein: 6g, Fat: 6g, Fiber: 1g

285.Rugelach with Blueberry and Pecan Filling

Prep Time: 15 mins Cook
Time: 20 mins Total
Time: 35 mins
Servings: 24 rugelach

Ingredients:
- 2 cups of all-purpose flour
- 1/2 tsp salt

- 1 cup of unsalted butter, chilled and slice into mini pieces
- 8 ozs cream cheese, chilled and slice into mini pieces
- 1/4 cup of granulated sugar
- 1 tsp vanilla extract
- 1 cup of blueberry preserves
- 1 cup of chop-up pecans
- 1 egg, beaten (for egg wash)
- 2 tbsp turbinado sugar (for sprinkling)

Instructions:
1. In a mixer, combine the flour, salt, butter, cream cheese, granulated sugar, and vanilla extract up to a dough forms.
2. Refrigerate for 1 hr after dividing the dough into four equal halves and wrapping every in plastic wrap.
3. Preheat the oven to 375 Ds Fahrenheit (190 Ds Celsius) and line a baking sheet with parchment paper.
4. Roll out one portion of the dough into a circle on a floured surface.
5. 1/4 cup of blueberry preserves Must be spread over the dough, leaving a tiny border around the edges.
6. Sprinkle the preserves with 1/4 cup of chop-up pecans.
7. Divide the dough into 6 equal wedges and roll every wedge beginning at the wide end.
8. Brush the rugelach with beaten egg and sprinkle with turbinado sugar on the prepared baking sheet.
9. Continue with the remaining dough portions.
10. Rugelach Must be baked for 18-20 mins, or up to golden brown.
11. Before serving, let them cool on a wire rack.

NUTRITION INFO (per serving - 1 rugelach):
Cals: 180 kcal, Carbs: 16g, Protein: 2g, Fat: 12g, Fiber: 1g

286.Tahini Brownie Bites with Sea Salt

Prep Time: 15 mins Cook
Time: 20 mins Total
Time: 35 mins
Servings: 24 brownie bites

Ingredients:
- 1/2 cup of unsalted butter, dilute
- 1 cup of granulated sugar
- 2 Big eggs
- 1 tsp vanilla extract
- 1/2 cup of tahini
- 1/2 cup of all-purpose flour

- 1/4 cup of cocoa powder
- 1/4 tsp baking powder
- 1/4 tsp sea salt (+ more for sprinkling)

Instructions:

1. Preheat the oven to 350°F (175°C) and coat a mini muffin pan with cooking spray.
2. Whisk together dilute butter and sugar in a combining basin up to well combined.
3. Stir in the eggs one at a time, followed by the vanilla essence.
4. Stir in the tahini up to smooth and fully combined.
5. Separately, combine the flour, cocoa powder, baking powder, and 1/4 tsp sea salt in a separate basin.
6. Add the dry ingredients to the liquid components gradually, stirring up to just blended.
7. Fill every cavity of the mini muffin tin about 3/4 full with the batter.
8. Top every brownie bite with a pinch of sea salt.
9. Bake for 15-20 mins, or up to a toothpick inserted into the center yields a few moist crumbs.
10. Let the brownie bites to cool for a few mins in the muffin tray before transferring to a wire rack to cool completely.

NUTRITION INFO (per brownie bite):

Cals: 120 kcal, Carbs: 13g, Protein: 2g, Fat: 7g, Fiber: 1g

287.Israeli Stuffed Mushrooms with Quinoa and Spinach

Prep Time: 15 mins Cook

Time: 25 mins Total

Time: 40 mins

Servings: 4

Ingredients:

- 8 Big mushrooms, cleaned and stems take outd
- 1/2 cup of quinoa, rinsed
- 1 cup of vegetable broth
- 1 tbsp olive oil
- 1 mini onion, lightly chop-up
- 2 garlic cloves, chop-up
- 2 cups of fresh spinach, chop-up
- 1/4 cup of feta cheese, cut up
- Salt and pepper as needed
- Fresh parsley for garnish

Instructions:

1. Preheat the oven to 375°F (190°C) and coat a baking dish with cooking spray.
2. Set aside after cooking quinoa in veggie broth according to box/pkg directions.

3. Warm the olive oil in a pan over medium heat. Sauté the chop-up onion up to it is transparent.
4. Cook up to the spinach wilts, then stir in the chop-up garlic.
5. Take out from the fire and toss in the cooked quinoa and cut up feta cheese. Season with salt and pepper as needed.
6. Place every mushroom in the prepared baking dish and stuff with the quinoa-spinach Mixture.
7. Bake for 20 mins, or up to the mushrooms are cooked, in a preheated oven.
8. Before serving, garnish with fresh parsley.

NUTRITION INFO (per serving):

Cals: 170 kcal, Carbs: 22g, Protein: 7g, Fat: 6g, Fiber: 4g

288.Falafel Buddha Bowl with Hummus and Avocado

Prep Time: 20 mins Cook

Time: 20 mins Total

Time: 40 mins

Servings: 2

Ingredients:

- 1 cup of dried chickpeas, soaked overnight
- 1 mini onion, roughly chop-up
- 3 garlic cloves
- 1 cup of fresh parsley leaves
- 1 cup of fresh cilantro leaves
- 1 tsp ground cumin
- 1 tsp ground coriander
- 1/2 tsp baking soda
- Salt and pepper as needed
- 2 tbsp olive oil
- 2 cups of cooked quinoa or brown rice
- 1 cup of hummus
- 1 ripe avocado, split
- Fresh lemon juice
- Cherry tomatoes, split cucumbers, and shredded carrots for garnish

Instructions:

1. Combine soaked chickpeas, onion, garlic, parsley, cilantro, cumin, coriander, baking soda, salt, and pepper in a mixer. Pulse the ingredients up to a coarse Mixture formed.
2. Form the ingredients into tiny falafel patties and pan-fry them in olive oil up to golden brown and crispy on both sides.
3. Divide the cooked quinoa or brown rice evenly between two serving bowls.
4. Top the grains with falafel patties, hummus, and split avocado, then sprinkle with fresh lemon juice.

5. Garnish with cherry tomatoes, cucumber slices, and carrot slivers.
6. Enjoy the falafel Buddha bowl immediately!

NUTRITION INFO (per serving):
Cals: 650 kcal, Carbs: 72g, Protein: 21g, Fat: 33g, Fiber: 19g

289.Shakshuka with Swiss Chard and Labneh

Prep Time: 10 mins Cook
Time: 30 mins Total
Time: 40 mins
Servings: 4

Ingredients:

- 2 tbsp olive oil
- 1 onion, chop-up
- 2 garlic cloves, chop-up
- 1 red bell pepper, chop-up
- 1 yellow bell pepper, chop-up
- 1 bunch Swiss chard, chop-up
- 1 tsp ground cumin
- 1 tsp ground paprika
- 1/2 tsp ground cayenne pepper (non-compulsory, for heat)
- 1 can (14 ozs) crushed tomatoes
- Salt and pepper as needed
- 4-6 Big eggs
- 1/2 cup of labneh (strained yogurt)

Instructions:

1. Warm the olive oil in a Big skillet over medium heat. Cook up to the onions are transparent.
2. Combine in the chop-up garlic and red and yellow bell peppers. Cook up to the peppers have melted slightly.
3. Cook up to the Swiss chard has wilted in the skillet.
4. Add the cumin, paprika, and cayenne pepper (if using). Cook for one more min.
5. Pour in the crushed tomatoes, season with salt and pepper, and simmer for about 15 mins, or up to the sauce thickens.
6. With a spoon, make mini wells in the sauce and carefully crack the eggs into the wells.
7. Cook the eggs, covered, for 5-7 mins, or up to the whites are set but the yolks are still runny.
8. Shakshuka Must be served hot with dollops of labneh on top.

NUTRITION INFO (per serving):
Cals: 250 kcal, Carbs: 18g, Protein: 11g, Fat: 16g, Fiber: 4g

290.Malabi with Passionfruit and Coconut

Prep Time: 5 mins Cook
Time: 10 mins Total
Time: 4 hrs 15 mins
Servings: 6

Ingredients:

- 1/2 cup of cornstarch
- 4 cups of coconut milk
- 1/2 cup of sugar
- 1 tsp vanilla extract
- 1/4 cup of passionfruit pulp (fresh or canned)
- Toasted coconut flakes for garnish

Instructions:

1. In a separate bowl, whisk together the cornstarch and 1/2 cup of coconut milk up to completely dissolved.
2. Heat the remaining coconut milk and sugar in a saucepan over medium heat up to the sugar melts.
3. Pour in the cornstarch Mixture and continue to stir continually up to the liquid thickens.
4. Take out from the heat and combine in the passionfruit pulp and vanilla extract.
5. Let the malabi to cool to room temperature in individual serving bowls or a big serving dish.
6. Refrigerate for at least 4 hrs, or up to firm.
7. Garnish with toasted coconut flakes before serving.

NUTRITION INFO (per serving):
Cals: 320 kcal, Carbs: 40g, Protein: 2g, Fat: 18g, Fiber: 1g

291.Rugelach with Apricot and Coconut Filling

Prep Time: 15 mins Cook
Time: 20 mins Total
Time: 35 mins
Servings: 24 rugelach

Ingredients:

- 2 cups of all-purpose flour
- 1/2 tsp salt
- 1 cup of unsalted butter, chilled and slice into mini pieces
- 8 ozs cream cheese, chilled and slice into mini pieces
- 1/4 cup of granulated sugar
- 1 tsp vanilla extract
- 1/2 cup of apricot preserves
- 1/2 cup of sweetened shredded coconut
- 1 egg, beaten (for egg wash)

- 2 tbsp turbinado sugar (for sprinkling)

Instructions:

1. Preheat the oven to 375 Ds Fahrenheit (190 Ds Celsius) and line a baking sheet with parchment paper.
2. In a mixer, combine the flour, salt, butter, cream cheese, granulated sugar, and vanilla extract up to a dough forms.
3. Refrigerate for 1 hr after dividing the dough into four equal halves and wrapping every in plastic wrap.
4. Roll out one portion of the dough into a circle on a floured surface.
5. 2 tbsp apricot preserves on top of the dough, leaving a tiny border around the borders.
6. Sprinkle 2 tbsp sweetened shredded coconut over the preserves.
7. Divide the dough into 6 equal wedges and roll every wedge beginning at the wide end.
8. Brush the rugelach with beaten egg and sprinkle with turbinado sugar on the prepared baking sheet.
9. Continue with the remaining dough portions.
10. Rugelach Must be baked for 18-20 mins, or up to golden brown.
11. Before serving, let them cool on a wire rack.

NUTRITION INFO (per rugelach):
Cals: 160 kcal, Carbs: 15g, Protein: 2g, Fat: 10g, Fiber: 1g

292. Tahini Swirl Brownies with Sea Salt

Prep Time: 15 mins Cook
Time: 25 mins Total
Time: 40 mins
Servings: 12 brownies

Ingredients:

- 1/2 cup of unsalted butter, dilute
- 1 cup of granulated sugar
- 2 Big eggs
- 1 tsp vanilla extract
- 1/2 cup of all-purpose flour
- 1/3 cup of cocoa powder
- 1/4 tsp baking powder
- 1/4 tsp salt
- 1/4 cup of tahini
- Sea salt flakes for sprinkling

Instructions:

1. Preheat the oven to 350°F (175°C) and coat a square baking pan with cooking spray.

2. Whisk together dilute butter and sugar in a combining basin up to well combined.
3. Stir in the eggs one at a time, followed by the vanilla essence.
4. In a separate basin, whisk together the flour, cocoa powder, baking powder, and salt.
5. Add the dry ingredients to the liquid components gradually, stirring up to just blended.
6. Spread the brownie batter evenly in the prepared baking sheet.
7. Drizzle tahini over brownie batter and gently swirl with a toothpick or knife.
8. Sprinkle with sea salt flakes on top.
9. Cook for 20-25 mins, or up to a toothpick inserted into the center comes out with a few moist crumbs.
10. Let the brownies to cool completely in the pan before slicing and serving.

NUTRITION INFO (per brownie):
Cals: 240 kcal, Carbs: 27g, Protein: 3g, Fat: 14g, Fiber: 1g

293. Israeli Stuffed Cabbage Rolls with Rice and Lentils

Prep Time: 30 mins Cook
Time: 1 hr Total
Time: 1 hr 30 mins
Servings: 6

Ingredients:

- 12 Big cabbage leaves
- 1 cup of cooked rice
- 1 cup of cooked green lentils
- 1 onion, lightly chop-up
- 2 garlic cloves, chop-up
- 1 tbsp olive oil
- 1 tsp ground cumin
- 1 tsp ground coriander
- 1/2 tsp ground cinnamon
- 1/4 tsp ground allspice
- 1 can (14 ozs) diced tomatoes
- 1 cup of vegetable broth
- Salt and pepper as needed
- Fresh parsley for garnish

Instructions:

1. In a Big pot of boiling water, blanch the cabbage leaves for 2-3 mins, or up to tender. Set aside after draining.
2. Warm the olive oil in a pan over medium heat. Cook up to the onions are transparent.
3. Combine chop-up garlic, ground cumin, ground coriander, ground cinnamon, and ground allspice in a combining bowl. Cook for one more min.

4. To the skillet, add cooked rice, cooked lentils, salt, and pepper. Combine up to well blended.
5. Roll every cabbage leaf firmly, tucking in the sides, with a dollop of the rice-lentil Mixture.
6. Pour the diced tomatoes, juice, and vegetable broth into a separate pot. Season with salt and pepper as needed.
7. Cover and boil the stuffed cabbage rolls in the tomato-broth Mixture for 45 mins to an hr, or up to the cabbage is soft.
8. Before serving, garnish with fresh parsley.

NUTRITION INFO (per serving):
Cals: 240 kcal, Carbs: 40g, Protein: 9g, Fat: 4g, Fiber: 10g

294.Falafel Salad Bowl with Tahini Dressing

Prep Time: 20 mins Cook

Time: 20 mins Total

Time: 40 mins

Servings: 4

Ingredients:

- 1 cup of dried chickpeas, soaked overnight
- 1 mini onion, roughly chop-up
- 3 garlic cloves
- 1 cup of fresh parsley leaves
- 1 cup of fresh cilantro leaves
- 1 tsp ground cumin
- 1 tsp ground coriander
- 1/2 tsp baking soda
- Salt and pepper as needed
- 1/4 cup of all-purpose flour (or chickpea flour for gluten-free)
- Oil for frying
- 4 cups of combined salad greens
- Cherry tomatoes, halved
- Cucumber slices
- Red onion slices
- Pickled turnips (non-compulsory)
- Tahini dressing (see below)
- Tahini Dressing Ingredients:
- 1/4 cup of tahini
- 2 tbsp lemon juice
- 2 tbsp water
- 1 garlic clove, chop-up
- Salt and pepper as needed

Instructions:

1. Combine soaked chickpeas, onion, garlic, parsley, cilantro, cumin, coriander, baking soda, salt, and pepper in a mixer. Pulse the ingredients up to a coarse Mixture formed.

2. Transfer the Mixture to a combining basin and toss in the flour up to it comes together.
3. Form the ingredients into tiny falafel patties and cook them in high oil up to golden brown and crispy.
4. In a separate bowl, whisk together the tahini, lemon juice, water, chop-up garlic, salt, and pepper to make the tahini dressing.
5. Arrange combined greens, cherry tomatoes, cucumber slices, red onion slices, and pickled turnips (if using) in salad bowls.
6. Drizzle the salad with tahini dressing and top with falafel patties.
7. Serve the falafel salad bowls right away.

NUTRITION INFO (per serving):
Cals: 420 kcal, Carbs: 38g, Protein: 14g, Fat: 25g, Fiber: 10g

295.Shakshuka with Roasted Red Peppers and Spinach

Prep Time: 10 mins Cook

Time: 30 mins Total

Time: 40 mins

Servings: 4

Ingredients:

- 2 tbsp olive oil
- 1 onion, chop-up
- 2 garlic cloves, chop-up
- 2 roasted red bell peppers, chop-up
- 2 cups of fresh spinach leaves
- 1 tsp ground cumin
- 1 tsp ground paprika
- 1/2 tsp ground cayenne pepper (non-compulsory, for heat)
- 1 can (14 ozs) crushed tomatoes
- Salt and pepper as needed
- 4-6 Big eggs
- Fresh parsley for garnish

Instructions:

1. Warm the olive oil in a Big skillet over medium heat. Cook up to the onions are transparent.
2. Combine in the chop-up garlic and roasted red bell peppers. Cook for a couple of mins.
3. Cook up to the spinach leaves are wilted in the skillet.
4. Add the cumin, paprika, and cayenne pepper (if using). Cook for one more min.
5. Pour in the crushed tomatoes, season with salt and pepper, and simmer for about 15 mins, or up to the sauce thickens.
6. With a spoon, make mini wells in the sauce and carefully crack the eggs into the wells.

7. Cook the eggs, covered, for 5-7 mins, or up to the whites are set but the yolks are still runny.
8. Before serving, garnish with fresh parsley.

296. Malabi with Orange Blossom and Pistachio

Prep Time: 5 mins Cook
Time: 10 mins Total
Time: 4 hrs 15 mins
Servings: 6

Ingredients:

- 1/2 cup of cornstarch
- 4 cups of whole milk
- 1/2 cup of sugar
- 1 tsp orange blossom water
- 1/4 cup of chop-up pistachios

Instructions:

1. Combine the cornstarch with 1/2 cup of milk in a mini bowl up to completely dissolved.
2. Heat the remaining milk and sugar in a saucepan over medium heat up to the sugar melts.
3. Pour in the cornstarch Mixture and continue to stir continually up to the liquid thickens.
4. Take out from the heat and add the orange blossom water.
5. Let the malabi to cool to room temperature in individual serving bowls or a big serving dish.
6. Refrigerate for at least 4 hrs, or up to firm.
7. Garnish with chop-up pistachios before serving.

297. Rugelach with Raspberry and Pecan Filling

Prep Time: 15 mins Cook
Time: 20 mins Total
Time: 35 mins
Servings: 24 rugelach

Ingredients:

- 2 cups of all-purpose flour
- 1/2 tsp salt
- 1 cup of unsalted butter, chilled and slice into mini pieces
- 8 ozs cream cheese, chilled and slice into mini pieces
- 1/4 cup of granulated sugar
- 1 tsp vanilla extract
- 1/2 cup of raspberry preserves
- 1 cup of chop-up pecans
- 1 egg, beaten (for egg wash)
- 2 tbsp turbinado sugar (for sprinkling)

Instructions:

1. Preheat the oven to 375 Ds Fahrenheit (190 Ds Celsius) and line a baking sheet with parchment paper.
2. In a mixer, combine the flour, salt, butter, cream cheese, granulated sugar, and vanilla extract up to a dough forms.
3. Refrigerate for 1 hr after dividing the dough into four equal halves and wrapping every in plastic wrap.
4. Roll out one portion of the dough into a circle on a floured surface.
5. 2 tbsp raspberry preserves Must be spread over the dough, leaving a tiny border around the edges.
6. Sprinkle 2 tbsp chop-up pecans over the preserves.
7. Divide the dough into 6 equal wedges and roll every wedge beginning at the wide end.
8. Brush the rugelach with beaten egg and sprinkle with turbinado sugar on the prepared baking sheet.
9. Continue with the remaining dough portions.
10. Rugelach Must be baked for 18-20 mins, or up to golden brown.
11. Before serving, let them cool on a wire rack.

298. Tahini Banana Muffins with Chocolate Chips

Prep Time: 15 mins Cook
Time: 20 mins Total
Time: 35 mins
Servings: 12 muffins

Ingredients:

- 1/2 cup of tahini
- 1/2 cup of honey or maple syrup
- 2 Big ripe bananas, mashed
- 1/2 cup of milk (dairy or plant-based)
- 1 tsp vanilla extract
- 1 3/4 cups of all-purpose flour
- 1 tsp baking powder
- 1/2 tsp baking soda
- 1/4 tsp salt
- 1/2 cup of chocolate chips

1. Preheat the oven to 350 Ds Fahrenheit (175 Ds Celsius) and line a muffin pan with paper liners.
2. Whisk together tahini, honey (or maple syrup), mashed bananas, milk, and vanilla extract in a combining bowl up to well blended.
3. In a separate dish, whisk together the flour, baking powder, baking soda, and salt.
4. Add the dry ingredients to the liquid components gradually, stirring up to just blended.
5. Incorporate the chocolate chips.
6. Divide the batter evenly among the muffin cups of, filling them about two-thirds full.
7. 18-20 mins, or up to a toothpick inserted into the center comes out clean.
8. Let the muffins to cool for a few mins in the pan before transferring to a wire rack to cool completely.

NUTRITION INFO (per muffin):
Cals: 240 kcal, Carbs: 35g, Protein: 5g, Fat: 10g, Fiber: 2g

299. Israeli Stuffed Tomatoes with Couscous and Mint

Prep Time: 20 mins Cook

Time: 20 mins Total

Time: 40 mins

Servings: 4

Ingredients:

- 4 Big tomatoes
- 1 cup of couscous
- 1 1/4 cups of vegetable broth
- 1/4 cup of chop-up fresh mint
- 1/4 cup of chop-up fresh parsley
- 1/4 cup of chop-up fresh dill
- 1/4 cup of chop-up green onions
- 1/4 cup of chop-up cucumber
- 1/4 cup of chop-up bell pepper
- 2 tbsp lemon juice
- 2 tbsp olive oil
1. Salt and pepper as needed
2. *Instructions:*
3. Take out the tomatoes' tops and scoop out the seeds and pulp, leaving a hollow shell. Place aside.
4. Bring the vegetable broth to a boil in a saucepan. Cover and take out from heat after stirring in the couscous. Let for 5 mins, or up to the couscous has absorbed the liquid.
5. Transfer the couscous to a Big combining basin and fluff with a fork.

6. To the couscous, combine in the mint, parsley, dill, green onions, cucumber, and bell pepper.
7. Whisk together lemon juice, olive oil, salt, and pepper in a mini bowl.
8. Toss the couscous Mixture with the dressing up to completely incorporated.
9. Fill every tomato hollow with the couscous Mixture.
10. The stuffed tomatoes can be served at room temperature or chilled.

NUTRITION INFO (per serving):
Cals: 280 kcal, Carbs: 42g, Protein: 7g, Fat: 10g, Fiber: 6g

300. Falafel Tabbouleh Bowl with Lemon-Tahini Dressing

Prep Time: 30 mins Cook

Time: 20 mins Total

Time: 50 mins

Servings: 4

Ingredients:

- 1 cup of dried chickpeas, soaked overnight
- 1 mini onion, roughly chop-up
- 3 garlic cloves
- 1 cup of fresh parsley leaves
- 1 cup of fresh cilantro leaves
- 1 tsp ground cumin
- 1 tsp ground coriander
- 1/2 tsp baking soda
- Salt and pepper as needed
- 1/4 cup of all-purpose flour (or chickpea flour for gluten-free)
- Oil for frying
- 2 cups of cooked quinoa or bulgur wheat
- 1 cup of chop-up cucumber
- 1 cup of cherry tomatoes, halved
- 1/2 cup of chop-up red onion
- 1/4 cup of chop-up fresh mint
- Lemon-Tahini Dressing (see below)
- Lemon-Tahini Dressing Ingredients:
- 1/4 cup of tahini
- 1/4 cup of water
- 2 tbsp lemon juice
- 1 garlic clove, chop-up
- Salt and pepper as needed

Instructions:

1. Combine soaked chickpeas, onion, garlic, parsley, cilantro, cumin, coriander, baking soda, salt, and pepper in a mixer. Pulse the ingredients up to a coarse Mixture formed.

2. Transfer the Mixture to a combining basin and toss in the flour up to it comes together.
3. Form the ingredients into tiny falafel patties and cook them in high oil up to golden brown and crispy.
4. In a separate bowl, whisk together the tahini, water, lemon juice, chop-up garlic, salt, and pepper to make the Lemon-Tahini Dressing.
5. Assemble the falafel tabbouleh bowls in individual serving bowls by layering cooked quinoa or bulgur wheat, chop-up cucumber, halved cherry tomatoes, chop-up red onion, and fresh mint.
6. Drizzle with Lemon-Tahini Dressing and top with falafel patties.
7. Immediately serve the falafel tabbouleh bowls.

NUTRITION INFO (per serving):
Cals: 480 kcal, Carbs: 53g, Protein: 17g, Fat: 23g, Fiber: 12g

301. Shakshuka with Swiss Chard and Harissa

Prep Time: 10 mins Cook

Time: 30 mins Total

Time: 40 mins

Servings: 4

Ingredients:
- 2 tbsp olive oil
- 1 onion, chop-up
- 2 garlic cloves, chop-up
- 1 bunch Swiss chard, chop-up
- 2 tsp harissa paste (adjust to your spice preference)
- 1 tsp ground cumin
- 1 tsp ground paprika
- 1 can (14 ozs) diced tomatoes
- Salt and pepper as needed
- 4-6 Big eggs
- Fresh cilantro for garnish

Instructions:
1. Warm the olive oil in a Big skillet over medium heat. Cook up to the onions are transparent.
2. Combine in the chop-up garlic and Swiss chard. Cook up to the chard begins to wilt.
3. Combine in the harissa paste, cumin powder, and paprika powder. Cook for one more min.
4. Pour in the diced tomatoes and juice, season with salt and pepper, and cook for about 15 mins.
5. With a spoon, make mini wells in the sauce and carefully crack the eggs into the wells.
6. Cook the eggs, covered, for 5-7 mins, or up to the whites are set but the yolks are still runny.

7. Before serving, garnish with fresh cilantro.

NUTRITION INFO (per serving):
Cals: 220 kcal, Carbs: 12g, Protein: 10g, Fat: 15g, Fiber: 4g

302. Malabi with Rosewater and Strawberry Sauce

Prep Time: 5 mins Cook

Time: 10 mins Total

Time: 4 hrs 15 mins

Servings: 6

Ingredients:
- 1/2 cup of cornstarch
- 4 cups of whole milk
- 1/2 cup of sugar
- 1 tsp rosewater
- 1/2 cup of strawberry sauce (store-bought or homemade)

Instructions:
1. Combine the cornstarch with 1/2 cup of milk in a mini bowl up to completely dissolved.
2. Heat the remaining milk and sugar in a saucepan over medium heat up to the sugar melts.
3. Pour in the cornstarch Mixture and continue to stir continually up to the liquid thickens.
4. Take out from the heat and add the rosewater.
5. Let the malabi to cool to room temperature in individual serving bowls or a big serving dish.
6. Refrigerate for at least 4 hrs, or up to firm.
7. Drizzle strawberry sauce over the malabi just before serving.

NUTRITION INFO (per serving):
Cals: 240 kcal, Carbs: 38g, Protein: 6g, Fat: 7g, Fiber: 1g

Printed in Great Britain
by Amazon

47484155R00073